MINNESOTA
FAMILY
WEEKENDS

MARTIN HINTZ

Trails Books

Black Earth, Wisconsin

Library of Congress Control Number: 2002114602
ISBN: 1-931599-22-X
Project Manager: Anne McKenna
Editor: Stan Stoga
Copy Editor: Todd Berger
Designer: Jennifer Walde

Printed in the United States of America by McNaughton & Gunn.

08 07 06 05 04 03   6 5 4 3 2 1

Trails Books, a division of
Trails Media Group, Inc.
P.O. Box 317
Black Earth, WI 53515
www.trailsbooks.com

To the Conleys, the Shaskeys, and the Wronkas, who opened the doors to Minnesota . . . and to Father James Whalen, who pointed out the "write" way.

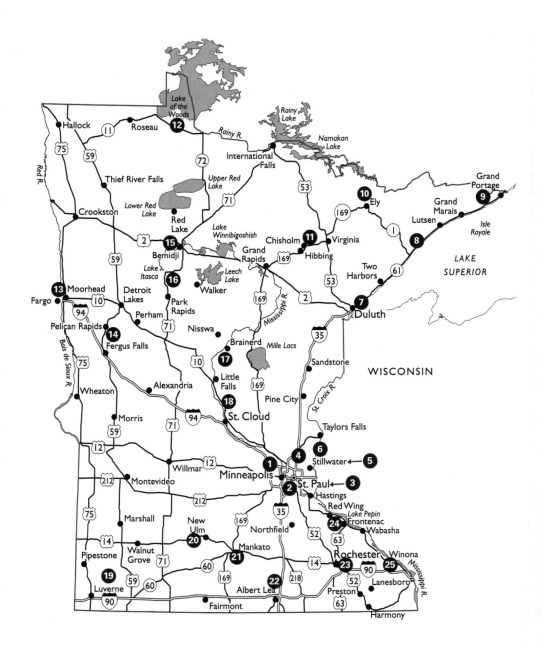

CONTENTS

INTRODUCTION

Minnesota! It's a wonderful mix of urban and rustic charm with something for all traveling tastes amid the sky blue waters. The state has cooked up a marvelous stew that the whole family can enjoy: king-sized servings of culture, outdoor recreation, human-made wonders, and nature at its best. Whether visitors spend a day, two days, or longer on their weekend jaunts, the state has attractions and activities that are tailor-made for families of all sizes and types.

No matter where the family is headed for the weekend, everyone is sure to come face-to-face with some part of Minnesota's colorful past and rich present-day diversity. For starters, the state is wonderfully influenced by the Native Americans who once controlled the region, influences tinged—as they are everywhere in America—with a bit of sadness, but also enhanced by the Native American will to survive years of hardship. Minnesota also offers innumerable tales of immigrant pluck: of Scandinavian courage on the frontier in the 19th century or the Hmong presence in today's urban settings. Minnesota has a marvelous political history, with the likes of liberal Hubert H. Humphrey and, yes, even wild-card wrestler-turned-politician Jesse Ventura. The state can also flex its economic muscle, with giants such as Cargill and General Mills, all held together by 3M tape.

Minnesota's cultural landscape is as eclectic as they come, a fact that family members of all ages and tastes will appreciate. The state has been home to children's writers such as Carol Ryie Brink, author of *Caddie Woodlawn*, and Laura Ingalls Wilder of *Little House on the Prairie* fame. It has also produced writers whose view of the American dream is far less benign—F. Scott Fitzgerald and Sinclair Lewis come readily to mind. And today, there is playwright August Wilson for a touch of soul. A wonderful library and bookstore system is evidence that Minnesotans appreciate their authors. The state features music by homegrown artists such as Prince and Bob Dylan. It offers *Grumpy Old Men* the chance to appear in films. It has festivals of all sorts, from elaborate affairs that attract people from all over the state to local shindigs that have family fun written all over them. It has ball games, restaurants, and museums. It has tall statues of lumberjack legend Paul Bunyan to admire, lift bridges to drive across, and universities with vibrant arts programs to enjoy.

But the state's abundant natural beauty is best of all, highlighted by Minnesota's incredible array of lakes. Shell, Buffalo, Pike, Diddle de Woodle, Washington, Little, Big, Sarah, Benton—the names roll on and on. There are so many, in fact, that many of them have been tagged with identical monikers. There are, for example, at least 156 Long Lakes and 83 Bass Lakes. Minnesota has more lakes than any other state, with some 15,000 such watery expanses to its credit. Of that number, 11,842 cover more than 10 acres.

And don't forget that Minnesota is the birthplace of the Mississippi River. It starts from a stream so narrow that small kids can leap across it, then gradually grows into one of the mightiest waterways on the planet. And it does this within the confines of the state. Viewing the Mississippi, whether at its headwaters or later, along the Great River Road, is an experience every family member will never forget.

This book is for families wishing to sample some of the sites and attractions that make Minnesota great, whether urban or rural, of historic value or recently created, natural or human-made. The 25 trips described herein cover all areas of the state and were carefully crafted so that families could comfortably spend two or three days in any of the regions. Of course, if you decided to stay longer, I'd be gratified and thrilled. It meant you and your brood experienced Minnesota in its ever-changing excitement and never-ending beauty. And that's the way it should be.

ACKNOWLEDGMENTS

For all their assistance, advice, and help in researching and preparing this manuscript, the author would like to thank Pam Percy, Deserae Constantineau, Steve Hintz, Kate Hintz, and Anthony Ross. Additional thanks go to Chuck Lennon of the Minnesota Division of Tourism and all the other industry personnel who indicated what should be seen and explained what there was to do in this wonderful state. Their input and suggestions were invaluable. And then there are all the other Minnesotans: the butchers, the bakers, and the candlestick makers who always seem glad to see you and your family arrive for a visit—no matter how long or short.

MINNEAPOLIS

Anybody with twins knows that they are never exactly alike. Each has its personality, with quirks that range from silliness to seriousness. It's the same with the Twin Cities of Minneapolis and St. Paul. Those in the know claim that Minneapolis is the brasher of the two communities, with an upbeat, in-your-face, edge-of-the-prairie mentality that proclaims loudly that everything is possible. They are probably correct, since the soul of Minneapolis is made of brawn and brain, capitalizing on what has always been a looking-West attitude, a true pioneer spirit. There is a youthful, kidlike exuberance to Minneapolis, as if everything is new and ready for a challenge.

Minneapolis is proud of its nickname: the "City of Lakes." With 22 large and small bodies of fish-filled water to enjoy, the nickname is certainly apt. There are Lakes Calhoun, Brownie, Harriet, Hiawatha, Nokomis, Lake of the Isles, and numerous others. Plus there are 170 parks tossed into the mix to endow the city with plenty of open space and greenery. The lakes present numerous recreational activities for families hot for adventure, whether over a weekend break or a longer stay. Bring the summer outdoor toys for some urban windsurfing or canoeing, as well as cycling and in-line skating. When the weather gets warm, entertainment heads outdoors in the form of concerts, plays, and movies in the city's parks. There are free concerts in several parks throughout June, July, August, and September, featuring Folk, Blues, Jazz, Big Band, children's music, and more. Contact the Minneapolis Park and Recreation Board for the current entertainment schedule (612) 661-4800.

During the winter months, over 30 outdoor ice rinks are maintained throughout the parks for ice skating, hockey, and broomball. Or enjoy a day of cross-country skiing on groomed trails. Some trails are even lighted for evening skiing. The largest regional park in Minneapolis is Theodore Wirth Park located at the intersection of Wirth Parkway and Plymouth Avenue North. Wirth Winter Recreation Area has something for the whole family, including rentals of snow tubes, ski equipment, and snowshoes. Cross-country skiing lessons are also offered. Downhill skiing is available for those looking for a faster pace.

Lake Harriet, one mile west of Lyndale Avenue, just north of 50th Street, is one of the area's most popular sites for canoeing, fishing, loafing, swimming, and just plain hanging out. Parking at the park is good, restrooms are clean, there isn't an entrance fee and there are plenty of spaces for summertime pic-nics. Folks walking with friends throughout most of the year, as well as bicy-cling, are two other activities enjoyed here by the locals. Bus routes 28 and 4 pass nearby if a visitor is in a local transportation mode. In addition, for more fun, Minnesota Public Radio has occasionally sponsored classical music and a picnic basket contest on the last Friday in June at the lake. The event is held in the Lake Harriet Bandshell, along the north shore. When the weather turns frostier, the grounds around Lake Harriet are also great for cross-country ski-ing in the winter. And kids will love the Lake Harriet Winter Kite Festival every year held in mid-January. Bring your own kite or buy an inexpensive one at the lake. The festival features music, an ice fishing expo, snowshoeing, and plenty of kite flying, of course.

If visiting Lake Harriet, be prepared to smile. The Minnesota Film and TV Board pitches the site as one of the prime Twin Cities outdoor attractions for making movies. As a result, commercials, shorts, and indie pixs are often shot around its shores, with the city skyline in the background. This might be just the chance for Junior to make it big. But stars of another kind are sighted on clear nights through the telescopes of the Minnesota Astronomical Society Sidewalk Astronomers. The club members turn out in good weather to look into the heavens and are happy to answer questions about what's happening "up there." Call the society to confirm times, (612) 649-4861.

Contact the Minneapolis Park and Recreation Board, 200 Grain Exchange, 400 S. 4th Street, Suite 200, Minneapolis, MN, 55415-1400, (612) 661-4800, for a roundup on activities throughout the city parks. The park system Web site is also helpful: http://www.minneapolisparks.org.

To take in other lakes within the city, a jaunt along The Grand Rounds is a fun way for the family to see one of the country's most scenic urban recre-ational byways. The Grand Rounds is a system of lovely trails, paths, and road-ways in a totally unique urban setting. There are seven byway districts offer-ing an unsurpassed view of Minneapolis by bike, "blades," foot, or vehicle. Twenty primary access points make the trail easy to find from interstates and major city streets. Along the 50-mile route, the family will see more than 50 interpretive sites, a dozen lakes, four golf courses, two waterfalls, a variety of gardens, at least one creek, and a river. Hospitality centers and information kiosks are also along the way. This stretch was designated a Minnesota State Scenic Byway in 1997 and became a national byway in 1998.

Highlights include Minnehaha Falls, adjacent to the Longfellow House In-terpretive Center off State Highway 55 and Minnehaha, and the James J. Hill Historic Stone Arch Bridge. The beautiful structure is the only stone bridge that crosses the Mississippi River. You can find the arch in the downtown River-front district south of the Hennepin Avenue Bridge. Hill was a railroad mag-nate in Minnesota's early history.

For flower lovers of all ages, the Lake Harriet Rose Garden on the west end of Lake Harriet is one of the more popular stops along the byway. Be sure to encourage the kids to stop and smell the roses. And then have them search out the Eloise Butler Wildflower Garden and Bird Sanctuary in Theodore Wirth Park, south of Wirth Lake along the parkway. The sanctuary opens April 1 and remains open until autumn, with hours from 7:30 a.m. to dusk daily. Contact the park at 763-522-4584.

To sample other parks within the area, the Suburban Hennepin Regional Park District, commonly called Hennepin Parks, is an independent, special park district established by the State Legislature in 1957. The system acquires and maintains reserves for the use of the citizens of suburban Hennepin County, Scott County, the metropolitan areas, and the state. For tons of information on the county's extensive facilities, contact the system at 12615 County Road 9, Plymouth, MN 55441-1299, (763) 559-9000; www.hennepinparks.org.

With the Mississippi River winding its snakelike way along the eastern border of town and the Minnesota River wriggling just to the south of the city's southern boundary, Minneapolis has enough natural beauty to inspire any landscape artist. For those who simply want to walk and enjoy the scene, meander down to the Mississippi Riverfront District. Originally the town of St. Anthony, the neighborhood is the birthplace of Minneapolis and is a great spot for a self-guided hike near the impressive St. Anthony Falls, which is the Mississippi River's only natural waterfall. Check out the old mills and weave through the historic buildings that are now shops and restaurants. Be sure the kids have saved their allowances for such a prowl. The temptations here are great.

Now it's time to open the history books and give the kids a bit of a lesson. Father Louis Hennepin was the first European to see the falls, arriving in 1680 after what probably seemed like a lifetime of paddling and portaging his canoe from Canada. For his efforts, he was captured by a band of Dakota, though he was held in relative comfort. The next year he was "rescued" by trader Daniel Greysolon, Sieur du Lhut, in whose honor the city of Duluth is named. Hennepin then roamed off into the wilderness to make more discoveries for his French king.

In 1803, under the Louisiana Purchase, the section of Minnesota south and west of the Mississippi River became part of the United States and settlers flocked to the region. Minnesota became a state in 1858, and Minneapolis was incorporated as a city in 1867. It became the Milling Capital of the World about a decade later as more than two dozen mills energetically operated off the power of the muscular falls to grind Midwestern grain into quality flour.

That's all in the history books now, yet Minneapolis relishes its roaring economic heritage and remains a corporate home to such Fortune 500 companies as General Mills, Northwest Airlines, and others of that international ilk. See, things do grow up. Just like in Peter Pan.

3

Take the Trolley

Here's a unique way to take the family on a sightseeing tour of Minneapolis. Among the benefits: taking a load off the feet and being able to gawk and not drive. The Minneapolis River City Trolley company presents 75-minute tours of downtown Minneapolis area and through the Chain of Lakes district. While not original trolleys, the vintage-looking vehicles offer a great opportunity for children to learn about the city in a fun and — thank heavens — affordable way. The trolley system operates from 10:00 a.m. to 4:00 p.m., daily from May through October. The Chain of Lakes tour runs weekends only after Labor Day.

Exact change is needed for fares. Rates for a single tour are $5 seniors and children (12 and under) and $10 for adults. An all-day pass costs $10 for seniors and children (12 and under) and $15 for adults. If you still need to see more, a three-day pass is $15 for seniors and children and $20 for grownups. The trolley runs every 20 minutes, with stops at St. Anthony Main, the Walker Art Center, the Minneapolis Convention Center, or at any of the identified stops along the way. Call the Trolley hotline at 612-204-0000 for more information.

Although the city's trolley system lasted only from 1867 to 1954, kids get a kick out of taking a ride on a real streetcar via the Como-Harriet Streetcar Line. The line is part of the volunteer-based Minnesota Transportation Museum The museum operates several Minnesota streetcars on two-mile, 15-minute round trips on the original Como-Harriet right-of-way from Lake Harriet to Lake Calhoun.

The line runs on weekends from May to October 27, starting at 12:30 p.m. and continuing to dusk. The cars leave the Linden Hills Station at Queen Avenue South and W. 42nd Street on the west shore of Lake Harriet. The roundtrip fare is $1.50 per person. Children under age 4 ride for free.

For details about the Minnesota Transportation Museum which manages the trolley line, contact the facility at its mailing address: 193 Pennsylvania Avenue E., St. Paul, MN 55101-4319, (800) 711-2591. You can also call the museum's facilities at the Jackson Street Roundhouse, (651) 228-0263; the Osceola & St. Croix Valley Railway, (715) 755-3570; or the Excelsior Steamboat, (952) 474-4801.

CENTRAL MINNEAPOLIS

Where Native Americans once came to trade, Minneapolis's city center is still a shopper's dream, especially for the buy-til-ya-drop contingent in the family. Teens go gaga on **Nicollet Mall**, a 12-block thoroughfare that presents shopping, shopping, shopping, with 400 stores and three million square feet of retail space. All the big names in exotica are here for a Rodeo-Drive-in-the-Midwest feel, as well as CD shops and trendy clothing stores for the young and those-who-used-to-be.

Gaviidae Common, 651 Nicollet Mall, is the premier shopping destination with Neiman Marcus, Talbots, Saks Fifth Avenue, Aveda Lifestyle Store, and a shopping bag of other high-end outlets. Gaviidae has a food court in which to rest tired feet while soda sipping. Several larger restaurants, such as Morton's Steakhouse, are also in Gaviidae. Call (612) 372-1222 to get the lowdown on all the stores.

For still more shopping, **Minneapolis City Center**, 40 South Seventh Street, has three levels of stores and small shops that cater to all one's needs, whether clothes, bath oils, incense, posters, fine china, or . . . well . . . get out the list. Call (612) 372-1200 for more details on window-shopping.

The city's downtown shopping area is linked via skywalks, so neither toddler nor teen has to indulge chilly toes in wintertime. While the miles of walkways might cut into the hot-chocolate trade, they do make it easy to get from block to block over the mushy, icy streets below. This is especially helpful when pushing a stroller or a wheelchair.

Strong walking shoes are important for strolling through the historic **Warehouse District**, another downtown neighborhood with cool galleries, antique outlets, exotic gift shops, and fancy and not-so-fancy eateries where the hipsters, yuppies, and upwardly mobile go to dine. But there are also some laid-back, inexpensive coffeehouses helping fill in every available square inch where kids can do croissants.

The Warehouse District's several art crawls during the year provide a good opportunity to explore the neighborhood. Be sure to check out the sculpture, paintings, fabric art, and installations in the old buildings here, saved only a few years ago from the wrecker's ball. Don't just stay on the first floors, but walk up the stairs or take the elevators to find real discoveries in the more remote lofts. The district generally lies between Hennepin Avenue on the south, Third Avenue North on the north, North First Street on the east, and North Seventh Street on the west.

Target Center, between Sixth and Seventh Streets at 600 First Avenue North, lies within the district and is home to basketball games and concerts. For tickets contact the arena at (612) 673-0900. For information on the district's activities, contact the Historic Minneapolis Warehouse District, 322 First Avenue North, (612) 334-3131; www.mplswarehouse.com. Families from around the Upper Midwest flock to Target Center to cheer their respective

St. Anthony Smiles on Minnesota

Settlers established the village of St. Anthony in 1848 on the east bank of the Mississippi River adjacent to St. Anthony Falls. By 1855, the beginnings of Minneapolis had sprouted on the west bank of the river, and that year the two communities were linked by a suspension bridge, the first span across the Mississippi River. In 1872, the two communities were united to form Minneapolis, whose name was created from the Dakota word minne, meaning "water," and the Greek word polis, meaning "city."

teams, so be prepared for a lot of noisemaking, greatly appreciated by the smaller fry.

When hungry tummies growl, take the gang to these places for a fun time out on the town: **Harvey's Bar and Grill**, 106 North Third Street, (612) 343-5930; **The Loon Cafe**, 500 First Avenue North, (612) 332-8342; or **Nikki's**, 107 Third Avenue North, (612) 340-9098. **Moose and Sadie's Coffeeshop**, 312 Third Avenue North, is a playful spot for a morning snack. Call (612) 371-0464.

ARTS AND THEATER FOR THE WHOLE FAMILY

Minneapolis struts its art like a peacock on parade, with oodles of activities for the young crowd to enjoy. The kids can see a plaster dog in a pop-art exhibition at the **Walker Art Center**, 725 Vineland Place, or take in a teen art show at the Walker, with mediums including video, spoken-word, music, web design, dance, film, photography, painting, or sculpture for youthful vibrancy and variety. Children three to eight can get a closer look at the displays during artist-led tours of the galleries on Sundays. These are limited-enrollment sessions, so make sure to order tickets through the center when vacation dates are confirmed.

On the first Sunday of every month, the center sponsors free, family-oriented activities, which range from short films to storytelling to collage making. "WAC Packs," filled with activities and games, can be borrowed for free at the center's front desk. For more information, call (612) 375-7622; or visit the Walker's Web site at www.walkerart.org.

On pleasant days, tour the **Minneapolis Sculpture Garden** across the street from the Walker. One of the most interesting pieces there, and sure to attract the kids' attention, is "Spoonbridge and Cherry." This art piece is in the shape of—what else but—a giant spoon and a massive cherry. The spoon is 52 feet long and the cherry alone weights 1,200 pounds. The **Cowles Conservatory** is adjacent to the sculpture garden, filled with rare flowers and always with a fine mist permeating the air. The conservatory's fountain is perfect for bridal photos, with more than one young ring bearer having been snatched back from leaping into the pool—just in time to save the tux.

While strolling around the sculpture garden, ask discerning kids if they agree with some observers that Louise Bourgeois' multilegged sculpture was inspired by her childhood crawls under the dining room table. Then ask how they think George Segal created "Walking Man." The answer is easy: He made a plaster cast of a real person in a long overcoat and then recast it in bronze. At the Walker, pick up a comprehensive flier, which relates some of the stories behind the sculptures in the 11-acre urban garden. J. Otto Seibold, who has illustrated such children's books at *Mr. Lunch Takes a Plane Ride* and *Mr. Lunch Borrows a Canoe*, created the flier.

The **Minneapolis Institute of Arts** is a humdinger of a museum with an 85,000-piece collection spanning centuries of high-class artistic presentations. The oldest object is a small figure from the Paleolithic Period, dating from about 20,000 B.C. The sandstone figure, called a "Venus-like" statue by museum curators, stands 5 1/4" high and 2 1/4" wide. It was probably a fertility piece, according to the MIA. Leaping to the present, or actually what passes as the future, one recent kid-popular exhibit showed off the costumes, models, and props from George Lucas's *Star Wars* series of movies. The exhibition, entitled "Star Wars: The Magic of Myth," showed how artifacts from the institute's permanent collection were similar to those used in the films. The exhibit also pointed out how *Star Wars* drew on ancient legends for its story line.

The institute opened in 1915 and underwent a major renovation in the late 1990s. The museum broadened the collection, added galleries, and remodeled existing space. These days, a vacationing family might run into teachers and docents leading packs of wide-eyed children through the institute, showing them the exhibited works. Tag onto the end of one of these tours and pick up background detail about the collections.

With an eye to parents with tiny tots, the institute's special **Family Center** has stroller parking, a nursing room, snack area, computers with children's art activities, and an activity area with soft sculptures. Art is displayed at a kid's-eye level. There are treasure hunts, musical programs, and tours geared toward youngsters. Kids may also like poking around the institute's gift shop. The well-stocked store has jewelry, books, and artsy gifts from around the world.

Even the littlest one likes the exotic Chinese rooms here, which include a scholar's study, a garden, and a reception hall. The institute acquired these period displays in China, and four Chinese artisans accompanied the items to the United States and reassembled them for the MIA. The artisans also installed the Chinese lions guarding the building entrance. The big beasties weigh in at eight tons each and are not hard to miss when driving up to the Institute at 2400 Third Avenue South, (612) 870-3131; www.artsmia.org. Admission to the general collection is free, though the institute sometimes charges an entrance fee for prominent temporary exhibitions.

The metro area has another 35 fine-art, history, and science museums that offer something for every age, such as the **Hennepin Center for the Arts**, 528 Hennepin Avenue South, (612) 332-4478, for upbeat, contemporary artwork. Purchase an Arts and Museum Pass at any of the museums and visit as many as you like. You can pay one price and visit the top cultural facilities in the Twin Cities. It's truly a good deal.

With a plethora of theater seats waiting for patrons, Minneapolis is on the main touring circuit for most of the big, splashy Broadway productions. The city's theaters attract visitors from around the Upper Midwest who come to see major presentations such as *Victor Victoria* and *The Lion King*. Major productions are staged at such marvelous venues as the **Historic State Theatre**, 805 Hennepin Avenue, (612) 339-7007, and the **Orpheum Theatre**, 910 Hennepin Avenue, (612) 339-7007.

Simply walking into the glittering main lobbies of either showplace can be astonishing, especially for little ones who probably have never seen so many glowing light bulbs in all their lives. Mirrors, thick carpeting, and dazzling chandeliers contribute to the sense of upscale place, of a magical world where imaginations are freed.

A number of other hip and trendy playhouses, such as the Hey City Theater, are also located along Hennepin Avenue. Night never seems to end in the hustling and bustling Hennepin Theatre District. The kids will enjoy a stroll along the brightly lit street, ablaze with theatrical dreams and aspirations.

The **Children's Theatre Company** offers a long menu of plays throughout the year, with past productions including *How the Grinch Stole Christmas, The 500 Hats of Bartholomew Cubbins,* and *Once upon an Island.* The troupe is considered one of the best in the country and often travels for overseas performances. In return, it hosts international companies in Minneapolis, which present shows that delightfully erase any nationality or border questions. Kids are just kids when having a great time. Theater groups from China and Russia have been among those coming to the city for these critically acclaimed shows. The productions are usually staged at the Minneapolis Institute of Arts. Call (612) 874-0400 for more information.

The city's regional thrust-stage theater jewel, the **Guthrie Theater**, presents well-reviewed presentations under the aegis of Joe Dowling, the Irish-born artistic director who came to Minneapolis from Dublin's world-famous Abbey Theatre. In 2002, the Guthrie unveiled plans for a fantastic new complex that will be another bright star in the Minneapolis string of entertainment gems. You can find the Guthrie at 725 Vineland Place, (612) 377-2224.

The theater regularly holds programs geared toward families and young adults, with matinees and informal discussion sessions with the actors that make for an interesting, educational vacation experience. Plays range from

An original production of *The Beggar's Strike* at the Minneapolis Children's Theatre Company. —Courtesy of the Children's Theatre Company

Shakespeare's *The Comedy of Errors* to the beloved *A Christmas Carol* by Charles Dickens. Also featured have been wonderful productions such as George Bernard Shaw's *Mrs. Warren's Profession, Six Degrees of Separation* by John Guare, Anton Chekov's riveting *Three Sisters,* and *Top Girls* by Caryl Churchill. Depending on the age and reading level of the kids, these productions—over ice cream/pizza/soda—are grist for family roundtable discussions about art and life.

In addition, to such large venues as the downtown theaters and the Guthrie, more than 30 smaller theater venues are sprinkled throughout the city, presenting shows of all kinds, including cabarets and comedies. While some present mature fare, a young adult can get a kick out of a show at the **Brave New Workshop Theatre**, 3001 and 2605 Hennepin Avenue South. The workshop was founded in 1958, making it one of the oldest satirical companies in the country. Call (612) 338-9467 for information on programs. The theater would be appropriate for the teens in the family, but the younger ones might not understand the humorous digs at politics and today's lifestyles.

THE SPORTING LIFE

Extended families, including grandparents, uncles, aunts, and cousins, as well as ma, pa, and the kids, find that a couple of days at a downtown hotel are fun for a reunion. Now, what if the hotel was housed in the same building as a water park? You can find this unique pairing at the **Depot**, which has a three-story, 185-foot high wet 'n wild water slide. The building, dating from 1899, was part of the main Milwaukee Road train station for generations. You can't miss the massive old structure, which still has plenty of ghosts lurking about from the days of the stream engine. The hotel is at 225 South Third Street, (612) 375-1700.

Minnesotans are ill at ease without ice around them, especially if they are hockey, figure or speed-skating fans. Subsequently the Depot folks knew that they had a good thing going by opening a year-round, glass-enclosed skating rink in the old train depot alongside the main hotel building, (612) 339-2253; www.depotrink.com. Weekenders are welcome to try their twirls and swirls on the ice.

The **Hubert H. Humphrey Metrodome**, home to two of the city's professional sports teams, the Minnesota Twins and Vikings, as well as the University of Minnesota's Golden Gophers football team, is on the eastern edge of downtown at 900 South Fifth Street. The facility is named after the former beloved mayor of Minneapolis and U.S. senator who went on to become vice president of the United States and a Democratic presidential candidate. Taking in a game is a good way to spend part of a visit to the Twin Cities. For schedules, call (612) 335-3370. To get the skinny on what happens behind the scenes at the Metrodome, take the gang on a tour of the facility. Guided walks around the facility are on Wednesdays, Thursdays, and Fridays from April through November. Call (612) 335-3309 for times and other details.

Many local baseball fans don't care for the Dome because they don't feel the sight lines are very good. Visiting outfielders also complain that it is hard to see the ball against the white roof. Be that as it may, attending a game is a blast. Just keep an eye on the young folks in the party because it is easy to get swept up in the rush to and from the seats. Always have an assembly point worked out in advance in such situations and be sure everyone has their seat numbers written down and carried with them at all times.

If other sports are on the calendar, the Minnesota Timberwolves National Basketball Association team and its women's counterpart, the WNBA's Min-

It's All in a Name

Minnehaha was the heroine of Henry Wadsworth Longfellow's famous poem *The Song of Hiawatha*, which he wrote in 1855. She married the handsome title character but eventually died of starvation. Although the poet never saw Minnehaha Falls in Minneapolis' Minnehaha Park, he immortalized the name in his poem.

Getting wet 'n wild at the Depot Water Park in downtown Minneapolis.
—Courtesy of the Depot Water Park

nesota Lynx, play at **Target Center** downtown. The Minnesota Wild professional hockey team does its ice thing over in St. Paul's Xcel Energy Center.

Whether the local heroes win or lose, **Nick's Sports World**, 625 Second Avenue South, claims it is the state's largest athletic supply outlet. The store is full to bursting with its pro and collegiate hats, jerseys, and related accessories for the Minnesota Vikings, Twins, Timberwolves, Lynx, Wild, Golden Gophers, and other teams. This is a real sports-lover's heaven, with enough stuff to cover the largest or smallest fan from topknot to tiptoe. Nick's stays open before and after all Metrodome events to capitalize on the crowds who hunger for that extra-special key-chain or coffee-mug memento. Call (612) 371-0412 or tap into Nick's Web site at www.nickssportsworld.com.

A TOUCH OF NATURE IN THE CITY

While Minneapolis might be the largest city in the state, the city has plenty of quiet places to explore. So, kids. Sssshhhhhh!!! The **Eloise Butler Wildlife Garden and Bird Sanctuary** in Theodore Wirth Park is one of the country's oldest wildflower gardens. Paths meander through marshland, prairies, and woods, providing an eye-catching, wide-ranging rainbow of colors. Guided walks are available on weekdays, with various programs offered on weekends. There are even full- and new-moon hikes under the stars, allowing the youngsters to play furry werewolf on the pathways. Wirth Park includes a five-acre bog with a floating boardwalk that carries the kids across the water to a "quaking" island made of sphagnum moss and shaded by 200 tamarack trees. Within the park, Wirth Winter Recreation Area provides an area for cross-country skiing and snowshoeing. The park is along Wirth Parkway and Plymouth Avenue North, (763) 522-4584.

The **Lake Nokomis Savanna Restoration and Prairie Garden** was planted in 1998 with a variety of grasses and exuberant wildflowers. Three perennial gardens were added near the intersection of Lake Nokomis Parkway and East 50th Street. Alert the kids that the "no picking" rule is in force. The gardens provide plenty of ideas to take home and try out on the back forty. The **Mississippi River Gorge** is another place to find solitude in the city, a place where even the bounciest baby will discover peace and calm. The trails along the eastern side of the gorge, particularly tucked into the bluffs, offer some of the best views in the autumn. West River Parkway is also a wonderful sight, regardless of the season. As forewarned, remember not to pick the flowers.

The **Minneapolis Park and Recreation Board** can provide details of programs in the city's vast park system. Schedules of activities can be obtained by calling (612) 370-4900.

PLACES TO STAY

Best Western Normandy Downtown, 405 South Eighth Street, (612) 370-1400 or (800) 372-3131

Best Western University Inn, 2600 University Avenue S.E., (612) 379-2312

Days Inn, 2407 University Avenue S.E., (612) 623-2288

Hilton-Minneapolis, 1001 Marquette Avenue South, (612) 376-1000

Hilton-Minneapolis North, 2200 Freeway Boulevard, (763) 566-8000 or (800)445-8667

Holiday Inn-Metrodome, 1500 Washington Avenue South, (612) 333-4646

Millennium Hotel, 1313 Nicollet Mall, (612) 332-0371 or (800) 222-8888; www.millennium-hotels.com

Minneapolis Marriott City Center, 30 South Seventh Street, (612) 349-4000

Nicolet Island Inn, 95 Merriam Street, (612) 331-1800

PLACES FOR FOOD

Brit's Pub, 1110 Nicollet Mall, (612) 332-3908

Brothers Delicatessen, 607 Marquette Avenue South, (612) 341-8007

Buca di Beppo, 1204 Harmon Place, (612) 288-0138

Grandmas Saloon & Grill, 1810 Washington Avenue S., (612) 340-0516

Hard Rock Café, 600 Hennepin Avenue, (612) 343-8081 (across the street from the Target Center)

Murray's, 26 South Sixth Street, (612) 339-0909

Pizza Luce, 119 North Fourth Street, (612) 333-7359

Pracna on Main, 117 S.E. Main Street, (612) 379-3200

William's Uptown Pub and Peanut Bar, 2911 Hennepin Avenue South, (612) 823-6271

PLACES TO SHOP

Al-Qalam Islamic Book Center, 2534 Central Avenue N.E., (612) 789-9506

American Swedish Institute Bookstore, 2600 Park Avenue South, (612) 871-4907

Ancient Traders Market, 113 East Franklin Avenue, (612) 870-7555

Antiques Riverwalk, 210 Third Avenue North, (612) 339-9352

Badiner Jewelers, Skyway Level, IDS Center, 80 South Eighth Street at Nicollet Mall, (612) 338-6929

Circa Gallery, 1637 Hennepin Ave South, (612) 332-2386

Creative Kids Stuff, Inc., 4313 Upton Avenue, (612) 927-0653

Flanders Contemporary Art, 400 First Avenue North, Suite 104, (612) 344-1700

Gallery 360, 3011 West 50th Street, (952) 925-2400

Ingebretsen Scandinavian Gifts, 1610 East Lake Street, (612) 729-9333

Intermedia Arts, 2822 Lyndale Avenue South, (612) 871-4444

The Lounge Gallery, 411 Second Avenue North, (612) 333-8800

Marshall Field's, 700 Nicollet Mall, (612) 375-2200

Neiman Marcus, 505 Nicollet Mall, (612) 339-2600

University of Minnesota bookstores: East Bank and Law School stores in Williamson Hall; West Bank store in Blegen Hall; Health Sciences Store in Moos Tower; www.bookstores.umn.edu

Wild Child Cotton Clothes for Kids, 4306 Upton Avenue South, (612) 926-5675

Wild Rumpus Books, 2720 W. 43rd Street, (612) 920-5005; www.wildrumpusbooks.com

FOR MORE INFORMATION

Family Times newspaper (monthly), Box 16422, St. Louis Park 55416, (952) 922-6186

The Greater Minneapolis Convention and Visitors Association, 33 South Sixth Street, Suite 4000, Minneapolis 55402, (800) 445-7412; www.minneapolis.org

Minneapolis Downtown, www.downtownmpls.com

SOUTHERN METROPOLITAN REGION

There's more to life in the southern environs of the Twin Cities than mall sprawl and land-gobbling housing developments. While green space sometimes seems to be a premium in the bedroom communities shadowed by the downtowns of Minneapolis and St. Paul, a determined traveler can find loads o' things to experience in southern Hennepin and northern Dakota and Scott Counties. Look out the car window, stop, and have fun.

FAMILY FUN IN APPLE VALLEY

The community of Apple Valley is only 20 minutes southwest of Minneapolis, with Cedar Avenue (Highway 77/County Highway 23) the main road through town. Even with the towers of the Twin Cities visible in the background, Apple Valley seems worlds away from "civilization." You can tell the kids that tigers, lions, and bears roam the vicinity—well, sort of. The critters aren't actually stalking down the streets, but simply call the 500-acre **Minnesota Zoo** their home. More than 2,000 animals have comfy residences within the sprawling complex, which consists of rolling, wooded hillsides and prairie land. The zoo site is one mile east of Cedar Avenue on County Highway 38.

The zoo is nationally noted for the natural settings that admirably showcase all the local furry, scaly, and hide-bound beasties. There are more than 350 species represented in the facility's marine, forest, tundra, aviary, and farm settings. Among the highlights of the zoo is the Northwest Airlines World of Birds Show, where parrots and other feathered entertainers do their stuff.

The zoo is open 363 days a year (closed Thanksgiving and Christmas Day)—leaving plenty of time for even the pokiest kid to roam the grounds and see the Siberian tigers in their natural habitat. A narrated monorail ride provides kids with a bird's-eye view of much of the zoo. Contact the zoo at 13000 Zoo Boulevard, (800) 366-7811 or (952) 431-9500; www.mnzoo.org.

If the weather turns too cold or rainy during any weekend visit, drop by the six-story IMAX theater on the zoo grounds with grandpa, grandma, the cousins, aunts, uncles, and other kids of all ages. Regularly changing films draw new, neck-craning crowds who love the action inside, whether they explore the Grand Canyon or sweep over a glacier. The films can be white-knuckle experiences for the littlest ones, but are sure to please anyone who has driven with dad on the freeway. Special zoo/IMAX combo and double-feature rates are available, but if guests simply want to visit the theater, single tickets for the IMAX can also be purchased. Hang on to the proverbial hat when that 12,000-watt, digital sound system cranks up. Call (952) 431-IMAX or visit the Web site, www.imax.com/minnesota.

In addition to the zoo, Apple Valley has plenty of other family activities. The **Apple Valley Family Aquatic Center** is loads of fun, especially for the young crowd. The center's Wild Water Playground pool has an average temperature of 83 degrees within its 18,000 square feet,—plenty of room for comfortable hmmm-neat swimming. It's a real rush swooshing down one of the three-story water slides and the steep-drop slides …at least for anyone in the teen level and under. Aw, heck, the whole place is perfect for the young-at-heart, like-to-get-wet crowd. Lifeguards and other attendants keep a close watch on the throngs. Before leaving the house or hotel, everyone should make sure they have along a favorite swimsuit.

If anyone in the family likes a less elevated, slower version of fun, the center has a sand and water playground. It's perfect for a budding young architect wishing to build sandcastles, mini-malls, or mansions. A volleyball court is also available for the bigger kids who want to show off their talents. The center sells an extensive array of gifts, providing a great opportunity to find holiday presents. If all that isn't enough, the center also hosts the **Ring-Around-The-Arts** festival on the first weekend in September, featuring artists from the area. They display and sell their creations, which make great gifts for friends and family back home. Many crafters have low-priced items geared toward junior treasure hunters. The center is at 14421 Johnny Cake Ridge Road, (952) 953-2300.

If the family wants to get away from the rush of daily life for a few days (this is suburbia, after all), the **Lebanon Hills Regional Park** offers 90 campsites tucked amid 2,000 acres. Bring a tent, a couple of campstools, hot dogs, and marshmallows and settle in for the night. It's located at 12100 Johnny Cake Ridge Road, (952) 454-9211. Call (651) 438-4737 for reservations. Teens and parents can also accept the challenge of the municipal **Valleywood Golf Course**, 4851 West 125th Street, (952) 953-2323, with its 18 holes considered among the toughest in the city.

LOTS TO DO IN BLOOMINGTON

With about 100,000 residents, Bloomington is Minnesota's third-largest city. More than a simple Twin City's suburb, the community has wild deer, a ten-mile strip of hotels, one of the state's major nature centers, the country's

Ice fishing on Hyland Lake in Bloomington. —Courtesy of Hennepin Parks

largest enclosed shopping and entertainment complex, and dozens of fine restaurants. It is northwest of Apple Valley via Cedar Avenue.

Let the junior historians in your group know that the city wasn't always so bustling, although it had been a crossroads for generations of Native Americans. The Ojibwe and Dakota lived along the area's rugged bluffs and hunted in the woodlands and river bottoms for centuries. Their children could play in the marshlands, while learning the grownup way of survival. By the turn of the 19th century, French-Canadian trappers were already well acquainted with the natural riches found in the region. Sans kids, however, they explored the length of the Minnesota River and paddled deep into the marshes along Ten-Mile Creek and the extensive chain of lakes that dapple south-central Minnesota.

When the land fell under the control of the fledgling United States, settlers, missionaries, and soldiers flooded into the area. The construction of Fort Snelling, at the confluence of the Minnesota and Mississippi Rivers, ensured the safety of European settlers in the Upper Midwest's nether regions. Irish-born Peter Quinn made friends with area Native American tribes and moved permanently to what would become Bloomington in 1842. Gideon and Samuel Pond soon followed, constructing the city's first school. The brothers' home is now on the National Register of Historic Places and is an interesting place to take the kids for a look back at pioneer life. The house is located at 401 East 104th Street, (952) 948-8881.

The city was incorporated in 1858, the same year that Minnesota became a state. The surrounding countryside, with its lush grasslands, was perfect for

Gathering of Communities

The Twin Cities metropolitan area includes more than six dozen communities, with a total population of 2.7 million.

raising horses. Dan Patch—the famous, record-setting pacer fabled in stories and song—made his home at one palatial estate.

When I-35W and I-494 were constructed in the 1950s and 1960s, Bloomington was off on its own race. Since the two roadways intersect in the city, it became a natural hub for business. And it was no small matter to be the home of the Met Center and Metropolitan Stadium, where the former Minnesota North Stars hockey team, the Minnesota Vikings, and the Minnesota Twins once held forth.

The ultimate one-stop-shop-until-you-drop **Mall of America** opened in 1992 on the site of the old stadium. Almost overnight, it became one of the country's major tourist attractions, annually attracting 40 million visitors and employing 12,000 persons. No need to panic about parking, the mall has 12,750 free parking places in adjoining ramps and lots. The place doesn't seem crowded, however; the sheer size of the place easily accommodates the masses.

If the kids seem rambunctious, tire them out with multiple half-mile walks around the facility (the mall has 4.3 miles of storefront space in all) while checking out the 520 specialty shops and the four anchor department stores: Bloomingdale's, Macy's, Nordstrom, and Sears. The mall's four main "streets" are named North Garden, West Market, South Avenue, and East Broadway. The kids will love **Al's Farm Toys**, on the third floor west, (952) 858-9139, for collectible Breyer Horses, toy tractors, chicken figurines, caps, construction toys, and loads of other kid stuff. Then there's the **Basic Brown Bear Factory**, (800) 396-BEAR, where you can select a teddy bear, stuff it, and then groom and dress the little beast. The shop has more than 30 characters and 40 outfits from which to chose. The store is located near the east entrance of the mall, on the first level not far from Sears.

Before plunging into the crowd of shoppers and lookers, make sure you put together a family plan. If the kids are on their own, set up a meeting place and a designated time to report in to mom or dad. Be sure that everyone's timepieces are synchronized and they know exactly where to be at the planned meeting time. While well laid out, the mall is a busy place and young folks need to be responsible and to check in when required.

So what's there for the kids to do once inside? You could have their teeth checked in the dentist's office or get their school physical at the doctor's office. You can't do better than that. But they'll have more fun at the seven-acre **Knott's Camp Snoopy** with its Ferris wheel, roller coaster, and other rock-about rides.

Knott's Camp Snoopy is as busy as an anthill during picnic season. Youngsters scamper amid the 400 planted trees, dart between the 30,000 plants and

Coming face-to-face with some denizens of Shark Cove at the Mall of America's Underwater Adventures. —Courtesy of Underwater Adventures

floral displays, and cavort on the verge-of-vertigo attractions such as the Mighty Axe and Paul Bunyan's Log Chute. Ghostblasters, a dark ride with plenty of thrills and chills within its secret recesses, is guaranteed to bring a scream (of delight) or two. Call (952) 883-8600 or visit www.campsnoopy.com.

For the oldsters, if wedding bells beckon during a shopping frenzy, the mall's Chapel of Love is available for the exchanging of vows. Since opening in 1994, more than 3,000 couples have tied the knot there.

The mall's hands-on **Underwater Adventures** is another popular indoor enticement. Some 3,000 denizens of the deep and the shallow—including alligator gar, sea turtles, and sharks—paddle, swim, and float in the aquarium's 1.2 million gallons of water. On-site programs include tours, classes, and visiting marine experts. At Sharky's Kids Club, participating youngsters receive two free tickets for future admissions, each with a paid adult admission. If the 7-to-12 age set still hasn't had enough of all that water, sleepovers are available. (952) 853-0612 or (888) DIVE-TIME; www.underwaterworld.com.

Speaking of sleeping over, no visitor to Bloomington ever need be without a place to stay. It offers Minnesota's largest concentration of hostelries, with at least 35 hotels near the Mall of America, with more than 7,000 guestrooms in all price ranges.

Even with all the build-up, Bloomington has reserved one-third of its area for parks and recreation. Those 45 square miles include a national wildlife refuge and the Hyland Lake Park Reserve. The **Japanese Garden** at Normandale Community College has a waterfall, arched bridges, and an eye-soothing lagoon. It's a quiet place to unwind after a hectic summer day tramping around the Mall of America.

The **Minnesota Valley National Wildlife Refuge**, 3815 East 80th Street, (952) 854-5900, which takes up most of Bloomington's southern border, consists of some 8,000 acres. Best of all, it is only a few blocks from the big mall. Indoor exhibits complement the outdoor prairie restoration and nature trails through the Minnesota River bottomlands. The refuge is one of the best areas in the Twin Cities for bike riding (bring your own cycles), cross-country skiing (in season), hiking, and bird watching. This is a great place to show young people how wildlife can be protected even in an urban environment.

The 1,000-acre **Hyland Lake Park Preserve** and adjacent Bush Lake are big draws for Twin Citians who love the outdoors. Kids appreciate the lighted cross-country ski trails for night forays into the woods, and they will also get excited about hitting the slopes at the fairly challenging downhill ski area in the park. These hills are especially suited for keeping limber and for practicing cool moves—perfect for the teen set.

The wildlife refuge and preserve serve another important duty: They air out the kids who might have spent too much time inside the confines of the overstimulating Mall of America. A trek amid the cattails and wildflowers does wonders toning down the energy released by the mall's bells and whistles.

FAMILY FUN IN EAGAN

This southern suburb was only designated a city in 1974, though the area became known as the "Onion Capital of the Nation" way back in the 1880s due to its bountiful harvests of the tear-jerking veggie. Those days are long gone, with the spread of new homes and shops covering the former farmland. The city's proximity to the Twin Cities and the international airport makes it a swell home base for Northwest Airlines and other major corporations. It is southeast of Bloomington via I-494 East to County Highway 31 South (Pilot Knob Road). Let the Scouts in the family act as guides. Just follow a map, and you'll arrive in fine shape.

Eagan hosts many festivals throughout the year. The **Candy Cane Corral**, held at the beginning of December, is one of the best kid-friendly events. Kids can scrounge for candy canes in a haystack, ride ponies, and visit Santa, that jolly old elf, when he arrives in his horse-drawn sleigh (weather permitting) at the **Diamond T Ranch**. During the nonwinter season, The Diamond T offers trail rides, riding lessons, and hayrides. The complex is located at 4889 Pilot Knob Road, (651) 454-1464.

Yet when the kids are more in the mood for a watery seahorse ride on a Saturday or Sunday, try out the water slides at the **Cascade Bay Water Park**, 3830 Pilot Knob Road, (651) 681-4777; www.cascadebay.com. Splish, splash, a whole lotta whooping goes on when the young ones come whizzing down the curvy slides into the cool pools—particularly refreshing on humid summer days. Take a bet on who will make it through the Hurricane and the Typhoon. The kids can then expend whatever energy is left by streaming each other with water cannons.

Football fans are also accommodated, with free roundtrip shuttle service to the Metrodome for hotel guests booking the EXTRAordinary Eagan Special during Vikings games. Call (800) EAGAN-20 for a free Eagan guide and coupons or check online at www.eaganmn.com.

SHAKE IT UP IN SHAKOPEE

Shakopee's **Valleyfair** might be described as an amusement park, but that's like saying the Himalayas are hills. The park is the largest in the Upper Midwest, spreading its 75 rides over 90 acres, along with stage shows, food stands galore, and who knows what else. It even has a special area, **Challenge Park**, for thrill seekers who want the tops in stomach-churning rides. These are guaranteed to supercharge any kids on the prowl for a ride with an extra dose of thrills and chills. How about the 250-foot Power Tower that has a turbo drop guaranteed to launch one's stomach into the brain? Thank heavens there are tamer rides that only turn hangers-on upside down. Valleyfair's **Whitewater Country** water park has 3.5 acres of splish-splashing activities for those hot days of midsummer. The whole huge facility is located at 1 Valleyfair Drive, (800) FUN-RIDE or (952) 445-7600; www.valleyfair.com. Shakopee is about 10 miles west of Eagan on Highway 101/13.

For those adventurers who prefer the strolling sports, such as golf, Shakopee can cater to their needs as well. The **Stonebrook Country Club** is a championship 18-holer spread over wetlands and hills. Golfers even need to take a ferryboat from the eighth hole to make the next shot. The teen golfer in the gang should enjoy that leg o' the links.

For much faster-paced action on your Shakopee visit, **Canterbury Park Racetrack** promises action for all ages. Kids love watching the thoroughbreds gallop around the track, while parents can try their hand at the betting booths. Canterbury also hosts other events, such as boat shows, computer exhibitions, dances, and art fairs. In October, the park's Spooky World is filled with live actors and special effects in several haunted houses graded by their "scream effect." That way, moms and dads can determine the nightmare level of the

Something Fishy in Minnesota

The most popular sport fish in Minnesota are walleyes, trout, northern pike, crappies, and bass. Many anglers prefer "catch and release" plans, whereby the fish can live to tell about the time it got away.

youngsters in tow. For winter, the track is home to snowmobile racing. It's located at 1100 Canterbury Road (Highway 83), (800) 340-6361 or (952) 445-7223; www.canterburypark.com.

Raceway Park, 6528 East Highway 101, has been part of the Shakopee scene for more than four decades. Late-model, hobby stocks, and other types of speedster vehicles whiz around the figure-eight–shaped track or semi-banked quarter-mile oval. As part of the NASCAR circuit, divisional races are run on Sunday evenings from April through September, much to the delight of kids who love cars. They'll remember the muscular roar of the heavy-duty engines long after race day. Call (952) 445-2257 or visit www.goracewaypark.com.

The **Minnesota Renaissance Festival** takes young guests from its physical site a mere three miles from downtown Shakopee and plops them down into the Middle Ages. Knights battle, jesters joke, kings rule, and ladies are in waiting. From mid-August through late-September weekends, the festival brings alive a colorful era of history that's been re-created in countless movies. Stroll through the festival shops and discover the perfect shield and sword to bring home to impress the neighbors. The Minnesota Renaissance Festival steps back in time at 12364 Chestnut Boulevard, (952) 445-7361. Don't be surprised if the youngsters play King Arthur for a week after a visit to the fest.

Yet if the family doesn't want to go that far back in time, there's always historic **Murphy's Landing**, 2187 East Highway 101, (952) 445-6901. Costumed interpreters present history as if it was their own life story, which makes for a subtle way to teach kids about the good old days. Depicting a boomtown settlement of the 1800s, the site is along the lazy Minnesota River. Forty historic buildings range from log cabins to Victorian-era homes. Events throughout the year include a fur-traders' rendezvous and a holiday folklore festival where the kids are encouraged to see how people lived in the area during the 18th and 19th centuries.

OTHER THINGS TO SEE AND DO

Burnsville, east of Shakopee on Highway 101/13, was settled by Irish farmers in the mid-1800s. From a few frontier stores in that era, the community blossomed into the state's fourth largest retail area for a total shop-till-you-drop experience. Visitors, no matter what age, can go back to the early days by rambling through **Antiques Minnesota**, with its 350 dealers peddling collectibles and honest-to-goodness valuable old stuff. For more modern stuff, the **Burnsville Center** hosts 170 stores, from large national chains to smaller independents. So you old-timers, break out the wallets (the kids should do the same with their piggy banks). In September, Burnsville hosts its annual Festive Fire Muster, with a parade of fire trucks. So if there is still money burning a hole in a visitor's pocket after all that shopping, the firefighters on duty will help save the day. What kid doesn't love the romantic sight of a fire engine?

Chanhassen, northwest of Burnsville via Highway 101/13, is home to the **Minnesota Landscape Arboretum**, where tiptoeing through the tulips is a state

A lucky lad getting knighted at the Minnesota Renaissance Festival in Shakopee.
—Courtesy of Mid-America Festivals

of mind for the youthful set. More than 60 plant collections and 22 display gardens are part of the extensive exhibits set amid the facility's 1,000 acres. When the garden's 200 crab-apple trees blossom in the spring, the perfume is delightfully heady. The arboretum can be discovered by walking, driving, or on skis (in the winter, naturally). A three-mile drive meanders amid the trees and tulip beds, with biking trails covering about 12 miles of cycling possibilities. Have the kids stop and really smell the roses. The arboretum is at 3675 Arboretum Drive, (952) 443-1400; www.arboretum.umn.edu.

Lakeville, abutting Burnsville on the south, calls itself a "city with small town charm and a big town heart." Four golf courses, the Ames Ice Arena, the

Ritter Farm Park nature preserve, and the nearby **Murphy-Hanrehan Park Reserve** (home of the state's only nesting area of hooded warblers) ensure outdoor adventure of all kinds for everyone in your clan. Augmenting those sites are the community's nine lakes and 57 parks, with more than 60 miles of pedestrian walkways and bike paths meandering around the waterways. For winter rambling, the parks have 25 miles of cross-country ski trails and warming huts to stave off the blustery winds. Kids enjoy the outdoors, but snuggling up next to something warm after a day in the snow is always appreciated. The preserve's operations office is at 15501 Murphy Lane Road, (952) 941-7922.

PLACES TO STAY

APPLE VALLEY
AmericInn Hotel and Suites, 1500 Glazier Avenue (Highway 77/County Road 42), (888) 489-STAY or (952) 431-3800; www.americinn.com

BLOOMINGTON
Best Western Thunderbird Hotel and Convention Center, 2201 East 78th Street, (952) 854-3411

Courtyard by Marriott-Mall of America, 7800 Bloomington Avenue South, (800) 321-2211 or (952) 876-0100

Radisson Hotel South and Plaza Tower, 7800 Normandale Boulevard, (800) 333-3333 or (952) 835-7800

EAGAN
Budget Host Inn, 2745 Highway 55, (800) Bud-Host or (651) 454-1211

Hampton Inn of Eagan, 3000 Eagandale Place, (800) HAMPTON or (651) 688-3343; hieagan@ncghotels.com

Holiday Inn Express Hotel and Suites, 1950 Rahncliff Court, (800) 681-5290 or (651) 681-9266; info@holidayinneagan.com

Homestead Studio Suites, 3015 Denmark Avenue, (651) 905-1778; mgregn@styhsd.com

Sleep Inn, 4510 Erin Drive , (800) 617-3262 or (651) 681-1770; jiseepinneagan@aol.com

SHAKOPEE
AmericInn Lodge and Suites, 4100 Twelfth Avenue, (952) 445-6775 or (800) 634-3444; www.americinn.com

Budget Host Inn, 2745 Highway 55, (800) BUD-HOST or (651) 454-1211

Park Inn and Suites, 1244 Canterbury Road, (952) 445-3644

PLACES FOR FOOD

APPLE VALLEY
Grizzly's Grill N' Saloon, 15020 Glazier Avenue, (952) 431-3216

Old Chicago Pasta and Pizza, 14998 Glazier Avenue, (952) 891-4600

Perkins Family Restaurant, 7620 West 150th Street, (952) 432-0626

Rascals Apple Valley Bar and Grill, 7721 West 147th Street, (952) 431-7777

BLOOMINGTON
North and South Food Courts, Mall of America, 60 East Broadway

Alamo Grill, Mall of America, (952) 854-7456

Cafe Odyssey, Mall of America, (952) 854-9400

Planet Hollywood, Mall of America, (952) 854-7827

Rainforest Café, Mall of America, (952) 854-7500

EAGAN
Al Bakers, 3434 Washington Drive, (651) 454-9000

Carbonne's Pizza, 1665 Yankee Doodle Road, (651) 452-6000

Sidney's, 3330 Pilot Knob Road, (651) 454-6400

SHAKOPEE
Applebee's, 1568 Vierling Drive East, (952) 233-3400

Culver's, 4058 12th Avenue East, (952) 233-4141

Papa Murphy's Pizza, 1106 Vierling Drive East, (952) 445-8118

Sambroso Mexican Restaurant, 1120 First Avenue East, (952) 445-0900

PLACES TO SHOP

BLOOMINGTON
Mall of America, 60 East Broadway, Bloomington, MN 55425,
(952) 883-8800; www.mallofamerica.com

Stores to follow are located in the Mall of America:

Abercrombie & Fitch, (952) 851-0911

Air Traffic, (952) 858-9599

Al's Farm Toys, (952) 858-8949

American Eagle Outfitters, (952) 854-4788 or 851-9011

Hot Topic, (952) 858-9150 (Hot Topics are also located in Blaine, Minnetonka, Burnsville, and Eden Prairie)

Wet Seal, (952) 851-0966 (also in Burnsville and Eden Prairie)

BURNSVILLE
Air Traffic, Burnsville Center, County Road 42 & 35W, Burnsville, (952) 435-2868

SHAKOPEE
Lady Di Antiques, 126 South Holmes Street, (952) 445-1238

Shakopee Trading Post, 723 First Avenue West, (952) 496-2263

FOR MORE INFORMATION

Apple Valley Tourism Bureau, 7300 West 147th Street, Suite 101, Apple Valley 55124, (800) 301-9435 or 952-432-8422; www.avmnchamber.org

Bloomington Convention and Visitors Bureau, 7900 International Drive, Suite 990, Bloomington 55425, (800) 346-4289 or (952) 858-8500; www.bloomingtonmn.org

Burnsville Convention and Visitors Bureau, 101 West Burnsville Parkway, Suite 150B, Burnsville 55337, (800) 521-6055 or (952) 898-5646; www.burnsvillemn.com

Eagan Convention and Visitors Bureau, 1474 Yankee Doodle Road, Eagan 55121-1801, (800) EAGAN-20 or (651) 452-9872; www.eaganmn.com

Lakeville Convention and Visitors Bureau, 20730 Holyoke Avenue, Lakeville 55044, (888) 525-3845 or (952) 469-2020; www.visitlakeville.org

Shakopee Area Convention and Visitors Bureau, 1801 East County Road 101, Box 717, Shakopee 55044, (800) 574-2150 or (952) 445-1660; www.shakopee.org

ST. PAUL

St. Paul had an inauspicious beginning as a riverboat stopover called "Pig's Eye Landing," recalling the nickname of local French-Canadian merchant Pierre "Pig's Eye" Parrant, who had a small store here. When Father Lucian Caltier built St. Paul's chapel in 1840, local leaders figured the moniker of the good saint would probably attract more business to the settlement than trader Parrant's rough-around-the-edges appellation. And so it was, when the town was incorporated in 1849 and received its city charter in 1954. Today, the only reminder of "Pig's Eye" Parrant is a hometown beer named in his honor. Nevertheless, the kids should have little trouble remembering his nickname.

The city's fathers and mothers of today now more readily point to the creative people at Minnesota Mining and Manufacturing (3M) who invented and produced the Post-It note, Scotch Tape, and a host of other household products that kids will readily recognize, rather than to good ol' Pig's Eye. St. Paulites can also be proud of the many other advances the city has made since it was first settled.

Today, the city covers 56 square miles, including three square miles of inland water or quality park action. It is the county seat of Ramsey County and the capital of Minnesota. The imposing state capitol is high above the city at the north end of Wabasha Avenue. Often, budding young artists and photographers are seen on the surrounding parkland sketching, painting, or taking photos for class art projects. Nearby are the Cathedral of St. Paul and the home of railroad financier James J. Hill, completing a powerful triumvirate of church, state, and business that made St. Paul such a powerhouse in the Upper Midwest over the generations. The small fry will definitely be impressed by the size of both sites.

ST. PAUL: PAST AND PRESENT, OLD AND NEW

St. Paul has always had its eye on the past while looking to the future. Beginning in the 1960s, the city began an extension downtown renovation, with such major building projects as the Capitol Centre, a 12-block spread of new apartments and office buildings; the Town Square Project; Galtier Plaza; the 37-story World Trade Center; and the renovation of the Landmark Center. Work is still ongoing all throughout the downtown, along the river, and into the neighborhoods. A new $10 million skyway-tunnel pedestrian link between the **RiverCentre** convention district and the downtown skyway system was completed in the summer of 2002. This makes for perfect exploring by excited children. The main section of the tunnel features colorful murals and other public art. The additions make it even easier to roam the entire downtown when blustery weather roars down from the North Woods on chilly winter days. Lead the kids through the extensive network of skyways that make livin' easy in St. Paul, regardless of the time of year. They won't even get sunburned.

Nowhere is the city's colorful past and vibrant contemporary scene as evident as in its ethnic makeup. The city is a mishmash of cultures, with a large percentage of residents claiming Irish heritage; the community's St. Patrick's Day parade in March is one of the largest in the Midwest. Others are German and Scandinavian, with more and more African Americans, Hispanic, and Native American citizens moving to town. Hmong and Thais, as well as refugees from Ethiopia and Somalia, present a young, new look to the city's face.

The multinational student bodies of the University of Minnesota–St. Paul Campus, St. Catherine's, Hamline, Concordia, St. Thomas, Macalester, and other institutions of higher learning bring even more mental, cultural, athletic, and youthful vibrancy to the scene. The neighborhoods around each of these schools, such as the Grand Avenue area around Macalester, are wall-to-wall with coffeehouses, cheap eats, trendy stores, bookshops, and small theaters geared toward the college set, their visiting parents, and wide-eyed younger siblings. The streets are often crowded with high school seniors and their moms and dads taking a few days off to explore St. Paul on college visitation trips.

SAMPLING THE PAST

To start off a family vacation in St. Paul, begin with a bit o' class and show the kids what hotels used to look like. Take the crew to the elegant Saint Paul Hotel, 350 Market Street, and experience the lobby tea service there. It's a chance to dress up and behave accordingly. Despite some possible protestations from the bouncier set, they'll get into the swing of things when the hotel's luxurious blend of hot chocolate arrives at tableside. Adults can indulge in the tea, served on bone china. Victorian teas—actually five-course meals—are held 3–5 p.m., Fridays and Saturdays, with a different theme each month. Romantic harp music provides the background ambience under the glittering Waterford chandeliers. Reservations are required. Call the hotel at (651) 292-9292.

If your youngsters find the Saint Paul Hotel a touch on the sedate side, take them to **Mickey's Dining Car**, a downtown holdover from years past. You can still provide them with a bit of historical nourishment, but this time accompanied by a burger and fries. The eatery is located at 36 West Seventh Street, (651) 222-5633.

For a touch of real history, escort the crew through the Minnesota Historical Society's **Minnesota History Center** museum at 345 West Kellogg Boulevard. The structure, built of Rockville granite and Winona limestone, overlooks downtown St. Paul. Among the many exhibits, "Sounds Good to Me: Music in Minnesota" explains how music affects the listener. Kids also can shop in the society's two stores and take a snack break in Cafe Minnesota where breakfast, lunch, and Sunday brunch are also served. For details on exhibits, tours, and the society's extensive library, call (651) 296-6126 or have the computer-literate members of the household use the historical society's Web site at www.mnhs.org.

Tours of the nearby **State Capitol** drop the family into the heart of Minnesota's legislative world, with its marble halls, bright chandeliers, and massive woodwork. Metered parking is available at Lot Q, north of the building at Cedar Street and Sherburne Avenue. Parking spaces can also be found in Lot D next to the State Office Building at Cedar Street and Constitution Avenue. But if a full day of touring is planned, use Lot Q or the Centennial Ramp orange level on Constitutional Avenue between Cedar and Roberts Streets. That way, there won't be worries about snag-

The Minnesota Music exhibit at the Minnesota Historical Society's History Center.
—Courtesy of the Minnesota Historical Society

ging a parking ticket and getting a ragging from the backseat gang. The capitol building is north of downtown at 75 Constitution Avenue, easily reached from I-94 and I-35E. Call (651) 296-2881 to confirm times for tours, which are held weekdays and Sundays.

During a refurbishment of the capitol building, art conservator Dan Tarnoveanu removed 22 layers of paint in the facility's old rathskeller cafe. He uncovered some lovely decorative work that brought the place back to its 1905 glory. Young artists in the family may find that process fascinating. Many sayings in German decorate the ceiling and walls honoring the thousands of German immigrants to the state. The cafe now has a new kitchen and extended hours for breakfast, lunch, and take-out.

After roaming the hallowed halls of the historical society and the capitol, drive the kids along nearby Summit Avenue. The thoroughfare was once home to noted author F. Scott Fitzgerald and is now considered to be one of the longest stretches of well-kept Victorian homes in the country. Someday, the youngsters might be reading some of the author's magnificent prose, and maybe some of the older ones are doing just that now. So a drive down Summit helps put some

Minnesota's First Newspaper

Some people consider the state's first newspaper to be the *Minnesota Register,* which claimed on its masthead it was printed in St. Paul on April 27, 1849. Actually, it was printed in Cincinnati, Ohio, two weeks earlier than that date. The Ohio-based publisher was vying with another upstart paper, the *Pioneer,* to be the first to reach the streets. And so the *Register's* first issue came out a day earlier than that of the *Pioneer,* which was printed in Minnesota. That paper was the forerunner of today's *Saint Paul–Pioneer Press.*

reality into Fitzgerald, highlighting that he was a real person who spent his early years in St. Paul. Although not open to the public, the house where Fitzgerald wrote his first novel *This Side of Paradise* is located at 599 Summit Avenue.

FORT SNELLING

The children will love stepping back even further into St. Paul's history with a visit to Fort Snelling, a restored stone fortress dating to the 1820s. The complex was once the center of trading and military activity along the Upper Mississippi River. When the United States took over the Upper Mississippi River valley after the Revolutionary War and solidified its political hold through the Louisiana Purchase, Fort Snelling was one of a chain of forts that extended from Lake Michigan to the Missouri River. The fort, named after its commander, Colonel Josiah Snelling, was completed in 1825. Snelling's men built roads, a gristmill, and a sawmill, and farmed the area. As more settlers poured into the area, the town that sprouted nearby grew into today's vibrant city of St. Paul.

Touring the old fort takes youngsters into the past: They can learn about frontier life as seen through the eyes of the men and women living there. The "soldiers" are costumed interpreters who evoke the rough day-to-day life of another era. Children can shoulder a musket, participate in a sing-along, try their hand at mending clothes, and even sip tea with an officer's wife. There is plenty of cannon firing, along with squalling fifes and pounding drums, to keep any tousled sleepyheads wide awake.

Family Fun Days are held on Memorial Day and Labor Day weekends, with "An Evening at Fort Snelling" programs scheduled once a month for families. Special hands-on activities involve kids in a variety of frontier experiences and crafts. For the souvenir-conscious, gift shops are located in the Fort Snelling History Center, as well as in the historic fort. Maps of the fort, books, foods, and frontier toys can be purchased. In the fort's store, youngsters can dicker with the shopkeeper for items and down a frosty root beer. Plan on spending at least a half day here in order to explore all there is to see and do within the

Kids getting a lesson about Minnesota's frontier days at historic Fort Snelling.
—Courtesy of the Minnesota Historical Society

compound's thick walls. A full day is not out of the question, if the gang really gets into the fun.

There is more to Fort Snelling than the old fortification. **Fort Snelling State Park** includes the forested riverbanks along the Mississippi and Minnesota Rivers, with their cottonwoods, ash, and willow framing the paths here. A naturalist leads interpretive programs year-round at the Pike Island information center, focusing on the geology, animals, and plants in the area. Snowshoe hikes are held in the winter to show life in the urban wilds when Old Man Winter is up and about. The treks are not so strenuous that kids or older adults couldn't make them. In the spring and summer, other courses demonstrate how to find edible wild plants. The park has 150 picnic sites; fishing; miles of hiking, biking, and ski trails; a polo grounds; a golf course; and canoe access on Snelling Lake. For more information, contact the park manager, Highway 5 and Post Road, (651) 727-1961. The park is located on the opposite side of the Mississippi River from St. Paul, across the highway from the Fort Snelling National Cemetery and the international airport. Watch for the signs along Highway 5: The multitude of highway curves, loops, and off-on ramps in this stretch of roadway can be tricky.

BACK TO THE PRESENT

For more "modern" activities, the **Minnesota Children's Museum** is the place to hang out for several hours. Youngsters can climb, jump, pull, push, and learn as they gallop through the museum's six galleries. Two additional galleries host such temporary displays as "Playing Together: Games," which ex-

Hot Idea Takes Flight

In 1862, Count Ferdinand von Zeppelin had some extra time on his hands while stationed at Fort Snelling as a German military attaché. He dreamed of a lighter-than-air craft and in 1864 made his first hot-air balloon ascension at the fort. He returned to Germany and continued to refine his invention. Eventually, the name "zeppelin" became associated with the giant airships that traveled the skies for a brief period in the early 20th century.

plored the history of games. The show was developed by the Children's Museum of Memphis and toured the country.

All the museum's ongoing exhibits are geared toward kids, from toddlers to 10 year olds, earning kudos for its range of learning experiences. It is considered one of the top 10 such kids' facilities in the United States. Kids love crawling through the giant anthill or building something really neat in the Inventor's Workshop. The entire family is encouraged to join the fun. The Bedtime Books program on Thursday evenings is particularly popular with some parents: The program features storytellers and readings designed to get kids dozing. All parents have to do is then lug the sleepers back to the hotel.

The museum, 10 West Seventh Street, is at the corner of Seventh and Wabasha Streets in downtown St. Paul, easily reached either I-94 or I-35E. Call (651) 225-6000 for recorded information or (651) 225-6001 to talk with a staff person.

The **Science Museum of Minnesota**, also in the downtown area, at 120 West Kellogg Boulevard, houses nearly two million artifacts in its 370,000 square feet of exhibit space. Families on holiday can spend time in the Omnitheater or the 3-D laser theater, then roam the galleries for hours to marvel at the dinosaur bones and reproductions of giant body parts. A trip to the Science Museum of Minnesota is not complete without a stop in the Explore Store. Kids will enjoy browsing through a wide variety of science-related books, posters, educational pieces, and mementos of the popular museum. The Elements Café offers vittles for the hungry mammals and an incredible view of the Mississippi River. Call (651) 221-9444; www.smm.org.

THE PERFECT PARK

Everyone enjoys wandering the trails around St. Paul's Como Lake with Spot or Fido or having a family picnic on the expansive grounds. Relaxing at a concert in the Lakeside Pavilion after a full day of golfing makes for a value-added chance to unwind. Musical shows and plays are often regularly featured here through the summer. You can also rent bikes and paddleboats at the pavilion.

When leaving the pups at home, stop at the **Como Park Zoo**. Numerous education sessions for toddlers, school-age kids, and adults have helped make the complex one of the most viable in the Upper Midwest. And the animals learn,

Crawling through a giant anthill maze at the Minnesota Children's Museum.
—Courtesy of the Minnesota Children's Museum

too. In an effort to get animals to voluntarily participate in their medical care, trainers teach them to lift their paws or flippers in return for a treat. This makes it less stressful when doctors are checking on the creatures or tending to a wound or illness. Zoo guests can watch this husbandry training at 1 p.m., Tuesday through Sunday at Seal Island.

The zoo participates in trades and loans of animals with other zoos around the world, so there are always new things to see. In 2002, the St. Paul facility received a two-year-old giraffe on loan from the San Diego Zoo for breeding purposes. Two female Siberian tigers were secured from the Indianapolis Zoo.

For questions, be sure to visit the Customer Service Office in the visitor center, situated between the Wolf Woods parking lot and the Primate House on the Zoo grounds. The office is open daily. It's also a good place to go when looking for lost children. Often-needed restrooms are located in the African Hoofed Stock Facility, in the Como Conservatory near Seal Island and in the amusement ride area. A few portable toilets are spotted around the grounds where construction is taking place. Strollers are available for rent at the Zoodale Gift shop in the visitor center. Call (651) 487-8233.

The facility is open 365 days of the year, with hours from 10 a.m. to 6 p.m., April 1 to September 30. Winter hours are 10 a.m. to 6 p.m., October 31 to March 31. Be aware that during bad weather, some exhibits may be shuttered. The zoo and parking are free.

There's always something additional at the **Como Park Conservatory**, the largest glass-domed botanical garden in the region. Located in St. Paul's Como Park, the garden occupies one-half acre under glass, and includes the seasonal one acre **Como Ordway Memorial Japanese Garden** designed by Nagaski's Masami Matsuda to the north, and the Enchanted Garden and Frog Pond Landscape to the east. The Conservatory is open year-round, with a varied schedule of events and workshops for kids and adults. During the winter months, this is a great place to go to get out of the Minnesota cold. With temperatures set warmer to accommodate the multitude of tropical plants, the family might mistake the place for Florida—just for a second. The Japanese garden is open from May 1 through September 30. The Conservatory has a dollar donation for juniors and adults, 13 to 64 years old and a 50-cent donation for kids (6 to 12) and seniors over 65. Toddlers under 5 are free.

The refurbished Cafesjian's Carousel is a popular attraction in the park. To find this magnificent example of wood carving and plain old-fashioned fun, follow signs in the park to the Conservatory. The carousel pavilion is just to the south. Built in 1914, the carousel is open only seasonally, however. Once based at the Minnesota State Fair, the carousel was going to be dismantled and sold in the late 1980s. But area donors saved it and it was placed in St. Paul's downtown and then moved to an indoor site at Como Park in 2000. Tickets are $1.50 for riders 1-year-old and over. Everyone must have a ticket.

Other park favorites include the redone **O'Neil's Amusement Rides**, open again in 2003 after being closed for an extended renovation. The young ones and teens love the Putt'er There Mini Golf, as well. For ma, pa and the bigger kids, the 18-hole Como Park course offers additional challenges.

Historical Como Park and Zoo is located off Lexington Parkway and Horton Avenue in St. Paul. The zoo office address is 1250 Kaufman Drive North and the Conservatory office address is 1325 Aida Place. The park extends on both sides of Lexington Avenue, with the lake and pavilion located east of Lexington. For additional details, call the 24-hour information line at 651-487-8200 or customer service at 651-487-8201. The park Web site has maps and directions from all parts of the Twin Cities. Visit www.stpaul.gov/depts/parks/comopark.

The City of Saint Paul, Division of Parks and Recreation has many other great places to visit and fun activities for the whole family to enjoy. There are over 160 parks and open spaces, 41 recreation centers, three 18 hole golf courses, 24 bicycle and pedestrian paths, one indoor pool and two outdoor pools, a public beach, and a sports dome.

The Division of Parks and Recreation offers athletic, recreational, educational, environmental, and social activities among its many programs for all kids of ages. For further information call the main office at (651) 266-6400 or visit www.stpaul.gov/depts/parks.

SUMMERTIME FUN

After spending two decades tearing up the grounds of Wisconsin State Capitol, the **Taste of Minnesota** moved to Harriet Island Regional Park on the Mississippi River. Celebrating its 21st anniversary year in 2003, the event continues to be one of the best freebies in the Twin Cities. Always starting July 3 and running for a week, the festival offers lots of music, with sounds leaning toward oldies. But the dozens of food booths and nightly fireworks, beginning around 10:30 p.m., are often worth the visit. Be sure to bring sunscreen, bug spray and loads o' bucks for the grub. You must purchase tickets for food, beverages, and rides, which have been $5. Food tends toward the quick and easy, requiring napkins. Sometimes, an extra load of disposable towelettes comes in hand to clean tiny sticky fingers. The older kids can fend for themselves.

Where at the Capitol, you might have circled for hours looking for a parking spot, the new site offers plenty of space. Paid lots range along Plato Boulevard and Water Street on the approach to the facility. There might be some street parking but don't bet on it, especially if you have tykes and elders along for the ride. They probably don't appreciate what might be a long haul walking to the entrance. Parking is also available in downtown ramps at River-Centre, the Science Museum, Victory Ramp and others. These are just a short walk to the Wabasha Street Bridge, which connects to the walking path leading to the site. The park address is 107 Water Street, St. Paul.

Here are a few easy directions for orientation. From Minneapolis in the west, get on eastbound I-94. Take the 5th Street exit to downtown St. Paul. Follow 5th Street to St. Peter Street and turn right. Travel two blocks to Kellogg Boulevard and turn left. Go one block and turn right onto the Wabasha Street Bridge. Cross the Mississippi River and turn left (east) on Water Street immediately across the bridge. Turn left on Levee Road and follow the signs. From the east, take westbound I-94. Head south on US Highway 52 (Lafayette Bridge) and exit at Plato Boulevard. Turn right on Plato and follow it until the park comes into view. From the north on I-35E, head south on Highway 52 and exit at Plato Boulevard. Turn right onto Plato and follow it until you see Harriet Island. From the south., Highway 52 crosses I-494 about eight miles east of the Mall of America. Head north on 52 and exit at Plato Boulevard. Turn left onto Plato and follow it until to the grounds.

Once there and organized, you still need to keep an eye on any of the kids less than four feet tall because the crowds surge back and forth between the food and music. Twenty-somethings often don't watch where they are going and toddlers' toes can be trampled. The wide-open river site, however, should alleviate a lot of the bumping and crowding that was a hassle in past years. This is a great place for teens to preen and meander. Even grandma might find someone for a coquettish wink and a nod. To be safe, find a central location for reunions if the boppers get to be free from ma and pa for a while. For information about the event, contact the Taste at 651-722-9980; http://www.tasteofmn.org.

The **Minnesota State Fair** is one of the nation's largest, attracting 1,693,460 persons in 2002. It showcases the best the state has in agricultural products, school and 4H projects, livestock, and plain ol' fun such as the amateur talent contest, as well as the grandstand shows.

There's a long history to all this, with four years of territorial fairs before the first Minnesota State Fair was held in 1859, the year Minnesota was granted statehood. Before moving to its current site, the early fairs were held on a lot near what became downtown Minneapolis.

A good place to start at the fair is to stop at one of the many information booths and load up on free maps and brochures. Don't forget the accessibility guides and entertainment schedules. Even if you try hard questions, it is tough to stump the folks who work in the info areas.

The fair is usually held the final week of August and runs through Labor Day, therefore capturing the last few dollars remaining from the family's summer vacation pool. With the low admission, allowing a full day of fun, the fair remains the bargain of the year...if you don't count the ears of corn eaten, carnival rides taken, and choppers and dicers purchased from the vendors. Everyone entering the fairgrounds needs a valid ticket. During the fair, tickets are $8 for adults ages 13-64, $7 for seniors ages 65 & over and kids ages 5-12. Kids under age 5 are free. There are also many discount packages available. It's wise to get identification bracelets for the kids...just in case somebody wanders off. You can pick up a bracelet at the Care & Assistance Center, the guest services office in the Visitors Plaza, and at all information booths.

The fairgrounds are located mid-way between the cities of Minneapolis and St. Paul, just north of Interstate 94 and south of State Highway 36. Contact these good old boys and girls at 1265 Snelling Avenue North, St. Paul, MN 55108 for more information. Call (651) 642-2200. The fair's Web site, http://www.mnstatefair, is helpful in determining updated rates. It will also outline entertainment schedules and fill you in on all the other details necessary to ensure a good time mingling with the cows, sheep, and chickens.

In 2002, the National Park Service began building a **Mississippi National River and Recreational Area** (MNRRA) visitor facility inside the main entrance of the Science Museum. It provides information on the impact the river has on the area's recreational activities, environment, culture, and economy, so kids completing school reports and parents planning vacations can find what they need. The facility also has loads of information on the 385 parks operated by the NPS around the country. The 72-mile MNRRA starts at the confluence of the Mississippi River and the Crow River near the cities of Dayton and Ramsey and stretches south to Hastings. Any outdoors lover, whether young or old, will appreciate taking advantage of this public service. The MNRRA main office is located at 111 West Kellogg Boulevard. Call (651) 290-4160.

For a creepy, crawling expedition, albeit one with a historical bent, take the crew on a tour of the **Wabasha Street Caves** and other wild-and-wooly sites dating from when St. Paul was a wide-open, mobster-friendly town in the 1920s and 1930s. Don't worry, the gangster guides are simply actors showing off the caves, which are now used for banquets and conventions. In the old days, bad guys and their gals supposedly holed up here. Two-hour tours take

Minnesota's Front Yard

The State Capitol Mall is often called Minnesota's front yard. The 36-acre green space links the capitol building with the state office building, the judicial building, and the Minnesota History Center on John Ireland Boulevard.

in sights around town, while a separate 45-minute tour covers only the caves. The caves are at 215 Wabasha Street South, (651) 292-1220.

Explore the Mississippi River via one of the excursion boats managed by the **Padelford Packet Boat Company**, reminiscent of frontier days. Daily excursions leave at noon and 2 p.m. in June, July, and August, and 2 p.m. every Saturday and Sunday in May and September. Fall color cruises are available in October. The boats depart from Boom Island in Minneapolis and Harriet Island in St. Paul. The family can sprawl on the top deck of the boats to soak up the sun or hunker inside the main cabins if the weather is on the nasty side. No matter what, this is one of the best ways for everyone to get out of the house and see the river and the Twin Cities from a different angle.

On Wednesdays in July and August, the company also operates a showboat, with such silliness aboard as "Dr. Jekyll and Mr. Hyde," a show where the audience is encouraged to cheer the hero and razz the villain, a fact much appreciated by the backseat gang on holiday. All is in good fun, and the roles are played by University of Minnesota theater students. Boarding for the showboat tours are at 5 p.m., with a dinner following the cruise. There is also a mid-day lunchbox trip and an afternoon matinee. Theater-only shows are also available. Call (651) 227-1100.

For another kind of stage show, this one a bit more serious, pay a visit to the **Penumbra Theater**, 270 Kent Street, home to one of America's top rated African-American theater companies. Many works by St. Paul's resident prizewinning playwright August Wilson are performed here. Youth theater and children's programs are also on tap. Watching such productions can be an eye-opening wonder for young theater fans. Call (651) 224-3180 for shows and times. The family will probably enjoy watching the taping of a live radio show. Take the crew to the **Fitzgerald Theater**, 10 East Exchange Street, to see Garrison Keillor's "A Prairie Home Companion" on stage. The venerable old theater has great sight lines, even from the balcony, which makes it perfect for the kid set trying to get a good view. Later, when the show is picked up and aired by National Public Radio, the kids can hear their own applause. Finally, you can take in a performance at the glittering **Ordway Center** for the Performing Arts, 345 Washington Street, (651) 224-4222.

One of the Padelford Packet Boat Company's vessels plying the Twin Cities' waterways.
—Courtesy of the Padelford Packet Boat Company

WINTER CARNIVAL AND PEANUTS

Two other St. Paul institutions that will appeal to the kids certainly bear mentioning. If you venture forth in the winter, enjoy 10 days of torchlight parades and goofy excitement of **Winter Carnival**, typically held the last week in January and the first week in February. Characters called Vulcans race around town in vintage red fire engines to harass the forces of the ice king and his court, signifying the mythological battle between hot and cold. During Winter Carnival, downtown St. Paul is ablaze with thousands of twinkling lights. Ice-skating rinks seem to pop up in every park and empty lot. Rice Park, in the heart of the city, is home to dozens of magnificent ice sculptures carved by international competitors. The displays are lighted at night to create a dazzling display of shimmering color. Bundled-up tykes, toddlers, and teens alike can take in the Winter Carnival parade, which kicks off the event. Make sure the little ones have their mittens. Hot chocolate rewards should await the family when the procession is over.

Everyone notices the "Peanuts" statues that pop up all over the city from June through September, celebrating the late Charles M. Schulz, the St. Paul native and creator of the famed comic strip. Each year, a different character is featured. Lucy Van Pelt got the nod in 2002, with Snoopy in 2000 and Charlie Brown in 2001. Artists decorate the statues, which are then auctioned off for scholarships at the College of Visual Arts in St. Paul and the Art Instruction Schools in Minneapolis. In early 2002, there were plans afoot for permanent bronze sculptures of Schulz characters to be placed in Landmark Plaza in

First Railroad in Minnesota

The state's first railroad, the Minnesota & Pacific, was built in 1862 to connect St. Paul to St. Anthony a few miles away. This was the first leg of a line that became the Great Northern Railway, which, at its peak, reached from St. Paul to the Pacific Ocean. The founder and owner, James J. Hill, became known as the Empire Builder. His house still stands across from the Roman Catholic cathedral in St. Paul, on bluffs overlooking the downtown.

downtown St. Paul. This would be a great opportunity to photographically capture the kids alongside some of their favorite comic-strip characters.

PLACES TO STAY

Best Western Kelly Inn–State Capitol, 161 St. Anthony Avenue, (651) 227-8711 or (800) 528-1234

Exel Inn of St. Paul, 1739 Old Hudson Road, (651) 771-5566 or (800) 367-3935

Holiday Inn RiverCentre, 175 West Seventh Street, (651) 225-1515

Hotel Saint Paul, 350 Market Street, (800) 292-9292 or (651) 292-9292

Radisson Riverfront Hotel Saint Paul, 11 East Kellogg Boulevard, (651) 292-1900 or (800) 333-3333

Red Line Inn and Conference Center, 1870 Old Hudson Road, (651) 735-2333 or (800) 733-5463

PLACES FOR FOOD

Big Apple Bagels, 849 University Avenue West, (651) 209-6020

Cafe Latte, 850 Grand Avenue, (651) 224-5687

Cahoots Coffee Bar, 1562 Selby Avenue, (651) 644-6778

El Burrito Mercado, 175 Concord Street (651) 227-2192

Elements Café, at the Science Museum of Minnesota, (651) 221-9444

Izzy's Ice Cream Cafe, 2034 Marshall Avenue, (651) 603-1458

Lee's and Dee's Bar-B-Que Express, 161 Victoria Street North, (651) 225-9454

Pazzaluna, 360 St. Peter Street, (651) 223-7000

Ruam Mit Thai, 475 St. Peter Street, (651) 290-0067

St. Paul Grill, 350 Market Street, (651) 222-GRILL

Swede Hollow Cafe, 725 East Seventh Street (651) 776-8801

PLACES TO SHOP

Asian Books and Gifts, 422 University Avenue, (651) 224-4331

Bound to Be Read, 870 Grand Avenue, (651) 646-BOOK (2665)

Captured Visions Gallery, 201 Western Avenue North, (651) 228-9579

Cooks of Crocus Hill, 877 Grand Avenue, (651) 228-1333

Creative Kidstuff, 1074 Grand Avenue, (651) 222-2472 or (888) 635-1045

Explore Store, Science Museum of Minnesota, 120 W. Kellogg Blvd., (651) 266-6400

Irish On Grand, 1124 Grand Avenue, (651) 222-5151

Marshall Field's–St. Paul, 411 Cedar Street, (651) 292-5000

Orbit Gallery, 5 West Seventh Place, (651) 293-0884

Red Balloon Children's Bookshop, 891 Grand Avenue, (651) 224-9508; redballbks@aol.com

Sonnen's Pet Shop, 406 St. Peter Street, (651) 222-2425

FOR MORE INFORMATION

Minnesota Historical Society, 345 West Kellogg Boulevard, St. Paul 55102-1906, (651) 296-6126

Minnesota Office of Tourism, 100 Metro Square, 121 East Seventh Place, St. Paul 55101, (651) 296-5029 or (800) 657-3700; www.exploreminnesota.com

St. Paul Convention and Visitors Bureau, 175 West Kellogg Boulevard, Suite 502, St. Paul 55102, (651) 265-4900 or (800) 627-6101

NORTHERN METROPOLITAN REGION

The northern suburbs of the Twin Cities form a horizon-to-horizon stretch of bedroom communities linked to the two downtowns by I-94, I-35W, I-35E, and their concrete tributaries such as U.S. Highways 169 and 10; State Highways 81 and 242; and County Highways 14, 47, 65, 109, and 610. Fridley, Brooklyn Park, Maple Grove, Coon Rapids, Anoka, Blaine, Shoreview, and neighboring suburbs make up this sprawling urban area. But these towns have a lot more going for them than merely strip malls and fast-food eateries.

Granted, they have their bustling commercial centers and strips of stores, including **Brookdale Center**, 1108 Brookdale at the junction of Bass Lake Road and Highway 152, Brooklyn Center, (763) 566-3373; and **Northtown Mall**, at University Avenue Northeast and Highway 10, Blaine, (763) 786-9704, among others. Yet there are also art centers, sports arenas, picnic sites, and historical attractions that make for a quick get-out-town breakout for vacationers of all ages whose time is as tightly budgeted as jeans on an adolescent rock star.

A car is an absolute necessity for touring the North Metro area. Subsequently, bring a map . . . or two . . . or three. The family will love you for it. The old adage that "you can't get there from here" is not quite true, but the distances between the things young visitors want to see and do can eat up hours—even with dependable transportation. After all, these are the "burbs." The sites-to-see are spread out, often 5 to 10 miles apart. Be assured that, even with the lure of mall shopping and strolling, no kid would want to walk from place to place—nor would parents.

PUTT-PUTTING AND SPLISH-SPLASHING

The time-challenged weekend family can have just as much fun on a semi-urban getaway adventure as it can on a multihour jaunt hundreds of miles away from home. Go-cart tracks and water parks are two ways in which this part of Minnesota can provide the fun. So you may as well begin the trip with a flourish—and earplugs. Get the teenagers—and maybe yourself—over to **Pro**

Kart Indoors, 1201 97th Avenue N.E., Blaine, (952) 808-RACE, for a motorized adrenaline rush. The big go-karts here can be driven by 16-year-olds, though 14- and 15-year-olds can drive for an extra fee. For the mini-karts on a one-hour course, kids have to be at least 54 inches tall and eight years old. The keen-eyed attendants know all the tricks when a youngster tries to stretch out, pretending to be taller. Standing on tiptoes does not count.

Family membership card packages are available for two adults and two kids. These are handy for discounts if a full card of racing is on tap. All races are eight minutes in length. This is a perfect way to entertain the gang if some cousins or grandma and grandpa are along for the ride. The oldsters, however, may wish to hang around the gift shop and check out the NASCAR souvenirs and apparel. If someone doesn't see what they want at first glance, the service-oriented clerks can take special orders.

When not booked for corporate or special events, Pro Kart Indoors offers public driving on its tough oval course. Each cart is outfitted with a 6.5-horsepower motor that gives the illusion of lots of speed. All drivers wear protective

Making a splash at the Bunker Hills Wave Pool in Coon Rapids.
—Courtesy of the Anoka County Parks and Recreation Department

Learning about the Good Old Days

The Gibbs Farm Museum, a state historical site, is open from May 1 through October 31. The original farm dates to 1849, the year Minnesota became a territory. Following a trail that crossed the farmland, Dakota used to stop at the farm and became friends with owners Herman and Jane Gibbs. Using costumed reenactors, the museum facility now depicts the lives of the area's Native Americans and the farm folk of that era. A patch of tallgrass prairie is also on the site. Gibbs Farm is located at 2097 West Larpenteur in Falcon Heights, northwest of the Minnesota State Fairgrounds. Call (651) 646-8629.

helmets and are strapped into a padded seat. Every cart has a protective bumper rail, so there won't be any real bone-shaking fender benders on tight turns. League racing is open to the public, providing the gang a chance to compete against others in the family. Trophies are awarded to the top three finishers in the various events.

After all the oil, grease, and fumes of go-carting, run the gang through a car wash. Well, not a real car wash, of course. Take 'em to the **Bunker Hills Wave Pool** for a hosing down. The pool, at Foley Boulevard and Highway 242 in Coon Rapids, is managed by the Anoka County Parks and Recreation Department. The pool area is smoke free, and guests are asked not to bring lawn chairs, coolers, or refreshments. However, guests can receive a hand stamp for readmission on the same day, allowing use of a picnic area nearby for lunch. Call (763) 767-2895; www.bunkerhillswavepool.com.

The 25,000-square-foot pool has what they call a "zero-depth" entry, so the littlest of kids can simply walk into the water. Tubes are available for rental in two-hour sessions starting on even hours of the day, if bodysurfing is not the day's sporting style. The maximum number of tubes allowed in the pool at any one time is 200, rented on a first-come-first-served basis. Lifeguards are on duty at all times and safety breaks are held every hour where everyone has to pop out of the pool for five minutes. Grumbling aside, this is a good way to keep track of all those bobbing heads.

Coast Guard–approved life jackets are allowed if parents supervise, but keep the rubber ducky or inflated shark at home. No other flotation devices are allowed. The average temperature is kept around 73 degrees, with waves generated every five seconds over 15-minute periods, followed by a 10-minute break before the next onslaught of rushing water.

The Wave Pool hosts Twilight Tuesday Nights for young people, with bands and other entertainment geared to teens who can splash to their hearts' content without toddlers in the way. Of course, the facility's concession stand does a booming business on nights like this. Other amenities in the pool area include lawn areas for sunning and two sand volleyball courts.

Bunker Hills Regional Park has RV and tent campgrounds, five miles of asphalt trails for hiking or biking, picnic pavilions, a golf course, horse stables offering trail rides, and a prairie area open for touring. Subsequently, a vacationing family can spend a long weekend in the area and never duplicate a single minute of fun-filled activities. The park entrance is a short leg north of the junction of Foley Boulevard and County Highway 242 in Coon Rapids, (763) 862-4970. In the winter, call (763) 757-3920.

So what about water-based fun in winter? Not many want to splash around in a wave pool when a paddling partner might be a polar bear on holiday. The **Tropics Indoor Water Park** readily provides the answer because the place is always a wonderful 84 degrees, even if a seasonal blizzard roars outside. The park is located in the Shoreview Community Center, 4580 North Victoria Street, Shoreview, (651) 490-4700; www.tropicswaterpark.com. From I-694, exit at Lexington Avenue (County Highway 51), drive north to County Highway 96 and turn right. Then take a left on Victoria Street. Bring all the swimsuited cousins and get a group rate.

The water park has a 210-foot-long slide and a teacup fountain that looks remarkably like a mushroom-shaped showerhead. Guests can play water volleyball or water basketball and even wrestle a rubber shark. Taking one vacation day here gets the backseat gang so squeaky clean they won't have to suds again for a week.

THE SPORTING LIFE

Many families come to the North Metro to have a ball, and some come specifically to play ball, particularly football (soccer, for you North Americans). Sports-minded folks then spread out to the other attractions throughout the area for more escapades as time allows.

The **National Sports Center/Blaine Soccer Complex** has 52 playing fields and is listed in the *Guinness Book of World Records* as the largest soccer complex in the world. Among the soccer events drawing the crowds are the NSC Cup Youth and Adult Tournament, the All-American Girls Soccer Tournament, the Schwan's Cup USA, the 4x4 Soccer Festival, the NSC 5v5 Holiday Classic, and other matches. The center is also home to the Minnesota Thunder, the state's professional soccer team, whose season runs from May through October and whose matches always attract large crowds.

There's a lot more going on at the center, as well. The complex sprawls over 172 acres, including an ice arena, sports hall, and bike-racing facilities in addition to picnic grounds and a 170-bed dormitory. With all these accommodations and services, the facility has hosted numerous national and international sporting events such as the International Special Olympics, North

The National Sports Center in Blaine, where soccer is king.
—Courtesy of the National Sports Center Foundation

American Indigenous Games, and World Champion Cycling Trails. While roaming around the place, be sure that everyone in the family has an autograph book. Track star Jacki Joyner-Kersee, basketball great Michael Jordan, and numerous other sports heroes and heroines often are on the scene to watch the action. A dedicated fan might get the signatures of the entire United States and Cuban national wrestling teams or the Japanese national rugby team.

The **National Youth Golf Center** is also located at the NSC, with a par-44, 18-hole course designed and maintained by the PGA. Kids enjoy the course and are always up to challenging their folks. The center is affiliated with First

Early Schools

In the 1820s, the first school for white children opened for the families of troops stationed at Fort Snelling. In the 1830s, missionary schools were established for Native American children. In 1849, the territorial legislature passed a law to set up the first public schools. In 1851, the position of a territorial superintendent of schools was established.

Tee, an organization made up of the country's major professional golf associations to encourage youngsters to enjoy the game. Low course fees help.

The NSC is located at 1700 105th Avenue N.E., (763) 785-5600. The site is about one mile east of Highway 65, on the northern edge of the Anoka County–Blaine Airport.

For other golf opportunities, there are darn good courses across the North Metro with plenty of roughs for a family of duffers wanting to do some wandering in the brush: The **Bridges of Mounds View**, 2850 82nd Lane N.E., Blaine, (763) 785-9063; **Brookland Executive Nine**, 8232 Regent Avenue North, Brooklyn Park, (763) 561-3850; **Rush Creek Golf Club**, 7801 County Road 101, Maple Grove, (763) 494-8844; **Greenhaven Golf Course**, 2800 Greenhaven Road, Anoka, (763) 427-3180; and a golf bag full of other tournament-level facilities. Don't forget to replace the divots.

QUIET TIME

Out here in these suburban boonies, families won't get much of a North Woods experience if they're looking for a hideaway deep in a quiet, piney glade alongside a placid stream. Yet there are major parks with loads of green space and trails for hiking, cycling, bird watching, and picnicking. Some of the cross-country ski trails here are lighted in the winter. Get the kids outside and let 'em burn off their excess energy.

The **Elm Creek Park Reserve**, 13080 Territorial Road, in Maple Grove, has an off-leash dog-exercise area where the family Fido can romp. A permit is required, however, so call (763) 424-5511 to confirm details. Don't forget to clean up after the critter, certainly a job for Junior. Also in Maple Grove, **Fish Lake Regional Park** is a popular outdoors draw with its boating and fishing opportunities, as well as in-line skating for the landlubber crowd whether teething or toothless. The park can be found at 14900 Bass Lake Road, (763) 420-3423. For bikers, the **Hennepin Parks Trails Corridor**, a 5.6-mile paved trail system, connects Coon Rapids Dam Regional Park to Elm Creek Park Reserve. The trail runs from Brooklyn Park to Maple Grove. Call (763) 424-5511 for more information. You can also trek across the 1000-foot-long walkway on top of the Coon Rapids Dam. A walk across the Mississippi River is an adventure, regardless of the age of everyone in the family.

For some indoor fare, the **American Wings Air Museum** takes kids into the world of flight, particularly that of the armed services. The museum is dedicated to promoting aviation, with exhibits on pilot equipment and military clothing, as well as flags and photographs. The museum is located at 2141 Rhode Island Lane, Blaine, (763) 786-4146; www.americanwings.org. The museum is on the grounds of the Anoka County–Blaine Airport, so airborne visitors can land the family plane almost in front of the place.

The **Brooklyn Park Historical Farm**, 4345 101st Avenue North, Brooklyn Park, consists of 10 acres of displays demonstrating what farm life in Minnesota was like in the late 1800s. The complex has a large farmhouse, barn, chicken coops, farm equipment, and other exhibits. Interpreters act out the roles of a typical farm family of that era and will answer questions about what life was like then. Call (763) 493-4604.

After spending most of a day at a water park, go-cart track, or any number of other fun factories, everyone is probably in the mood for a good meal and maybe a movie. The **MegaStar Cinema**, 12575 Elm Creek Boulevard, Maple Grove, (763) 494-3333, is a great place to satisfy both wishes. In addition to an on-site restaurant, this 16-screen film house has VIP boxes similar to those in sports stadiums. Two 20-seat suites, sectioned off from the rest of the theater by soundproof glass, offer reclining leather seats, a wet bar, and sound and temperature controls. This arrangement is perfect for an extended family get-together, but, with all the amenities, it will be difficult to keep all eyes glued to the movie.

Or perhaps a couple of hours of bowling after dinner would fit the time-off ticket. For instance, the **Mermaid Entertainment and Event Center**, 2200 U.S. Highway 10, Mounds View, is a lodging complex with 70 hotel rooms; an indoor pool and tummy-tingling water slide; a 32-lane bowling alley; a full-service restaurant with breakfast, lunch, and dinner options; and a nightclub for the parental units after-hours. Call (763) 784-7350.

PLACES TO STAY

BLAINE

Super 8 Motel, 9410 Baltimore Street N.E., (763) 786-8888 or (800) 800-8000; www.super8.com

BROOKLYN CENTER

AmericInn Motel, 3050 Freeway Boulevard, (763) 566-7500 or (800) 634-3444; www.americinn.com

Comfort Inn, 2550 Freeway Boulevard, (763) 561-0900 or (800) 456-4000

Hilton Minneapolis–North, 2200 Freeway Boulevard, (763) 566-8000 or (800) 445-8667

BROOKLYN PARK
Budget Host–Brooklyn Park, 6280 Lakeland Avenue North, (763) 533-6455 or (800) 283-4678

FRIDLEY
Best Western Kelly Inn, 5201 Central Avenue N.E., (763) 571-9440 or (800) 528-1234

HAM LAKE
Ham Lake Campground, 2400 Constance Boulevard, (763) 434-5337

MAPLE GROVE
Maple Grove KOA Campground, 10410 Brockton Lane, (763) 420-2255 or (800) 562-0261

Red Carpet Inn, 7295 Forestview Lane, (763) 493-2277 or (800) 251-1962

MOUNDS VIEW
Days Inn, 2149 Program Avenue, (763) 786-9151 or (800) 777-7863

SHOREVIEW
Hampton Inn North, 100 Gramsie Road, (763) 482-0402 or (800) 426-7866

PLACES TO EAT

ANOKA
Anoka Food Co-op and Cafe, 1912 Second Avenue, (763) 427-4340

Kam Wong's Chow Mein, 3641 Round Lake Boulevard, (763) 422-9193

Punky's Cafe, 650 East Main Street, (763) 323-8241

BLAINE
Big Bite Pizza, 10811 University Avenue N.E., (763) 757-0000

Old Chicago, 198 Northtown Drive, (763) 783-8566

BROOKLYN CENTER
50's Grill, 5524 Brooklyn Boulevard, (763) 560-4947

BROOKLYN PARK
Carbonne's Pizzeria, 1408 85th Avenue North, (763) 315-2239

Fanion African and Asian, 7648 Humboldt Avenue, (763) 566-3030

COON RAPIDS
BK Family Restaurant, 11496 Martin Street, (763) 755-3412

FRIDLEY
Stuart Anderson's Cattle Company, 5696 University Avenue N.E., (763) 571-5087

MAPLE GROVE
Chipotle Mexican Grill, 7750 Main Street North, (763) 494-5005

PLACES TO SHOP

ALBERTVILLE
Outlets at Albertville, I-94 at County Highway 19 (westbound Exit 202/eastbound Exit 201), (763) 497-1911; www.outletinfo.com

ANOKA
Amish Center, 224 East Main Street, (763) 712-1350

Amore Antiques, 2008 Second Avenue, (763) 576-1871

Pure Bliss, 211 East Main Street, (763) 323-8160

BLAINE
Mrs. B's Dolls, 10130 Central Avenue N.E., (763) 786-6825

BROOKLYN PARK
Bob Evans Gifts, 8501 Wyoming Avenue North, (763) 425-2214

MAPLE GROVE
Davlins' The Woods, 15825 95th Avenue, (763) 416-9663

OSSEO
Mary D's Dolls and Bears and Such, 423 Third Street S.E., (763) 424-4375

FOR MORE INFORMATION

Minneapolis Metro North Convention and Visitors Bureau,
6200 Shingle Creek Parkway, Suite 248, Minneapolis 54430,
(763) 566-7722; www.justaskmn.com

STILLWATER

Lying in the beautiful St. Croix Valley, yet little more than 30 minutes east of the Twin Cities, Stillwater is an ideal spot for families who want a bit of the rural life without venturing too far from urban creature comforts. Twin Citians consider a jaunt here to be perfect for a day trip or a short weekender.

This is an area that the Dakota and Ojibwe once called their home. The dense forests were filled with game, and the mighty St. Croix River was fish-rich and accessible to the Native Americans who lived high on the bluffs and fertile land above the river bottoms. After a treaty in 1837 allowed white settlers to move into the area, it didn't take long for the native people to move elsewhere.

About the same time, the region's vast tracts of timber attracted hordes of newcomers intent on striking it rich. Soon rough-and-ready lumbermen floated their log rafts downstream on the St. Croix to the mills that turned out lumber by the millions of board feet. In fact, the establishment of the Stillwater Lumber Company in 1843 officially marks the "founding" of Stillwater, almost six years before the Minnesota Territory was established by Congress. The first Minnesota Supreme Court met in town in 1849. They must have sent a lot of desperadoes upriver because the Minnesota Territorial Prison was constructed in town between 1851 and 1853. Sadly, the last remaining building at the Territorial Prison site burned to the ground in September, 2002, though two more recently built prisons lie just south of Stillwater. The city, along with St. Paul, became the territory's first incorporated communities in 1854.

These days, the city is much more genteel than when saloons and honky-tonks ruled. Today, the family can take in the **Rivertown Art Fair, Farmer's Market, Music on the Waterfront**, and the **Fine Art and Jazz Festival**. But to retain a certain open-ended air, the city manages 222 acres of parkland, so there is plenty of green space to go around. Lumberjack Days is another of the city's festivals, held in July. The festival memorializes those early woodsmen who once made then-rowdy Stillwater quite the place for rest and recuperation.

OUTDOORSY FUN

Stillwater is located near a handful of wonderful state and national recreational facilities, ideal for the family in a hurry or looking for an inexpensive and convenient foray into the world of nature. Hiking, biking, canoeing, cross-country skiing, bird watching, and just loafing under the trees are among the many outdoor opportunities that can be experienced in the area. The **Gateway State Trail** is a multiuse trail stretching more than 18 miles from St. Paul to about five miles north of Stillwater. Other nearby recreational areas include **St. Croix Bluffs Regional Park**, 10191 South St. Croix Bluffs, (651) 430-8240; **Afton State Park**, 6959 Peller Avenue South, Hastings, (651) 436-5391, to the south; and **Lake Elmo Regional Park** to the west. Stretching along the St. Croix to the north are **William O'Brien, Interstate**, and **Wild River State Parks**. All of these provide lots of camping and outdoor-recreation opportunities for families seeking the perfect getaway, yet close enough to get back to town for pizza when the mood strikes.

Canoeing is fun along the St. Croix River, with everyone suited up in life vests. Paddling along the waterway is a great way to build family teamwork. Several canoe and kayak rental outlets are in the Stillwater area, with drop-off and pick-up service. The **St. Croix National Scenic Riverway** extends more than 150 miles, protected along its entire length by strict federal conservation rules. Don't forget to bring a picnic lunch and plenty of bottled beverages. Be sure to pick up after yourselves. For more information on the riverway, contact the National Park Service, 401 Hamilton Street, St. Croix Falls, Wisconsin, (715) 483-3284.

Winter doesn't slow the outdoor adventure around Stillwater, where hardy residents love ice fishing, snowmobiling, skating, and skiing. Sledding is great fun on downtown Stillwater's **Chillicoot Hill**, just the thing before heading indoors to one of the many local eateries for cups of hot chocolate and tall tales about roughing it on the slopes. Kids can't seem to get enough of the hills, the cocoa, and the stories.

A favorite attraction among the more agile teens and young adults is the climbing wall inside Stillwater's old grain elevator. Check with P.J. Asch Otterfitters for instructions, as well as day passes for the more experienced climbers. Climbing parties for groups can also be arranged. It's located at 413 East Nelson Street, (651) 430-2286; www.pjaschotterfitters.com.

SAMPLING STILLWATER

Stillwater remains a river city, regardless of its civilized veneer. Families can harken back to the heyday of steamboating on the St. Croix, which ran roughly from 1860 through 1890, with a trip aboard a fancy excursion boat. Take in the sights from the deck of one of the five riverboats operated by the **St. Croix Boat and Packet Company,** which features a variety of lunch and dinner cruises, many with musical accompaniment. The dock is located at 525 South Main Street, (651) 430-1236; www.andiamo-ent.com.

Yet railroads also were important for the city's growth, with the first line reaching Stillwater in 1871. Youngsters and their parents can still enjoy those long-ago, delightful days of rail pampering aboard the **Minnesota Zephyr**, 601 North Main Street, (800) 992-6100; www.minnesotazephyr.com. The fancy

A riverboat about to glide under the lift bridge at Stillwater's Lowell Park.
—Courtesy of Deb Chial Photography

dining train takes guests on a three-and-one-quarter hour run along the St. Croix Valley. Even though kids more in tune with the latest grunge music may raise their eyebrows at the sound, the Zephyr Cabaret lays out plenty of great old hits from the 1940s and 1950s as the train frolics and rolls along.

One of the best ways to see the city is via the **Stillwater Trolley Company**, which offers 45-minute narrated tours that run hourly from May through October. The little red trolleys are based at the Freight House Restaurant along the river downtown and trundle past many of the community's historical buildings. See if the architecturally minded in the family can tell the differences among the Greek Revival, Second Empire, Craftsman, Prairie, Queen Anne, and Italianate styles of homes. The trolley company is located at 400 Nelson Street, (651) 430-0352.

Many of Minnesota's wealthiest lumber barons and bankers, as well as ordinary folks, built a hodgepodge of beautiful homes that now make Stillwater such a delightful visual experience. If you do your own driving to look at the houses, don't be frustrated with the many dead-end streets that halt at the edge of a ravine or along the river's edge. That's how the city was laid out. Have your assigned young navigator sound the alarm when a precipice presents itself.

If the tykes tire of touring, teen girls love poking around the dress and jewelry shops on or around Main Street. One of the most popular, **Relaxation Station**, has funky clothes, sterling silver necklaces with inlaid stonework, rings,

Stillwater Becomes Known

The community of Stillwater earned its name due to the calm waters of nearby Lake St. Croix. The name was suggested by local residents in 1843 because the area reminded them of their former home in Stillwater, Maine.

and earrings. The shop is at 223 East Chestnut Street, (651) 439-1548; www4.web sitegalaxy.com/thefunkyrelaxationstation.

Kids also love feeding the ducks on the St. Croix River, using bags of cracked corn purchased at the **Stillwater Farm Store**, 401 South Main Street, (651) 439-6143. You can also take the kids out to **Aamodt's Apple Farm**, 6428 Manning Avenue, (651) 439-3127, a few miles west of downtown, where they can learn about apple growing and the wonders of picking fruit. The farm also offers hay and sleigh rides in the autumn and winter.

Speaking of feeding, the hamburgers and malts at Darla's Malt Shop, 131 South Main Street, are excellent rewards for a young one's patience in indulging their elders on tours around town. The diner has a drive-up window, but it's more fun eating inside and reveling in the 1940s atmosphere. Call (651) 439-9294.

BOOKTOWN

Families seeking a little intellectual nourishment will be thrilled to see that Stillwater has been recognized as a Booktown, one of only about 20 such communities in the world and the first in North America to receive that honor. The designation indicates that books and booksellers play a major role in the economic life of a community. And that's certainly the case with Stillwater, with an array of new, used, and antiquarian book outlets lining its streets.

According to resident bookworms, there are more than 450,000 books for sale in the city's downtown shops. Prices range from under $5 to more than $2,000, depending on the title, as well as its age and condition. Determined shoppers from around the world regularly visit Loome Antiquarian Booksellers, 201 North Main Street, (651) 430-9805; www.loomebooks.com, to browse through its 150,000 volumes. Nineteenth-century maps of small towns across the country are also available, a fun purchase for vacationing families interested in taking home a souvenir of real value.

For those with a religious bent, Loome Theological Booksellers issues monthly catalogs for its international buyers, as well as encourages drop-bys for that special find. Bargain hunters enjoy prowling the choir loft in the store, a former church. The area is bursting with rare secondhand or out-of-print philosophy texts, religious treatises, and ecclesiastical histories. The shop is located 320 North Fourth Street, (651) 430-1092; www.loomebooks.com.

Two stores in particular have a nice array of historical and contemporary children's books. The kids can plop down on the carpet or curl up in a chair

Along the Saint Croix River at Stillwater. Minnesota Office of Tourism photograph.

while checking out a favorite tome at St. Croix Antiquarian Booksellers, 223 East Chestnut, (651) 430-0732; grgoodmn@msn.com. For an added bonus in The Valley Booksellers, 217 North Main Street, (651) 430-3385, the youngsters can enjoy looking at an aviary of rare birds, including Australian diamond-back doves, orange cheek waxbills, and several exotic finches, such as zebra and society. The store's Web site is www.valleybookseller.com.

Cutting Up the Wood

The first sawmill was built in Stillwater in 1844. Barely 10 years later, the massive rafts of logs floated down the St. Croix to town made Stillwater the lumber center of Minnesota. One such raft stretched for more than nine miles.

PLACES TO STAY

AmericInn Motel and Suites, 13025 60th Street North, (651) 439-1100 or 800) 634-3444; www.americinn.com

Best Western, 1750 West Frontage Road, (651) 430-1300 or (800) 647-4039; www.bestwestern.com

Country Inn and Suites, 2200 North Frontage Road, (651) 430-2699 or (800) 456-4000; www.countryinns.com

Holiday Inn Express, 2000 Washington Avenue, (651) 275-1401 or (800) HOLIDAY; www.holidayinn.com

Lowell Inn, 102 North Second Street, (651) 439-1102; www.lowellinn.com

Lumber Baron's Hotel, 101 West Water Street, (651) 439-6000 or (800) 456-4000; www.lumberbarons.com

Super 8 Motel, 2190 West Frontage Road, (651) 430-3990 or (800) 800-8000; www.super8.com

PLACES FOR FOOD

Broadway Pizza, 1980 Market Drive, (651) 430-9888

Dock Cafe, 425 East Nelson Street, (651) 430-3770

Dreamcoat Cafe, 215 Main Street, (651) 430-0615; www.dreamcoatcafe.com

Famous Dave's, 14200 60th Street North, (651) 439-5200; www.famousdave.com

Gasthaus Bavarian Hunter Restaurant, 8390 Lofton Avenue, (651) 439-7128; www.gasthausbavarianhunter.com

Mad Capper Saloon and Eatery, 224 South Main Street, (651) 430-3710

Timber Lodge Steakhouse, 1820 Market Drive, (651) 430-9988

PLACES TO SHOP

The Chef's Gallery: A Hardware Store for Cooks, 324 South Main Street, (651) 351-1144; www.thechefsgallery.com

Grand Games, 317 S. Main Street, (651) 351-9449

Mid-Town Antique Mall, 301 South Main Street, (651) 430-0808 or (651) 430-1843; www.midtownantiques.com

Musicmaker's Kits, 14525 61st Street Court North, (651) 439-9120; www.musickit.com

St. Croix River Exchange Building, 317 South Main Street; it houses Fish 'n Ships, (651) 462-2997, www.fishandships.com; Gifts & More, (651) 275-9288; and Grand Games, (651) 351-9449

FOR MORE INFORMATION

Greater Stillwater Chamber of Commerce, 201 South Main Street, Stillwater 55082, (651) 439-4001

St. Croix River Valley Innkeepers, 303 North Fourth Street, Stillwater 55082, (651) 998-0185; www.innsofthevalley.com

ST. CROIX VALLEY

The St. Croix River is the big draw in these parts, the reason that loggers swarmed into the area more than 150 years ago and the reason families today flock to its scenic wonders and abundant outdoor activities. Of course, the short drive from the Twin Cities doesn't hurt matters either.

In 1837, the Ojibwe ceded timber-cutting rights in the heavily forested St. Croix Valley to the United States. Almost overnight, the region was flooded with keen-eyed entrepreneurs and their surveyors seeking the best stands of pine to claim. Soon afterwards, a trading post and lumber mill were established on the west bank of the river, the first in a series of structures to accommodate the new industry. After the first wave of Yankees, hundreds of Swedish immigrants flooded into the valley to work in the forests and at the mills. It was not long before Taylors Falls became a thriving young community and the area prospered.

During the boom, the river always exerted its considerable influence. Near the town, the rushing waters narrowed and made a sharp bend, causing waterfalls and rapids that often became plugged with cut timber floating downstream. One jam, formed by an estimated 150 million board feet stacked 50 feet high, choked the river for miles. It took 200 men about six weeks and tons of dynamite to undo the jackstraw mess. To correct the problem, the Nevers Dam was built a couple of miles north of Taylors Falls in 1890; it provided more waterpower to push the timber through the narrows. In 1912, with the woods depleted for hundreds of miles around Taylors Falls, the final log went through the dam's gates, and the logging era virtually ended.

MODERN WATER POWER

Old-time lumberjacks would be amazed to see that the river is still very popular with today's visitors, although for far different reasons. And the timber barons would be astonished to find how water is used as the driving force behind at least one major present-day attraction—and how it brings thrills and chills to thousands of visiting families. Behold **Wild Mountain**, a 100-acre-plus, all-seasons recreational facility one hour northeast of the Twin Cities.

Getaway families really turn on to several thrilling water slides operating throughout the summer. The Super Chute is an open-flume slide that concludes with a big splash into a pool. The shorter set can ride with an adult. The Hydrotube is fully enclosed, creating an illusion of more speed and con-

Summertime fun at Wild Mountain Water Park.
—Courtesy of Wild Mountain Ski and Snowboard Area

tributing to louder shrieks of excitement. The Big Country consists of a series of ponds connected by chutes for a fast, wet-and-wacky ride. The Black Hole whizzes swimmers through an underground chute, finally tossing the guests into a pool with an explosion of water. The Lazy River is at the opposite end of the thrill scale with a leisurely float atop an inner tube along the park's 800-foot-long man-made river.

For most of the water rides, guests need to be at least 46 inches or taller to ride along with an adult. But the smaller members of the family aren't left out of the fun. A kiddy park has a giant frog slide and wading pool to keep the toddlers happy. An adult must be present to keep an eye on things.

Those visitors who don't have their swimsuits along can choose a dry ride atop a sled for a wild trip down a German-made alpine slide that stretches 1,700 feet from the crest of the mountain to its base. Adults may admire the view from up here, but the kids usually just want to hit the breakneck slope— one that includes 21 banked turns and at least one major dip.

When done with all the rides and slides, not-quite-tired guests love hopping aboard a Formula K Go-Kart that roars along at speeds up to 20 mph. Solitary riders must be at least 54 inches tall. Those under 36 inches need to ride with an adult. However, kiddy go-carts don't have any age or height rules. These tiny vehicles only go up to five miles per hour over a separate 300-foot-long track.

In the winter, Wild Mountain provides a heap of frozen water available for the skiers in your group. More than 20 major ski runs—for beginners through intermediate and on to advance and expert—accommodate the skill levels of thousands of skiers each season.

Kids new to the slopes quickly get into the groove with ski or snowboard lessons. Wild Mountain offers a three-class session in both sports for outdoors lovers who are 14 years old and up. The lessons help the tyro learn to use a chairlift, make turns, and control that all-important stop. Free 30-minute lessons are given to skiers ages 8 and up, and an hour-long course is available for snowboarders 12 and older. Group and private lessons are also available for a fee.

To attract families, Wild Mountain offers deals such as a spring season pass, which allows guests to ski or ride all the crazy rides they wish. Another special deal allows a free lift ticket for the lucky birthday person (just bring proof that it's the right day).

Wild Mountain is about seven miles north of Taylors Falls on County Highway 16, and parking is free. Although there is food service in the park, some guests prefer to bring their own picnics. Contact the park at Box 225, Taylors Falls 55084, (651) 257-3550 or (800) 447-4958. The facility also handles canoe rentals and excursion boat trips.

ROLLIN' DOWN THE RIVER

Even though the kids—and other family members as well—may be smitten with all the fiberglass fun, everyone would be well advised to experience up close the natural beauty of the St. Croix Valley. The best way to do that is via canoe, with rental outfits such as Wild Mountain providing the appropriate craft and safety accessories. Even if on a time budget, vacationers can indulge themselves in a lazy ride starting across the river from Taylors Falls in Wisconsin's half of Interstate State Park and continuing downstream to either Wisconsin's Osceola landing or Minnesota's William O'Brien State Park. These trips can last two to six hours, depending on the endpoint and how well paddlers can work with each other to develop the appropriate forward action. Remember, some cynics warn that loving couples should never canoe or paper walls together if they want their relationship to remain strong.

Minnesota's Waters

Most of Minnesota's rivers flow in one of three directions: north toward Hudson Bay, east toward the Atlantic Ocean, or south toward the Gulf of Mexico. Fifty-seven percent of the state is drained by the southward-flowing Mississippi River. The Hudson Bay–Nelson River system drains more than 30 percent through the Red River of the North and the Rainy River. Only about nine percent is drained by the Great Lakes–St. Lawrence system through the St. Louis River and the numerous smaller flowages into Lake Superior.

A hint: if paddling down to either point, leave the car at the endpoint, round up the kids, and hop aboard an express bus back to Taylors Falls to pick up a canoe. When the cruise is completed and all the bald eagles and deer have been spotted and counted, the family car is there waiting. Reservations are required, with the Osceola Express leaving at 11 a.m. and 1 p.m., and the O'Brien Express leaving at 10:30 a.m.

Two-day or weeklong trips are also available along the Upper St. Croix and Namekagon Rivers, along the **St. Croix National Scenic Riverway**. The nine-river national system was established in 1968 to preserve the pristine quality of the waterway. While some of the river rapids are challenging to the less-experienced canoeist, they are not classified as whitewater. Buses to any of several launch sites are picked up at the Wildwood RV Park and Campground, three miles south of Taylors Falls on Highway 8. Taylors Falls Canoe Rental can provide the appropriate craft at its landing, one mile south of Taylors Falls on Highway 8.

But if canoeing is not in the family lexicon, everyone can still enjoy an otter's-eye view of the St. Croix aboard the 150-passenger **Taylors Falls Queen** or the 250-passenger **Taylors Falls Princess**. Departing from the docks in town, much like the boats of old used to do, both vessels take riders past spectacular scenery and rock formations with such interesting names as the Devil's Chair, Turk's Head, and the Old Man of the Dalles. Another is a stone cross that supposedly was the inspiration for the river's name, Holy Cross, or St. Croix. Since 1906, these excursions have been the highlights of family trips to Taylors Falls. Climb aboard the boats at Interstate State Park on the Minnesota side of the river.

SOME LAND-LOCKED FUN

Covering 295 acres on either side of the river, **Interstate State Park** has 48 year-round campsites and three miles of hiking trails to explore. Among the interesting landforms here are the 200 or so potholes in the ancient rock, formed when small boulders and sand became caught up in whirlpools. The abrasive action of the stones drilled the holes. From Memorial Day to autumn, rangers guide tours around the potholes and have answers to just about anything the kids can ask. The half-mile trail is accessible to wheelchairs, but paths elsewhere are rugged and not recommended for those with too many physical challenges.

The entrance to the Minnesota side of the park is at the stoplight where Highways 8 and 95 intersect. A small gift store is located at the east entrance near the pothole area for the requisite souvenirs. Local tourism information can be picked up here, as well.

A permit is required to visit Minnesota's state parks. To purchase a sticker, contact the Department of Natural Resources Information Center, 500 Lafayette Road, St. Paul ((651) 296-6157 or (888) MINNDNR) to order a permit. The permit is good for one year from the month it is punched and entitles purchasers to unlimited visits to all 72 Minnesota state parks and recreation areas.

The Saint Croix Valley at Minnesota's Interstate State Park.
—Courtesy of Minnesota Department of Natural Resources

If visitors are registered owner of two vehicles, they can receive a $5 discount on the second vehicle permit. The second permit must be affixed to a vehicle registered to the same person who purchased the regular vehicle permit. Permit costs are $20 (annual vehicle permit); $15 (second vehicle permit); $12 (special permits - designated for people with a State of Minnesota handicapped license plate). Day passes are $4. The same fee applies to out-of-state visitors. Contact the park at (651) 465-5711.

For another perspective of the river and to learn more about the landscape, be sure to cross the Highway 8 bridge to St. Croix Falls, Wisconsin, and trek the trails in Wisconsin's half of **Interstate State Park**. An Ice Age interpretive center here tells how the land was formed eons ago, making perfect school-report material for the backseat gang. Although the park is Wisconsin's oldest, opening in 1900, the link with Minnesota is strong. Citizens on both sides of the river lobbied to open the site in order to preserve its natural beauty. Two-

Early Minnesota Hunters

Thick pine forests covered Minnesota thousands of years ago. The earliest inhabitants of the eastern portion of the region, Paleo-Indians, lived in these woods and fished the waters of Lake Superior. They chipped flint and other stones into spearheads and arrow points. These people were replaced by the Eastern Archaic people of the Copper Culture, who made their weapons and household implements from copper, which was plentiful throughout the Lake Superior region. People of the Northeast Woodland culture were the next to settle the area, inhabiting it between 1000 B.C. and A.D. 1600. They were hunters and gatherers, harvesting wild rice and picking berries. They built permanent villages throughout the area.

hundred-foot-high bluffs rear above the racing waterway, with hiking trails taking strollers to within inches of the drop-off.

The kids will have plenty of other things to do in the park. In addition to camping and hiking along the Summit Rock, River Bluff, Eagle Peak, Pothole, Skyline, or Meadow Valley Trails, they can fish from shore in the **Lake o' the Dalles**, a small body of water inside the park. A fishing pier for the physically challenged makes it easy for folks in wheelchairs to see if they can bring in a whopper bass. Swimming is also allowed here, with a beach house at the north end of the lake.

If the youngsters enjoy bird watching, the park's interpretive center has a checklist that helps keep track of which songsters are identified. In addition, bald eagles are often seen soaring over the waterway on their search for lunch, especially during the wintertime. There are also 10 miles of cross-country ski trails that just about everyone in the family should be able to traverse when the winter winds blow.

For more information on the park, contact the ranger at 1100 State Highway 35, St. Croix Falls, Wisconsin 54024, (715) 483-3747. A vehicle admission sticker is required or a day pass.

A visit to the **St. Croix State Forest**—about 50 miles north of Taylors Falls—provides a taste of Minnesota of the old days prior to the loggers' arrival, when a vast blanket of trees spread across the landscape. The forest is tucked into a bend of the St. Croix River in east-central Minnesota. Pile the backseat gang into the covered wagon or SUV and travel east from Hinckley on Highway 48 or from Sandstone along Highway 123 and County Highway 30. Bring hiking boots along with the all-important camping equipment.

The St. Croix State Forest offers loads of family recreational opportunities with its Boulder Campground, Tamarack River Equestrian Camp, and miles of hiking trails, some of which double as snowmobile trails in the winter. One of the best snowmobile routes runs from the campground along the hilly west bank of the rolling Tamarack River, past the equestrian campground and then over the river. Once across, take the trail along the river south to Squaw Point where the Tamarack joins the St. Croix River. Teens especially will like this type of snow challenge. Many local kids under 13 get their start here snowmobiling with their families, learning about safety and proper driving techniques.

Two other great treks are within the border of the forest. The **Willard Munger State Trail** will eventually run from the urban rush of the Twin Cities to Duluth. Here in the state forest, it passes alongside Churchill and Graces Lakes, which are two lovely gems full of fish waiting to nibble on a fishing fan's bait. Once the trail leaves the state forest, it continues on 10 miles to St. Croix State Park trail center. Plan your hiking speed and length accordingly, depending on the ages of the youngsters along for the trek.

The **Gandy Dancer Trail** is built along an abandoned railroad right-of-way through Polk and Burnett Counties in Wisconsin, passing through Pine

Horseback riders on the Tamarack Trail in the Saint Croix State Forest.
—Courtesy of Minnesota Department of Natural Resources

County in Minnesota and then back into Wisconsin's Douglas County. The kids will see a wide range of plant life, from prairie flowers to pine trees, as well as deer, squirrels, rabbits, and plenty of other forest creatures, provided they are quiet and respectful of the wilderness. If Fido comes along, he has to be on a leash. Oh, and don't forget to bring drinking water.

For maps and other details on these trails and all the outdoor opportunities in the forest, contact the area forester, 312 Fire Monument Road, Hinckley 55037, (320) 384-6146.

TAYLORS FALLS

The community of Taylors Falls, situated in the middle of the St. Croix Valley, has been inextricably linked to the timber industry and the St. Croix River since its beginnings. The town was named after Jesse Taylor, an early settler who saw the enormous potential of the entire region and staked his claim on much of the west bank of the river. He brought in more men and a partner, Benjamin F. Baker, to begin work on a mill upstream from the trading post. Taylor built log cabins, and other structures before selling out in 1846. Frame houses eventually replaced the cabins, stores opened, and a downtown district was laid out in 1850. Taylors Falls also grew into one of the major steamboat stops on the St. Croix.

Two of the more interesting buildings in Taylors Falls now comprise the **Old Jail Bed and Breakfast.** In 1869, a one-story tavern was built fronting a cave in the river bluff that was used to cool the beer. In 1852, the owners purchased a two-story stable and livery from the Chisago House Hotel to use as apartments. They set the new purchase on top of the saloon which, over the years, evolved into a grocery store, chicken-plucking company, beauty shop, and a mortuary. Next door to the tavern, the Taylors Falls jail and its four snug cells were built in 1884. This building was sold in 1923, and it eventually housed other firms, including an ice house and a shoe repair shop.

Local businesswoman Helen White renovated the entire property and turned it into a hostelry in 1981, making it the state's first licensed bed-and-breakfast. For rates and availability, contact the inn at 349 Government Street, Taylors Falls 55084, (651) 465-3112.

PLACES TO STAY

CHISAGO CITY/LINDSTROM
Super 8 Motel, 11490 Lake Lane, (651) 257-8088 or (800) 800-8000; www.super8.com

DRESSER, WISCONSIN
Valley Motel, 211 State Highway 35, (715) 755-2781 or (800) 545-6107

One of the many quaint buildings in Taylors Falls. Minnesota Office of Tourism photograph.

FOREST LAKE
AmericInn Motel, 1291 Broadway Avenue West, (651) 464-1930 or (800) 634-3444; www.americinn.com

Country Inn and Suites, 1954 Broadway Avenue West, (651) 982-9799

Forest Lake Motel, 7 Sixth Avenue N.E., (651) 464-4077

NORTH BRANCH
Super 8 Motel, 6010 Main Street (State Highway 95), (651) 674-7074 or (800) 800-8000; www.super8.com

OSCEOLA
AmericInn, 38675 14th Avenue, (651) 674-8627 or (800) 634-3444; www.americinn.com

River Valley Inn and Suites, 1030 Cascade Street (State Highway 35), 715-294-4060 or 888-791-0022

ST. CROIX FALLS, WISCONSIN
Dalles House, 720 Vincent Street, (715) 483-3206 or (800) 341-8000

Holiday Inn Express, 2190 U.S. Highway 8, (715) 483-5775 or (877) 422-4097

TAYLORS FALLS
The McLane House, 519 Bench Street, (651) 465-4832

The Springs Inn, 361 Government Street, (651) 465-6565 or (800) 851-4243

Wildwood RV Park and Campground, U.S. Highway 8, three miles south of Taylors Falls, (651) 257-3550

PLACES FOR FOOD

ST. CROIX FALLS, WISCONSIN
Dalles House Restaurant, 720 Vincent Street, (715) 483-3246

St. Croix Cafe, 103 North Washington Street, (715) 483-9079

Twin Falls Embers, 2186 U.S. Highway 8, (715) 483-5443

Wayne's Fine Food, 1961 U.S. Highway 8, (715) 483-3121

TAYLORS FALLS
Chisago House Restaurant, 361 Bench Street, (651) 465-5245

Coffee Talk, 479 Bench Street, (651) 465-6700

The Drive-In, 572 Bench Street, (651) 465-7831

Rocky River Bakery, 306 Bench Street, (651) 465-7655

PLACES TO SHOP

ST. CROIX FALLS, WISCONSIN
Ben Franklin, 125 North Washington Street, (715) 483-3050

Loni River Gifts, 125 North Washington Street, (715) 483-1936

Luhrs-Bjornson Art Work, 241 North Washington Street, (715) 483-9612

FOR MORE INFORMATION

Polk County Information Center, 710 State Highway 35 West, St. Croix Falls, Wisconsin 54014, (900) 222-7655

St. Croix Falls Chamber of Commerce, Box 178, St. Croix Falls, Wisconsin 54024, (715) 483-3580; stcroixfallschamber.com

DULUTH

Duluth hugs the foot of a long line of 800-foot-high bluffs on the western shore of frosty Lake Superior, the largest body of fresh water in the world. It is a community shaped by the lake, being one of the longest and most narrow cities in the United States, stretching 23 miles along the rocky shoreline. Duluth is the fourth largest city in Minnesota and has long been an economic powerhouse on the Upper Great Lakes. Young scholars can use these details for those dreaded "what I did this summer" class reports.

The area has been inhabited for at least 10,000 years. The Dakota and Ojibwe were well established in the region by the 1600s. They fished, hunted, and collected maple sap to boil down to syrup and sugar, moving by canoe up and down the lakeshore with ease. Daniel Greysolon, Sieur du Lhut, was the first French explorer to arrive in the neighborhood in 1636. The city was named in his honor.

Today, the international commercial hub of Duluth offers a great lesson in economics for the backseat gang. The city is hooked up to the outside world via the Great Lakes and the Saint Lawrence Seaway system, whereby freighters can reach the Atlantic Ocean in about eight days. This 2,342-mile route connects the Midwest to markets from Africa to Asia. During the shipping season, more than 1,200 vessels use the port, hauling millions of tons of bulk and general cargo. Children often get a kick out of looking at the ship flags and trying to guess the nation of origin.

A VIEW OF DULUTH FROM ON HIGH

Skyline Parkway is a grand way to get the entire lay of the land. Enger Park offers the best view along the thoroughfare that runs 30 miles across the top of the bluffs overlooking Duluth, bluffs which were once the shoreline of Lake Superior. For the family geography notebook, the lake today is 350 miles long and 160 miles wide, covering an area of 31,820 square miles. Its average depth is 475 feet. The rock tower in Enger Park, near the golf course, provides even more of an eagle's-eye view of this watery scene.

From Skyline, look down at **Minnesota Point**, a 6.5-mile strand of sand formed by the current of the St. Louis River as it flows into the lake. The view, from high above the city, is a grand place to see the Duluth Ship Canal, dug

Loading Up on Ore

By 1888, 2,200 ships annually berthed in Duluth, carrying upwards of two million tons of cargo. Ten railroads served the port. When Duluth's ore docks were built in 1893, the city became a major terminal for iron ore heading to giant steel mills in Indiana, Ohio, Michigan, and Illinois. Even today, Duluth remains a busy port, with taconite, a low-grade ore, its chief export.

through the point in 1871. The cut allows the giant freighters access to Duluth's inner harbor. Have a contest on who can spot the most ships in a given amount of time. Bring binoculars for a better look.

Duluth's best-noted landmark is the Aerial Lift Bridge that now connects the mainland to the point. The bridge rises every time a ship needs to pass, thereby holding up traffic for a few minutes. The locals are used to it, despite their grumbling when having to wait for the bridge to lower. Fourth of July fireworks over the bridge are spectacular, with their explosive sparkling and thunderous roaring shaking the horizon.

While on Skyline, turn everyone's eyes farther to the east to spot Duluth's sister city: Superior, Wisconsin. The communities bill themselves as the Twin Ports and for generations have shared the economic booty that resulted from their desirable geography. One of the best ways to see the sites and sights of Duluth is aboard an old-fashioned port trolley that runs daily from Memorial Day to Labor Day between the downtown, the waterfront, Canal Park, and other tourist-oriented locales. Or families can take a horse-drawn carriage ride through Canal Park and along the lakefront during the summer.

THE HARBOR AREA

No matter how you get there, be sure to take a stroll along the **Lakewalk**, which provides an up-close look at all the waterfront activity. Extending 4.2 miles along the shore, the boardwalk passes the Great Lakes Aquarium (more on this later) and the rose garden in Leif Erickson Park. Pause at the ship canal to watch weather-beaten freighters—most of them are longer than three football fields—maneuver under the Aerial Lift Bridge and then ever so carefully into their berths in the inner harbor. Once tied up, they'll load tons of clay or taconite ore, or unload cargo containers filled with everything from tractor parts to furniture. The ships' mighty screws churn up wakes that cause nearby sailboats to bob like corks in a rough sea.

The **Lake Superior Maritime Visitors Center** at Canal Park has a plethora of information on the history of Lake Superior, the shipping activity of the Twin Ports, and the work of the Army Corps of Engineers throughout the Upper Midwest. The center is adjacent to the Duluth Ship Canal, the Aerial Lift

Duluth's famous Aerial Lift Bridge in the down position.

Bridge, and the Lakewalk. Among the attractions within the high-tech, two-story building are full-sized replicas of ship cabins and a pilothouse, a giant steam engine from the retired Corps tug *Essayons*, working radar, and numerous ship models. The family can take in film showings and educational programs, as well as pick up fact sheets and brochures. The well-versed visitors center's staff helps guests make the most of their stay in Duluth-Superior. The center is handicapped-friendly, with an outside ramp and inside elevator for easy access. Parking is a short stroll away. And the best part of all for large families on a calendar crunch—the facility is free of charge and open to the public all year. Hours vary by the season. For tour reservations, call (218) 727-2497.

While in the harbor area, climb aboard the **SS *William A. Irvin*,** an ore boat turned into a museum. Where it once plied the lakes with its loads of ore, the boat is now docked permanently and open for tours in the summer. Moored alongside is a muscular old tugboat called the *Lake Superior*, which can also be visited after touring its larger neighbor. Kids can play pretend-captains for a time. Around Halloween, the Irvin becomes the "Ship of Ghouls" with plenty of action for anyone in the family who doesn't scare easily. The museum is located at 350 Harbor Drive, (218) 722-7876 or (218) 722-5573; www.decc.org/attractions/irvin.htm. Access is from the **Duluth IMAX Theater** and the **Duluth Entertainment Convention Center (DECC)**, 301 Harbor Drive, (218) 727-0022 or (218) 722-5573; www.decc.org/attractions.

Then give the gang a taste of the lake while on a harbor tour aboard a **Vista Fleet** excursion boat. The ticket office is located at DECC or by calling (218)

722-6218. Daily trips are scheduled from mid-May to mid-October. There are a variety of cruises the family can choose, from lunch and dinner excursions to sundaes on Sunday Fun Cruise and a Moonlight Cruise with Pizza.

The children can get a firsthand look at the warehouses and grain elevators in the port, sailing literally under the bows of the freighters. There are six major elevator systems in the harbor, a testimony to Minnesota's long agricultural history. They store wheat, soybeans, corn, barley, and other grains hauled in by train and truck from around the state, as well as the Dakotas, Nebraska, Iowa, and Wisconsin. A railroad hopper car can hold up to 3,600 bushels and can be emptied in 90 seconds.

Have the kids guess the height and capacity of the structures. Answers: most are more than 100 feet tall and hold more than one million bushels of grain. Elevator A, owned by General Mills, is the oldest active elevator in the city. Built in 1896, it holds 3.5 million bushels. Yet a more modern unit, the Harvest States Cooperatives elevator, stores up to 10 million bushels of grain. Now that's a lot of corn flakes.

Passing along the taconite ore loading docks is another lesson on movement of bulk products. The ore is mined on the nearby Mesabi Range in northeastern Minnesota and hauled by train to the harbor. Dock Number 6 is 2,304 feet long and 85 feet tall, with a maze of conveyor belts taking the ore from the dock's storage bins and dumping it into a ship's hold faster than a teenage daughter emptying her jewelry case on prom night.

Show off your knowledge for the kids and tell them that four trains can be unloaded every eight hours from the three tracks atop Dock Number 6, amounting to about 150,000 tons of ore. Each bin on the dock holds four cars' worth of taconite, or about 280 tons. To fill a 1,000-foot-long freighter, the seven-hour job takes 875 carloads.

The young folk should be impressed with such a wealth of parental knowledge. If they aren't, ask them to do some math and figure out how many tons per hour it takes to fill a freighter (11,500). First one with the right answer gets a pizza.

MORE KID-FRIENDLY ATTRACTIONS

The **Lake Superior Railroad Museum**, 506 West Michigan Street, provides a peek into the land version of the freight-hauling world. Kids can climb into the cab of a steam locomotive and gaze out the window of an old wooden caboose. On display is the state's first steam engine and an antique steam rotary snowplow. This is the place for anyone looking for info on how the railroads affected the Upper Midwest. Call (218) 733-7590.

The gang will also love a ride on the **North Shore Scenic Railroad**, which departs from the depot at 506 West Michigan Street, (218) 722-1273 or (800) 423-1273; www.pinternet.com. The train rumbles out of Duluth and edges along the shores of Lake Superior. The rides are narrated, with a 90-minute excursion to the Lester River or a six-hour trip to Two Harbors. There are also "Pizza Train"

Old Stumps Discovered

In 1994, dredging crews in Duluth harbor discovered hundreds of tree stumps rooted 15 feet below the surface of the water. Geologists estimated that the stumps were at least 1,600 years old and had been gradually covered as Lake Superior's water level rose over the years.

rides, "Murder Mystery" trips, and other expeditions. The Lake Superior and Mississippi Railroad also offers 90-minute rail trips along the picturesque St. Louis River. The gang can ride along in vintage cars to see all the sights, departing from the LS&M station at Grand Avenue and Fremont Street, across from the Lake Superior Zoo. Call (218) 624-7549, or log on to www.LSMRR.org.

Canal Park, along the waterfront, once a warren of tired old warehouses and dilapidated freight terminals, is now a vibrant district with restaurants and numerous entertainment attractions for the young people. Youth-oriented to the nth degree, **Bananaz** is a 52,000-square-foot family entertainment complex inside a renovated manufacturing plant. Paved walkways and old-time streetlamps inside the building provide an interesting ambience. Yet most kids won't notice the decor as they stampede toward the video games; a climbing wall; and flight, racing, and golf simulators. Willie's Garage, a 1950s diner inside the complex, is a fun place to haul the hungry when they tire of rock climbing. The facility is located at 329 South Lake Avenue, (218) 720-5868.

Also in the Canal Park area is the **Grand Slam Family Fun Center**, which combines fast- and slow-pitch softball, a mini-golf course, laser tag, and basketball courts. It's the best place in town to get the wild ones to burn off their pent-up energy. The facility is open year-round, so vacationers can enjoy a grand time in the Adventure Playground even when the temperature plummets outside. Try the center's Grand Slam Pizza Parlor when the hungries hit. The facility is at 395 Lake Avenue South, (218) 722-5667; www.funusa.net.

In a setting not quite as interactively wild as the fun center or Bananaz, young Duluth visitors can view fish nose-to-nose in the **Great Lakes Aquarium and Freshwater Discovery Center**, 353 Harbor Drive, the country's only freshwater aquarium. A giant sturgeon stares back balefully from its lair in one 120,000-gallon tank, with another 70 species making their homes in nearby exhibit areas. Call (218) 740-3474; www.glaquarium.org.

Yet if the family wants to get even closer to the fish, consider taking a charter fishing boat out on the lake after steelhead and lake trout, as well as Atlantic, chinook, and coho salmon. Half- and full-day charters are available, with all necessary equipment provided. Be sure to dress for the weather. A huge slab of Atlantic salmon is just the thing to bring home after a weekend in Duluth to impress the neighbors and to make an amazing show-and-tell for the grade-school set. Be sure, however, to get an appropriately sized cooler in order to pre-

A diver and a five-foot-long sturgeon delighting young visitors at Duluth's Great Lakes Aquarium and Freshwater Discovery Center. —Courtesy of the Great Lakes Aquarium

serve the catch. The Duluth Convention and Visitors Bureau can provide names and contact numbers for the 15 or so charter-boat captains based in the harbor.

Landward, kids can get close to the denizens of the **Lake Superior Zoological Gardens**, where black-footed ferrets, tigers, monkeys, and snow leopards show their stuff. Little ones love rummaging through the zoo's Tiger Paw gift shop to find inexpensive souvenirs to show pals back home. The zoo is at 72nd Avenue West and Grand Avenue, (218) 733-3777; www.Iszoo.org.

YEAR-ROUND ACTIVITIES

Duluth is an action-packed city, with hardly any downtime between the festivals, regattas, races, and other outdoors carryings-on. Almost every week has something to celebrate: the annual Bayfront Blues Festival, Festival of Lights at Christmas, Park Point Art Fair, Duluth National Snocross for snowmobilers, and the Duluth Air and Aviation Expo. A family seeking a weekend getaway can fill its dance card quickly around these parts.

In June, **Grandma's Marathon** highlights the spectacular scenery of the Duluth area and the North Shore. However, the runners most likely don't take a lot of notice of the greenery. The run celebrated its 25th anniversary in 2001,

---

Loads of Berths

Hundreds of general cargo ships dock at the Arthur M. Clure Public Marine Terminal owned by the Seaway Authority of Duluth. The Clure Terminal has 6,600 feet of berths, where up to seven vessels can dock at one time. The terminal has loading and unloading facilities for ships, railroad cars, and trucks. Special transfer equipment can move cargo on pallets or slings, and two rail-mounted gantry cranes work together to lift up to 150 tons at a time.

---

with weekend events including an all-you-can-eat spaghetti dinner, a health and fitness expo, and parties, parties, parties. For all the details, contact the marathon at Box 16234, Duluth 55816, (218) 727-0947; www.grandmasmarathon.com.

For a race with a little more edge, the city hosts its annual **Northshore In-line Marathon** early in September, with more than 4,000 in-line skaters zooming along a 26.2-mile route toward the waterfront finish line. There are kids' sprints if the teens want to show their speedster stuff. For an entry form, log on to www.northshoreinline.com, or call (218) 723-1503.

Not to be put off by the winter, Duluth residents and their guests celebrate Winterfest (weather permitting) with broomball, skiing, horse-drawn sleigh rides, and the **John Beargrease Sled Dog Marathon**. The race pits 60 teams against each other and nature to run a 500-mile course. While the racers are out there in the wilderness, the city's visitors can have fun at the cutest puppy contest and try their hand at mushing aboard a dogsled themselves. Even the kids can have a try at it. For information, contact the race office at Box 500, Duluth 55801, or call (218) 722-7631. Be sure the backseat gang dresses warmly.

After all that vacation hoopla, it's necessary to return home simply to rest up—and prepare for another visit.

PLACES TO STAY

Best Western Downtown, 131 West Second Street, (218) 727-6851 or (800) 528-1234

Buena Vista Motel, 1144 Mesaba Avenue, (218) 722-7796 or (800) 569-8124

EconoLodge Airport, 4197 Haines Road, (218) 722-5522 or (800) 922-0569

Fairfield Inn by Marriott, 901 Joshua Avenue, (218) 723-8607 or (800) 228-2800; www.fairfieldinn.com

Hampton Inn, 310 Canal Park Drive, (218) 720-3000 or (800) HAMPTON

Holiday Inn Hotel and Suites, 200 First Avenue, (218) 722-1202 or (800) 477-7089; www.holidayinnduluth.com

PLACES TO EAT

Gallagher's Country Cafe, 5671 Miller Trunk Highway (218) 729-7100

Grandma's Saloon and Grill, 522 Lake Avenue South, (218) 727-4192

Green Mill, 340 Lake Avenue South, (218) 727-7000

Lake Avenue Cafe, 394 Lake Avenue South, (218) 722-2355; lacae@duluth.infi.net

Old Chicago Pizza, 327 Lake Avenue South, (218) 720-2966

Pickwick, 508 East Superior Street, (218) 727-8901

Porter's, 207 West Superior Street, (218) 727-6746

PLACES TO SHOP

The Green Mercantile, 209 East Superior Street, (218) 722-1771

Hezibah's Sweet Shoppe, 394 Lake Avenue South, (218) 722-5049

J. Skylark Company, 394 Lake Avenue South, (218) 722-3794

Northern Lights Books and Gifts, 307 Canal Park Drive, (218) 722-5267 or (800) 868-8904

Snow Goose/The Goose Next Door, 600 East Superior Street, (218) 726-0927

Torke Weihnachten Christmas and Chocolates, 600 East Superior Street, (218) 723-1225 or (800) 729-1223

FOR MORE INFORMATION:

Duluth Convention and Visitors Bureau, 100 Lake Place Drive, Duluth 55802, (218) 722-4011 or (800) 438-5884; www.visitduluth.com

Duluth Seaway Port Authority, 1200 Port Terminal Drive, Duluth 55186-0877, (218) 727-8525; www.duluthport.com

NorthShoreVisitor.com; (218) 387-2368

Superior-Douglas County Chamber of Commerce and CVB, 205 Belknap Street, Superior, Wisconsin 54880, (715) 394-7716; www.superiorwi.net or www.visitsuperior.com

Wisconsin Indianhead Country, Box 628, Chetek, Wisconsin 54728 (800) 826-6966; www.wisconsinindianhead.org

THE SCENIC NORTH SHORE

The drive north from Duluth to Minnesota's border with Canada is a photographer's dream trip. Even a child with an inexpensive disposable camera can get fantastic vacation shots to show the pals back home. There are snapshot-perfect vistas virtually every mile along **Highway 61**, an attraction in itself and a route considered by experienced travelers to be among the most picturesque in North America. The deep black waters of Lake Superior to the south, and the raw hills, waterfalls, and thick woods on the north side of the highway keep the backseat gang's collective heads turning. In fact, the 24 miles of roadway between Duluth and Two Harbors has been designated as a federal scenic byway. Rightly so.

To aid motorists, green-and-white milepost markers are placed at intervals along the highway to guide motorists to state parks and other attractions on the North Shore. The markers are also a mileage reference; they begin with "0" in Duluth and continue on to the Pigeon River at "150." The markers are handy for gauging the progress of your journey, especially when the squirming kids keep asking how far it is to the next pit stop. For instance, a marker indicates that the village of Knife River is 20 miles from downtown Duluth, that Tettegouche State Park is 58.5 miles, and so on.

SUPERIOR HIKING TRAIL

Of course, there are other ways to get to Canada. The **Superior Hiking Trail** runs from Two Harbors to the border, wriggling along the North Shore on the edge of the hills above Lake Superior. The trail's proximity to towns makes daytrips possible, though the tough-minded and strong-legged can also hike the trail on long backpacking expeditions. Trail maps can be obtained at all North Shore state parks, with access points regularly marked about every 5 to 10 miles along Highway 61. Pick up the trailhead at Silver Creek Township Road 613, four miles north of Two Harbors on Highway 61. Keep the toddlers out of tennies and in strong boots if a hike is planned.

The endpoint, reached after a lot of up-and-down trekking, is at Jackson Lake Road, north of the hamlet of Hovland, some 15 miles northeast of Grand

Marais. The trail, with all its side-trip options, loops, and digressions, is about 200 miles. One of the nicest short jaunts, especially for kids not used to much walking, is the quarter-mile Cross River Trail, accessed at the Cross River rest area northeast of Schroeder along Highway 61. The hike is a comfortable, easy climb to some great views.

There are a couple of ways to take a one-way hike on the Superior Hiking Trail. The first is to catch the shuttle that transports hikers to their jumping-off point; they can then trek back to their vehicle. The second way is to hike first and grab the shuttle on its return.

The Superior Shuttle has a brochure listing pickup times, locations, and parking suggestions along the trail. Getting picked up outside the regular time costs extra and needs to be arranged in advance, so synchronize watches and be Johnny-on-the-spot at the designated site—or miss the coach. It can be a long walk home. There are special rates for kids under 16 and for dogs, so you can bring Fido along for the expedition. The shuttle operates independently of the association that manages and maintains the trail. Capitalizing on the influx of weekend vacationers, the Superior Shuttle runs its service on Friday, Saturday, and Sunday from early May to mid-October, as well as on Memorial Day and Labor Day. The shuttle can be contacted at 2618 U.S. Highway 61 East, Two Harbors 55616, (218) 834-5511 or (612) 554-6662.

Some hikers prefer walking from lodge to lodge on a multiple-day trip. Staying overnight in a comfortable hideaway is sometimes easier than camping

The heart of the North Shore: Highway 61 rolling alongside silvery Lake Superior. Minnesota Office of Tourism photograph.

A River, or Two, Runs into It

Many rivers empty into Lake Superior along the North Shore. Among them are the French, Knife, Encampment, Gooseberry, Beaver, East, Baptism, Little Marais, Caribou, Two Island, Cross, Temperance, Onion, Cascade, Devils Track, Brule, Reservation, Hollow Rock, and Pigeon.

along the route, especially if kids are along. In the winter, skiers often select routes providing day-long distances from resort to resort. Be careful not to overextend the experience for younger skiers and know the abilities of each family member before setting out; enticing cranky kids to continue on to a distant caravansary can be quite tiresome. Never hike or ski alone, as this is wilderness and trailmates are always helpful if an injury occurs. This is always a good point to emphasize to the younger ones in the family. There is hardly anything more scary than to be alone and lost or injured in the woods, an unforgiving place for the unwary.

KNIFE RIVER

The communities along Highway 61 are an interesting lot, worth a pause in your journey for exploration. The village of Knife River is noted for its delicious smoked fish, especially at Russ Kendall's **Smoked Fish House**, 149 U.S. Highway 61, (218) 834-5995, where a visitor can get salmon, herring, whitefish, or trout, plus home-smoked beef jerky. The latter item is a great way to keep the kids munching and quiet on a long ride north to vacationland. The original inhabitants of the area around the Knife River, the Ojibwe, used sharp stones found in the river as tools and weapons, hence the name. The village was founded by copper miners, and the town was also a center for the pulpwood industry. When those booms died out, the villagers turned to smelt fishing.

TWO HARBORS

Two Harbors is the seat of Lake County, with an economy based on tourism and the iron-ore industry. Stop at the city's **R. J. Houle Information Center** on Highway 61 for tourist fliers, brochures, and maps. Scooping up the literature can be a job for the kids. Attractions in the town of 3,500 are a comfortable walk; nothing is too far afield for even the pokiest little one with the shortest legs.

Freighters the length of several football fields utilize the community's docks, best viewed from Lighthouse Point or Van Hoven Park. Kids love touring the nearby *Edna G*, an 1896 coal-fired tugboat that was the last of its kind on the Great Lakes.

Two Harbors also has two interesting museums. The first is the **Depot Museum**, Waterfront Drive and South Avenue, (888) 832-5606 or (218) 834-4898, with its splendid array of historical artifacts from the region. The **3M Museum** celebrates the town where the famous corporation was founded; the museum is located in the now-multinational corporation's original office building at 210 Waterfront Drive, (218) 834-4898.

Two Harbors offers something for each person in the family. Many summertime visitors enjoy the lazy Thursday evenings in Owens Park, kicking back and listening to the band concerts. Bring mosquito spray, just in case Minnesota's state "bird" is out in force. The city's many stores, restaurants, and outfitters cater to the camping, hiking, biking, and skiing crowd, making it a good place to stock up on groceries before heading into the woods.

Open for touring all year, the **Two Harbors Lighthouse** was built in 1892. It is Minnesota's oldest operating lighthouse, earning a listing on the National Register of Historic Places. The keeper's house has morphed into the Lighthouse Bed and Breakfast, restored to an early-1900s look. The facility is located at 1 Lighthouse Point, (218) 834-4898. Ghost stories featuring haunted lighthouses are perfect for late nights around the campfire.

Just northeast of Two Rivers is **Silver Creek Cliff**, where Highway 61 runs through a 1,400-foot-long tunnel blasted through rock that is millions of years old. Because the original roadbed became unstable due to wave action on the cliff side, the roadway needed to be shifted away from the water. The only place to go was into the bluffs themselves in what was an engineering marvel of road building. Kids love the swooshing passage that carries them deep into the rock face and out again.

LOTS TO DO AT LUTSEN

About 65 miles farther north on Highway 61 lies **Lutsen Mountain**, often called the "Vail of the Midwest" by skiers in the know. The Sawtooth Mountain range here has a stomach-churning 1,000-foot drop that teenagers love and oldsters do too—well, most do. Four peaks are available for the downhill set, with 87 ski trails running at least two miles over Lutsen's 390 acres. The resort's vast size allows longer stays of up to a week or more without coming across many of the same runs twice, which makes for a perfect "no-boredom" stay, regardless of age and inclination. The region is buried each season under up to 10 feet of wonderful powder between Thanksgiving and April.

The **Lutsen Nordic Center** offers 27 kilometers of groomed cross-country ski trails accessible by area lifts. A lift ticket hauls the skier to the tops of mountains, allowing for a smooth, gradual descent to the base through heavily wooded glades of birch, maple, and pine. Smart skiers fill daypacks with food and extra wax, taking advantage of the well-set tracks where they can kick and glide for hours along the North Shore Ski Trail (where hikers walk in the summer). The Nordic Center's trail network links with more than a half dozen

Lutsen Lore

The community of Lutsen was an important port for Lake Superior tugs pushing giant rafts of logs to Duluth in the 1890s. The town was named by Swedish immigrants, recalling a village in Europe where King Gustavus Adolphus was killed in a battle with the Austrians in 1632.

other trail systems over a variety of terrain. Locals can suggest the best routes for beginner, intermediate, and advanced skiers.

At a mere four-and-one-half hour drive from the Twin Cities, Lutsen offers Midwestern skiers a tremendous bargain. They appreciate the fact that they can spend barely 40 bucks on gas, compared to almost $2,000 for airfares for four persons, plus shuttles, to some of the Rocky Mountain resorts. Tacking on the cost of slope-side condos, lift tickets, and food at Minnesota prices rather than Western rates makes the Lutsen range a real economic plus for families. Even more moola can be saved by going before Christmas or at midweek during the peak seasons of February and March. Many area lodgings offer great deals in order to fill rooms. Even when planning a short family getaway, these savings add up.

You can also save another 40 percent (plus avoid standing in line) by purchasing advance lift tickets online at www.lutsen.com. Heck, those savings are

Courtesy of Lutsen Mountains.

The Kinderschool at Lutsen Mountain.

convincing enough not to leave that grumpy, independent-minded 16-year-old at home. The trip can be offered in exchange for some babysitting of younger siblings while on vacation, allowing moms and dads the chance to head over to Papa Charlie's at the gondola base area for some R & R, pizza, bit o' bubbly, and a couple of games of pool. Live music is an added draw for the 18 and above crowd. For just a few of the plentiful accommodations in the area, see "Places to Stay" at the end of this section. Call Lutsen Mountain, (218) 663-7281, or visit the Web site listed above.

Lutsen's high energy level is not limited to the winter. In warmer weather, the kids will be thrilled to take a chairlift to the summit of Eagle Mountain at **Sawtooth Mountain Park**, then take the Alpine Slide downhill for a half-mile along a winding, concrete trough on a ride that will make them squeal and parents pale. For the short-stay visitor, Sawtooth also has hour-long horse rides on area trails and hand-led pony treks through a meadow—a great way to introduce the smallest kid to the wonders of riding. Mountain biking and hiking are also available, plus there's a deli and grill for the hungry.

STATE PARKS APLENTY

Minnesota lays out a wonderful menu of state parks along the North Shore, each with its own personality. Gooseberry Falls, Cascade River, Tettegouche, George H. Crosby, Split Rock Lighthouse, Grand Portage, Temperance River, and Judge C. R. Magney are easily reached along Highway 61. Tell the kids to get out those cameras.

One of the best is **Gooseberry Falls**, located about twelve miles north of Two Harbors. Five waterfalls here send shutterbugs racing for their cameras. Encourage the kids to get creative with camera angles to create photos for their own special memory book when they return home. The best waterfalls are right at the bridge traversing Highway 61, with water tumbling 30 feet over the Upper Falls into a pool, which then leads to the two-level Lower Falls before roaring another 60 feet downslope to boil fiercely at the base of the mountain. Call Gooseberry Falls State Park, 1300 U.S. Highway 61 East, at (218) 834-3955.

There are marvelous hiking opportunities around the park and along the Gooseberry River, passing along five major trails covered by an umbrella of aspen, birch, and conifers. While meandering along, be sure to have everyone pause occasionally and listen . . . listen to the waterfalls, the wind in the trees, the birds. There are some 142 species of birds that nest or fly through the park, according to skilled watchers who log these sorts of things. Subsequently, be sure to bring along a handy bird guidebook and binoculars. If the kids are interested, they may also want to record their findings.

To impress the children, you can tell them that Gooseberry Falls appears on maps dating from 1670 and that the area became a state park long afterwards, in 1937. The site currently consists of 1,662 acres. Information on the other state parks along the North Shore can be secured from the state's Department of Natural Resources, Division of Parks and Recreation. The DNR Information Center is located at 500 Lafayette Road St. Paul, Minnesota 55155-4040. Call (651) 296-6157 or (888) MINNDNR. TTY: (651) 296-5484 or (800) 657-3929. The DNR Central Office hours are 8:00 a.m. - 4:30 p.m., Monday - Friday. Closed holidays. The Web site is http://www.dnr.state.mn.us.

Always popular with history fans and lighthouse lovers, Split Rock Lighthouse in the state park of the same name is managed by the Minnesota Historical Society. High atop a wind-blown 130-foot cliff about 20 miles northeast of Two Harbors, the building has looked out over the lake for more than 90 years. The structure was built after a fierce storm in 1905 damaged 30 ships on the lake, many of them hitting rocks along the shoreline near the location of the future lighthouse.

Subsequently, the lighthouse was constructed between 1908 and 1910 to warn vessels away from the dangerous cliffs. Every 10 seconds in the old days, an incandescent oil vapor lamp cast its comforting glow 20 miles out over the lake to warn ships that they were approaching shore. The eerie call of foghorns was used as an alarm during foul weather. Tours take guests around the fog-signal building, the lighthouse keeper's homes and the lighthouse itself. The scene is reminiscent of the 1920s, as costumed interpreters talk about life as it was lived at the time. Split Rock Lighthouse is located at 3713 Split Rock Lighthouse Road, Two Harbors 55616, (218) 266-6372 or (888) 727-8386. Split Rock makes for more great ghost stories.

SOME MAJOR RESORTS

Vacationing families along the North Shore have their choice of roughing it by camping, enjoying a comfortable cabin stay, or being pampered at a full-service resort. If the last option is for you, check out the Lutsen Resort at Lutsen Mountain, with its lakeside dining, two pools, and a nine-hole golf course. Accommodations range from log cabins to classy condominiums. Lutsen caters to the kids as well, with outdoor activities and a large game room. Call (218) 663-7212 or (800) 2-LUTSEN; www.lutsenresort.com.

Other notable resorts in the Lutsen area include **Bluefin Bay** on Lake Superior, called "Minnesota's Favorite Resort" by *Minnesota Monthly* magazine and "Resort Property of the Year" by the Minnesota Innkeepers Association. The resort has a kid's program with hiking, candle making, rock collecting and painting, games, and other kid-oriented activities to keep them busy. As a bonus, Bluefin offers its own free shuttle to hiking and mountain-biking trails. **Caribou Highlands Lodge** has a Mountain Kids Camp for the 4- to 12-year-old set staying at its Lutsen property, as well as family scavenger hunts and bingo matches, pizza parties, and volleyball. **Eagle Ridge** has an Eagle Rangers kids program with hiking, games, and other programming for kids. Folksingers and storytellers are regular features during evening programs.

For details, contact Bluefin Bay, 7198 U.S. Highway 61, Tofte, (218) 663-7296 or (800) 258-3346, www.bluefinbay.com; Caribou Highlands Lodge, 371 Ski Hill Road, (218) 663-7241 or (800) 642-6036, www.caribouhighlands.com; Eagle Ridge at Lutsen Mountains, 565 Ski Hill Road, (218) 663-7284 or (800) 360-7666; www.eagleridgeatlutsen.com.

Let It Snow, Let It Snow

While lake-effect snow ensures an abundant supply of the white stuff around Lutsen, the ski resort at Lutsen does its bit to add more with snow-making machinery. The resort guarantees that 25 runs will be open by December 1, totaling at least 10 miles of trail. Forty runs stay open through mid-April, a long-standing tradition of more than 15 years running. But nature always does the best job. Snow clouds are formed as damp, heated air above the lake condenses as it rises. Winds push the clouds over the colder land, resulting in magnificent snowfalls.

The kids will love the area gift shops, many of which cater to a wilderness/frontier theme. Among the best is **Tom's Logging Camp and Trading Post** at Stony Point two miles south of Knife River and 16 miles northeast of downtown Duluth on Scenic Highway 61, which runs parallel to the main Highway 61 between Duluth and Two Harbors. Made of timbers, the building is reminiscent of an old-time trader's store with maple syrup, wild rice, Native American handicrafts, and similar items for sale amid the antiques. As a bonus, the facility has self-guided tours of a re-created logging camp, complete with a cook shanty, blacksmith shop, bunkhouse, and nature trail. Tom's is open from May 1 through October 20. For further details, contact the store's headquarters, 5797 North Shore Drive, Duluth 55804, (218) 525-4120; www.tomsloggingcamp.com.

Then it's back to the woods.

PLACES TO STAY

Bob's Cabins on Lake Superior, 664 Old North Shore Road, Two Harbors 55616, (218) 834-4583

Grand Superior Lodge, 2826 U.S. Highway 61, Two Harbors 55616, (218) 834-3796 or (800) 627-9565; www.grandsuperior.com

PLACES TO EAT

Betty's Pies, 1633 U.S. Highway 61, Two Harbors 55616, (218) 834-3367 or (877) 269-7494; www.bettyspies.com

Emily's Inn B&B, 218 Scenic Highway 61, Box 174, Knife River 55609, (218) 834-5922

Rustic Inn Cafe and Gifts, 2773 U.S. Highway 61, Two Harbors 55616, (218) 834-2488; www.rusticinncafe.com

Splashing Rock Restaurant at Grand Superior Lodge, 2826 U.S. Highway 61, Two Harbors 55616, (218) 834-3796 or (800) 627-9565

PLACES TO SHOP

B.E. Nelson Designs, 583 North Shore Scenic Drive, Larsmont, 218-834-4234

Loon Landing, 543 Scenic Drive, Two Harbors, (218) 834-8088; www.lakentet.com/~loonland

Playing With Yarn, 276 Scenic Drive, Knife River, (218) 834-5967 or (877) 693-2221; www.playingwithyarn.com

FOR MORE INFORMATION

A good general Web site is www.northshorevisitors.com.

Boundary Country Trekking, 173 Little Ollie Road, Grand Marais 55604, (218) 388 4487 or (800) 322-8327; www.boundarycountry.com

Lake County Historical Society, Box 128, 520 South Avenue, Two Harbors 55616, (218) 834-4898; www.northshorehistory.com

Lake Superior North Shore Association, Box 159, Duluth 55804; www.LakeSuperiorDrive.com. Email Susan Lampi, LSNSA Secretary-Treasurer at SusanLSNSA@aol.com

Lutsen Mountains, Box 129, Lutsen 55612 (218) 663-7281; www.lutsen.com

Lutsen-Tofte Tourism Association, Box 2248, Tofte 44615-2248, (888) 61-NORTH

Minnesota Department of Natural Resources, Division of Parks and Recreation, 500 Lafayette Road, St. Paul 55155, (651) 296-6157 or (888) MINNDNR (646-6367); toll-free inside Minnesota, (800) 657-3929; www.dnr.state.mn.us

Minnesota Department of Natural Resources Information Center, (800) 766-6000

Minnesota State Park campsite reservations, (800) 246-CAMP

North Shore Scenic Drive Association, Box 240, Knife River 55609, (no phone); www.northshorescenicdrive.com

North Shore State Parks, P.O. Box 1342, Grand Marais 55604; To reserve a campsite, call (800) 246-CAMP; www.northshoreguide.com/parks

R. J. Houle Visitor Information Center, 1330 U.S. Highway 61, Two Harbors 55616, (218) 834-4005 or (800) 554-2116; www.lakecnty.com

Superior Hiking Trail, 731 Superior Avenue, Two Harbors 55616, (218) 834-2700

Two Harbors Area Chamber of Commerce, 1026 Seventh Avenue, Two Harbors 55616, (218) 834-2600 or (800) 777-7384; www.twoharbors.com/chamber

GRAND MARAIS AND ISLE ROYALE

The far northeastern tip of Minnesota along Highway 61 as it nears Canada sure is remote. And so the backseat gang may have visions of black bears (which, to be certain, are out there to the west), huge fish rising to the bait (to the watery east), and red-jacketed Mounties at the border (to the north). The area is also stunningly beautiful, with an ocean of greenery waving on one side of the highway and the cold waters of Lake Superior lapping the shoreline on the other. This is a world far removed from urban pavement, without a fast-food joint in sight, a situation that the kids will have to endure.

That's exactly the way it should be, whether you are enjoying a fast getaway for a few days or a longer vacation. It's an area rife with opportunities for hiking, swimming, rock climbing, bird watching, fishing, skiing, sightseeing, and a lot more. The **Superior National Forest** spreads along 150 miles of the U.S.-Canada border, with more than three million acres in which to find adventure. Of those acres, more than 445,000, or 695 square miles, are surface water such as lakes and ponds, along with 1,300 miles of cool, trout-filled streams.

So, bring fly rods, fishing poles, swimsuits, walking sticks, rain (or sun) hats, and bug repellent for Minnesota's monster mosquitoes. Thus prepared, your family should be set for fun.

MARVELOUS GRAND MARAIS

But before plunging into the wilds, putter around Grand Marais for a day or so. The city, about 18 miles northeast of the Lutsen area along Highway 61, is the largest tourist center along this stretch of the scenic North Shore. One of the best things in town is the municipal indoor swimming pool complex, which includes a wading pool for kids. Head for the pools with pent-up little ones when cold weather or lashing rain prevents a trek in the woods.

Despite its remote locale, Grand Marais is considered one of Minnesota's top artist communities. The **Grand Marais Art Festival** in July brings together some of the state's best artists and hosts workshops, lectures, and demonstrations throughout the season. Call (888) 922-5000. The **North House Folk School**, 500 West Highway 61, teaches traditional crafts, timber framing, boat-building, woodworking, preparing foods, shelter building, and a host of other North Woods necessities. North House is on the west end of downtown Grand Marais and is easily spotted. Contact the folks here at (218) 387-9762 or (888) 387-9762; info@northhouse.org.

About 20 miles northwest of Grand Marais, determined hikers will find **Eagle Mountain**, Minnesota's highest point. Reached via County Highway 12 to County Highway 8, the trailhead for the route to the top of the mountain is located in the Pat Bayle State Forest. The peak is 2,301 feet above sea level. This is probably not the best trek for little kids, but in-shape teens wanting to prove a point should be able to make it to the top. Just remember all the wilderness hiking rules: never go alone, let someone know when and where you'll be at a certain time, dress for the weather, bring extra food and water, and have a small first-aid kit along.

If you're looking for a tamer touch of wilderness for the whole family, check out **Judge C. R. Magney State Park**, named after the late Minnesota Supreme Court justice and Duluth mayor who was an advocate of the state's park system. One of his most noteworthy comments was that "our state parks are

The sumptuous Great Hall at the historic Naniboujou Lodge.
—Courtesy of Naniboujou Lodge

everyone's country estate." Located 15 miles northeast of Grand Marais along Highway 61 at the Brule River, the park boasts 4,514 acres, with picnic grounds, a campground, and extensive hiking trails, making it a worthy pullover for a few hours or an overnight. The park provides plenty of room for the children to stretch their legs.

Show the kids the ancient lava flow visible near the parking lot along Highway 61, which can launch a story about how erosion and the forces of nature are still impacting the earth's surface. About 1.2 billion years ago, the North Shore was a cauldron of volcanic activity, with one great flow extending from Grand Portage to Lutsen estimated to have been 21,000 feet thick at one time. Tens of thousands of years of erosion and glacial activity followed, with the Sawtooth Mountains one of the reminders of the past. For details about the park, contact the manager, Judge C. R. Magney State Park, Grand Marais 55604, (218) 387-2929.

If the gang feels the need for some luxury in the midst of the wilderness, consider a stay at the **Naniboujou Lodge** on Highway 61 at the Brule River. This is an historic 1920s-era inn with Native American decor and a solarium. It's a great place to eat, with hearty breakfasts, special sandwiches that kids devour, and high tea. The facility is open May to October and on January, February, and March weekends. Naniboujou Lodge was originally an exclusive private club, with baseball star Babe Ruth, boxer Jack Dempsey, and author Ring Lardner among its charter members. Today, Naniboujou Lodge is open to the public. The lodge is on the National Register of Historic Places and boasts one of Minnesota's largest native-rock fireplaces: a 200-ton work which stands in the 30-foot by 80-foot Great Hall dining room. Contact the resort at 20 Naniboujou Trail, Grand Marais 55604, (218) 387-2688; www.naniboujou.com.

GRAND PORTAGE

Twenty miles northeast of the state park on—what else?—Highway 61 lies Grand Portage. Seven miles south of the Canadian border, the town earned its name from the Ojibwe and French-Canadian traders who linked their inland winter camps to their summer residences along the lake. Their 8.5-mile trek to Fort Charlotte on the Pigeon River led to the vast string of lakes to the west (now the Boundary Waters Canoe Area Wilderness) and eventually to the open plains of central Canada. Anybody walking the **Grand Portage Trail** these days will realize what effort it took to penetrate the wilderness in the days of the fur traders. The kids will get a kick out of the **Grand Portage National Monument** (just about everything around here carries the Grand Portage moniker), a restored Northwest Fur Company depot, complete with a stockade. The old fort, which stood here at the peak of the fur trade between 1730 and 1805, was once a hub of economic activity and is now a popular tourist attraction from mid-May through mid-October. **Grand Portage State Park** is nearby, featuring fantastic photographic opportunities at High Falls.

Grand Portage Rendezvous Days in late June is a festival that blends Native American traditions with those of the white man's frontier culture. Kids will love playing horseshoes and participating in the festival's walk-run race. Tribes from around the Midwest and Ontario demonstrate their dancing skills during the festival. There are usually kid's dancing competitions, too.

Travelers in the region during the winter can get trailside sites or even participate in the **Grand Portage Sled Dog Race**, which runs in January from Thunder Bay, Ontario, to Grand Portage. The race goes along the routes taken by those long-ago voyageurs and their Native American predecessors.

IDYLLIC ISLE ROYALE

It is the natural wonder of Isle Royale National Park that brings many vacationers to Grand Portage, as ferries to the park leave from town (travelers can also reach the park via ferries from Houghton and Copper Harbor, Michigan). The island is officially part of Michigan, though it's much closer to Minnesota; it lies approximately 17 miles southeast of Grand Portage and about 45 miles north of Copper Harbor. From Grand Portage, trips are available to either side of the island. They vary from about three to seven hours. For details on schedules and rates, call the Grand Portage–Isle Royale Transportation Line, (715) 392-2100 or visit their Web site, www.grand-isle-royale.com.

The island has been a national park since 1932 and is only open to the public from April to November. Be prepared to walk a great deal: no motorized vehicles are allowed on the island. The island is accessible to hikers, campers, fishing fans, canoeists, sea kayakers, and boaters. There aren't even any public telephones on the island. So you may want to have a cell phone handy. But don't rely too heavily on such modern gadgetry in this wildest of places; reserve cell phone use only for emergencies, which don't include, by the way, calls by your teenagers to their friends back home.

Isle Royale was formed by volcanic action that shook the world more than a billion years ago. The kids may already know these facts from their science and geography classes, but—according to geologists—a huge magma flow

Animals under Scrutiny

The moose and wolf populations on Isle Royale have been the subject of intense research by wildlife ecologists for nearly 50 years, the longest-running such study in history. Scientists are especially interested in the complex predator-prey relationships between the two groups. Because of its confined area, Isle Royale is an ideal laboratory for studying wildlife behavior.

Checking out the Menagerie Island (Isle Royale) Light. —Courtesy of the National Park Service

poured into a giant crack in the center of what is today's North America, running from Kansas to Lake Superior.

While the cooling lava hardened, the North American Continental Plate smashed into other rock plates and pushed the lava out from its sides. The pressure pushed the lava down the plate's midsection, creating a U shape with edges fractured into overlapping ridges. These land formations can still be seen today on the northern side of the island. The cracks eventually filled with sediment and slowly turned to rock. Ten thousand years ago, the last great ice age pushed down the existing land, draining the vast upper Great Lakes. As the glaciers melted, the waters of Lake Superior rose, surrounding the island. Isle Royale is 45 miles long and nine miles wide, encompassing 850 square miles, with 165 miles of hiking trails.

The early people who lived around the edges of the glaciers adapted to the conditions, collecting copper for their implements and making canoes to easily get across the water. The Native American lifestyle remained the same for generations until the arrival of the French drastically changed their way of doing things. The mineral-rich region became a political and social battleground between the French and the British, and, later, between the Americans and the native tribes of the region. Much of this history is put into perspective at Grand Portage National Monument, so it's wise to stop with the kids at the old fort before visiting the island.

Over the ensuing years, the island's topography has changed. The land was almost totally stripped of its timber cover as settlers logged the land. Miners searching for copper and iron dotted the island with their pits and then moved on. Families regularly sailed out from the mainland to set up camps and drop their nets offshore for whitefish. Even young children were enlisted to help. But by the end of the 1980s, the federal government finally ended commercial fishing in the park's waters.

As lighthouses were constructed around the perimeter of Isle Royale and sailing became easier and safer, vacationers discovered the island. In the 1920s, Detroit newspaperman Albert Stoll, Jr., and others pushed the idea of turning the island into a national park. President Herbert Hoover signed the law creating Isle Royale National Park.

THE ISLE ROYALE EXPERIENCE

Children can learn about the island through the **Junior Ranger Program**, available for young people aged 6 to 12. They work with rangers and parents to solve riddles about the island and its flora and fauna. Successful graduates earn a badge and a signed certificate. In fact, there are many educational programs and guided hikes on the island, open to adults and kids alike. Activities are scheduled at Windigo, Rock Harbor, and Daisy Farm, with tours to Passage Island and Lookout Louise. Most programs are free. Visitors can take nature walks, watch evening slide shows, and chat around campfires. A visit to the 1855-era lighthouse at Rock Harbor is a fun side trip.

A per-day user fee is required to visit the island; however, kids under 11 are free. Season passes are also available at the Windigo Ranger Station on the island. No pets are allowed. They can disturb the local animals and cause disease, particularly for the wolf packs that live on Isle Royale.

While there, you may want to avoid the outdoors at night by staying at **Rock Harbor Lodge**, managed by National Park Concessions. The facility, located along the shore at Rock Harbor, is open from May through September. The lodge's rooms with private baths can be a welcome relief after a few days tenting. Other lodge amenities include a dining room, grocery store, snack bar, and a souvenir shop packed with postcards and other gewgaws, plus a marina with rentable motorboats. Guided fishing and sightseeing tours are also available from here.

However, most visitors enjoy camping out. All shelters and campsites are on a first-come, first-served basis. There are several options for families to try: three-sided shelters that sleep up to six persons, tent sites accommodating one to three tents, and group sites for parties of seven to ten persons. To ease overcrowding, only limited stays are allowed. It is suggested that only lightweight backpacking stoves be used for cooking to reduce the potential of fire. If you do decide to build a campfire in one of the park's metal fire rings, remind the kids that campfires always need to be totally extinguished before leaving an

Fire Safety

Here are some fire safety tips for having a good time camping on Isle Royale, or anywhere else for that matter: use a lightweight stove for cooking and a candle lantern for light. Where fires are allowed, use an established fire ring. Keep fires small; use only sticks found on the ground that can be broken by hand. Burn all wood and coals to ash, and then extinguish campfires with water and scatter the cooled ashes.

area or retiring for the night. Be sure to have them help police the site, leaving it in good condition for the next visitors.

Do not let anyone in the group, especially children and older adults, drink untreated water other than from the taps at Rock Harbor and Windigo. Water should be boiled or filtered before use. Hikers must also plan their meals carefully. Some experienced outdoors lovers even put together a pre-trip cookout at home to practice preparing what they'll take on the trail so there are no surprises. Don't feed the local critters because they will grow accustomed to raiding your grub. Hang your food pack from a tree branch several feet above the ground. Campers must carry in their own food and carry out their refuse. Pit toilets are available at campsites, but if nature calls Junior on the trail, move at least 100 feet away from the path or any water sources. Dig a pit about six inches deep and then make sure your child covers everything when finished.

The whole family needs to wear hats, long-sleeved shirts, and pants during bug season. Black flies, gnats, and mosquitoes are plentiful in June and July. Bring repellent and netting, as well as repair material for tent tears. These beasties are persistent and can ruin a night's sleep, but they are part of the island experience. Learn to live with them. Kids should be prepped that they may be chomped on by no-see-ums that bite before they can be brushed away. Teach youngsters that putting damp mud on a bug bite often draws out the poison.

Using a warm, water-resistant sleeping bag is very important because of the changeable weather around the island. Hardly anything is worse than climbing into a damp bag on a cold night. Be sure that everyone has a foam pad on which to sleep; air mattresses can spring a leak and are really not that comfortable. Remember that cutting pine boughs for placing under a sleeping bag is not allowed.

Try to keep noise to a minimum; much of the fun on Isle Royale comes from enjoying the solitude. By being quiet, kids have a better chance to see the animals that live on the island, such as moose, fox, and other species.

The Isle Royale National Park Web site has numerous other suggestions for staying safe and having a great time on the island. Log onto www.isleroyale.national-park.com for details on registration, boating and canoeing, camping, sanitation, wildlife, and more. Remember that since the island is so isolated, a minor problem can easily and quickly become a major challenge or even degenerate into an emergency. So be prepared. For more details, contact Isle Royale National Park, 800 Lakeshore Drive, Houghton, Michigan 49931-1895, (906) 482-0984.

PLACES TO STAY

GRAND MARAIS

Best Western Superior Inn and Suites, East U.S. Highway 61, 104 First Avenue, (218) 387-2240 or (800) 842-8439

Devil Track Lodge, 205 Fireweed Lane, (218) 387-9414 or (877) 387-9414; www.deviltracklodge.com

Grand Marais RV Park and Campground, Box 820, U.S. Highway 61, on the Grand Marais harbor on Eighth Avenue West off U.S. Highway 61, (218) 387-1712; for reservations only, (800) 998-0959

Gunflint Motel, 101 West Fifth Avenue (Gunflint Trail), (218) 387-1454; www.gunflintmotel.com

Harbor Inn Motel, 207 Wisconsin Street, (218) 387-1191 or (800) 595-4566; www.obreal.org/harborinn

Lund's Motel and Cottages, 919 West U.S. Highway 61, (218) 387-2155 or (218) 387-1704

Nelson's Traveler's Rest Motel, Box 634, West U.S. Highway 61, (218) 387-1464 or (800) 249-1285; www.travelersrest.com

Old Shore Beach Bed and Breakfast, 1434 Old Shore Road, (218) 387-9707 or (888) 387-9707

Outpost Motel, 2935 East U.S. Highway 61, (218) 387-1833 or (888) 380-1833; www.outpostmotel.com

Russell's Cottages and Motel, 20 West Fifth Avenue (Gunflint Trail), 55604-0014, (218) 387-1108; www.grandmaraismm.com

Sandgren Motel, East U.S. Highway 61 and Second Avenue East, (218) 387-2975 or (800) 796-2975

Sawtooth Cabins and Motel, 510 West Second Street, (218) 387-1522

SeaWall Motel and Cottages, U.S. Highway 61 and Third Avenue West, (218) 387-2095 or (800) 245-5806

Shoreline, 20 South Broadway, (218) 387-2633 or (800) 247-6020

Tomteboda Resort Motel and Log Cabins, 1800 West U.S. Highway 61, (218) 387-1585 or (800) 456-5258; www.tomteboda.com

Trailside Cabins and Motel, 1100 West US Highway 61, (218) 387-1550 or (800) 585-2792

GRAND PORTAGE
Grand Portage Lodge and Casino, 70 Casino Drive off U.S. Highway 61, (218) 475-2401 or (800) 543-1384

PLACES FOR FOOD

GRAND MARAIS
Angry Trout Café, Box 973, Fifth Avenue West and U.S. Highway 61 across from start of the Gunflint Trail, (218) 387-1265

Birch Terrace Supper Club and Lounge, Box 1449, Sixth Avenue and U.S. Highway 61, (218) 387-2215

Blue Water Cafe, downtown at the harbor, (218) 387-1597; www.bluewatercafe.com

Dairy Queen and Brazier, Box 507, Second Avenue West and U.S. Highway 61, (218) 387-1741

Gunflint Tavern on the Lake, Box 985, 111 Wisconsin Street, (218) 387-1563; www.gunflinttavern.com

Harbor Inn Restaurant, at the harbor, (218) 387-1191 or (800) 595-4566; www.bytheharbor.com

The Harbor Light Supper Club, Box 398, U.S. Highway 61 west of Grand Marais, (218) 387-1142

Sven and Ole's, 9 West Wisconsin Street, (218) 387-1713; www.svenandoles.com

Victoria's Bakehouse and Deli, 411 West U.S. Highway 61, (218) 387-1747

PLACES TO SHOP

GRAND MARAIS
Dockside Fish Market, Box 921, Fifth Avenue West and U.S. Highway 61, (218) 387-2906

Grand Marais Lake Superior Trading Post on the Harbor, Box 370, at end of First Avenue West, (218) 387-2020; www.lstradingpost.com

The Market, Box 848, West Wisconsin Street, adjacent to Sven and Ole's; (218) 387-2118; www.magicwindow.com/themarket

Stephan Hoglund Design and Jewelry Studio, Box 850, Wisconsin Street, adjacent to the Gunflint Tavern; 218) 387-1752 or (800) 678-1891; www.stephanhoglund.com

The Market, Box 848, West Wisconsin Street, adjacent to Sven and Ole's; (218) 387-2118; www.magicwindow.com/themarket

Waters of Superior, 501 West Highway 61, (218) 387- 9766; www.watersof-superior.com

Wilderness Waters Outfitters, Box 368, West Highway 61, (218) 387-2725 or (800) 325-5842; www.wilderness-waters.com

FOR MORE INFORMATION

Grand Marais Art Colony, Box 626, Grand Marais 55604, (218) 387-2737 or (800) 385-9585; www.grandmaraisartcolony.org

Grand Marais Visitor Center, Box 1048, Grand Marais 55604, (888) 922-5000; www.grandmaraismn.com

Grand Portage information, www.grandportagemn.com

Grand Portage–Isle Royale Transportation Line, 1507 North First Street, Superior, Wisconsin 54880-1146, (715) 392-2100; www.grand-isle-royale.com

Isle Royale National Park, 800 East Lakeshore Drive, Houghton, Michigan 49931-1895, (906) 482-0984; www.isleroyale.national-park.com

ELY AND THE BOUNDARY WATERS

The wilderness of far northeastern Minnesota will challenge even the most dyed-in-the-wool campers in your family unit. Yet it's the perfect place to get away from gridlock grind and 20th-floor office workdays. These barely utilized woods and waters have been the perfect vacation spot for more than a century. Some of the trees here were teenagers when the Pilgrims landed at Plymouth Rock. So pack a compass and the kids, and head to the woods.

The **Boundary Waters Canoe Area Wilderness (BWCAW)** is the reason people flock to this region, and Ely is the jumping-off point for those venturing into the pristine woods and lakes. If the family is seeking an honest-to-goodness wilderness getaway, this part of Minnesota is just the ticket, and Ely is the place to find everything you need for a trip into the BWCAW. It's hard not to believe in the city's claim as the "Canoe Capital of the World."

The wilderness preserve is considered one of the most beautiful places on earth, so much so that *National Geographic* magazine suggested that it is one of the places to visit in one's lifetime. Who wants to argue with that? A trip here is not a mere weekend getaway, although it can be done by flying in and out of this remote northern borderland with Canada. Most people drive to the edge of the wilderness, making the four-hour or more trek from the Twin Cities to spend at least a week. Once here, why rush? Encourage the rear-window set to smell the piney perfume, look for moose, or catch a largemouth bass.

More than a million backcountry acres of lands and pine forests have been set aside for the BWCAW in the heart of the Superior National Forest. It is the largest wilderness preserve east of the Rocky Mountains.

The Ely area was Ojibwe stomping grounds before the 1700s, when French traders made their way to this pelt-heavy wilderness. After the traders moved on to other areas, gold prospectors moved in and settled the area. They didn't find gold but did discover high-grade iron ore in the 1880s and 1890s. Eventually, there were mines all around Ely in Savoy, Pioneer, Sibley, and Zenith. In fact, after several tries at other monikers such as Florence, the city was named after a miner, Samuel B. Ely. And remember: Ely is pronounced "eelee"; call it "e-lie" and the folks who run the Stoney River Café will charge you double. In the late-19th century, the need for timber to shore up the tunnels and for railroad ties spun off a major logging industry.

A bit of heaven on earth: the Gunflint area in the Boundary Waters Canoe Area Wilderness. Minnesota Office of Tourism photograph.

Today, the underground mines are silent and most are sealed off so no unsuspecting visitors take a tumble. However, open-pit mining for taconite ore, with a 20 percent iron content, is still a major industry southwest of Ely in Babbit, Mountain Iron, and Eveleth.

Tourism became another important stage in the region's economic development as early as 1916. Folks paid good money to haul themselves and their urchins on explorations of the lakes and islands of the borderlands. They needed guides, and the locals were glad to oblige.

ELY OUT OF DOORS

Regardless of age, there are numerous canoeing, hiking, biking, cross-country skiing, and snowmobile trails that a vacationing family can enjoy throughout the North Country around Ely. The Kawishiwi Ranger District of the **Superior National Forest** has plenty of possibilities for all skill and endurance levels of trekkers, from those wanting a simple quiet stroll to determined ramblers seeking a more rugged adventure. Most of the more remote trails are marked by blue diamond signage and waist-high cairns, or piles of rock. Drop by the ranger station permit center, located east of Ely on State Highway 169, to pick up trail maps and other helpful literature. The staff can answer most of the questions that even the most inquisitive kid can ask. You can find the main forest headquarters in town at 118 South Fourth Avenue East, Ely 55731, (218) 365-7600.

Before taking off, there are a few things to remember out in the woods. Don't hike alone and keep a very close watch on the little ones. Let someone know where you are going and when you expect to return. Take water, some high-carbohydrate snacks, matches, a small flashlight, insect repellent, a pocketknife, and a compass. Wear sturdy hiking boots. Dress for the weather; it is

Digging Deep

Ely's first open-pit mine, the Chandler, opened in 1888. More than 1,200 miners labored in the pits during its early years. The mining companies paid miners for work completed, not by the hour. The men averaged $1.80 to $2.20 a day in 1897. Over the years, miners extracted about 19 million tons of iron ore from the Ely mines.

easier to take off a layer than to be uncomfortable. Stay on the trails. And it's not fair to leave behind any grumpy teenagers.

You don't have to venture far from Ely to enjoy the best of what the BWCAW has to offer. Many miles of quality trails meander amid the pines around Ely, allowing outdoors lovers the chance to stretch taut muscles. The easy-to-intermediate pathways on Bear Island, just south of town, are free. They provide excellent opportunities to see deer, moose, and possibly even gray wolves. There are several other Kawishiwi trails that all but the smallest in the family can enjoy. The 5.6-mile **Bass Lake Trail** is six miles north of Ely, offering backpacking campsites, a waterfall, and plenty of overlooks. This trek takes from four to six hours. **Secret Lake Trail** and **Blackstone Lake Trail** are about 20 miles northeast of Ely. Both are great for day hikes, leading through bogs and on to high vistas. Be careful on the ledges, especially if younger, less-experienced climbers are along.

Other good trails around Ely include those in the **Hidden Valley Recreation Area**, off Highway 169 east of Ely; the **Thomas Winter Recreation Trails** west of town; the Trezona Trail northeast of the city; and the **Birch Plantation Ski Trail** located in the first Red Pine plantation in the Superior National Forest at County Roads 623 and 131.

Canoeists love the solitude found in the BWCAW, where there are more than 1,500 miles of water trails to explore. Remember that permits are required to enter the area; the permits limit traffic in the wilderness in order to protect the ecology of the region. No motorboats are allowed in the vast majority of the BWCAW. Encourage the children to leave their compact-disc players and headphones at home, so they can hear such things as trees rustling in the breeze and flies buzzing around them. They may be surprised to learn that not all groovy sounds emanate from electronic devices.

Remember that you'll need to carry in your food and haul out your garbage. Leave the bottles and cans at home. Kids will think it's Earth Day all over, and over and over. Information about these restrictions and other advice are available from the U.S. Forest Service, local resorts, and the 22 licensed, professional canoe-trip outfitters in the Ely area.

When winter rolls around, Ely switches gears under the seven feet of annual snowfall that's dumped on the community between December and April.

Imagine that! But since vacationers are not expected to shovel, winter week-end getaways can include cross-country skiing or snowmobiling instead of de-manding that your 16-year-old digs out a path from backdoor to garage.

No matter what outdoor activities your family craves, the area's numerous outfitters will help your budding Lewises and Clarkes get off on the right foot. They can assist in selecting entry points, campsites, and routes, as well as sug-gest where to catch the biggest fish. Outfitters work with kids, teens, and old-sters in their quest for walleye and remote campsites. There are many youth and Scout camps scattered throughout the neighborhood, giving young peo-ple a taste of the wilds and encouraging them to return when they become older. Many repeat vacationers to Ely received their love of the North Woods from early-in-life wilderness adventures as a wide-eyed child.

Snowshoers, canoeists, dogsledders (mushers), hikers, ice-fishing fans, and others heading here can be rigged out at **Gateway North Outfitters** and other area outfitters, which provide everything from life jackets to robust sandwiches designed to carb up the hardworking outdoors fan. Gateway North is located at 1892 West Shagawa Road, (218) 365-7000 or (800) 280-2359; www.gate-waynorthoutfitters.com. Two other outfitters of note in Ely are **Voyageur North**, 1829 North Sheridan Street, (800) 848-5530, and **Wilderness Adven-tures**, 943 East Sheridan Street, (800) 843-2922.

This is resort country, with a wide range of properties: from the rustic mom-and-pop places to the larger resorts that offer enough amenities to sat-isfy a sheik. Camping is also part and parcel of an Ely adventure. Watch out for black bears, and keep all foods locked in an auto trunk or suspended from a tree limb high above the ground. The creatures are usually harmless, unless a mother is defending her cubs. Just make a lot of noise on the trail to alert any wayward bruin that you are approaching.

Finally, adventurous families can captain a houseboat on various lakes throughout the district. Try Birch Lake with its 20 square miles of wilderness waters in the Superior National Forest near Ely. For bargain vacationers, spring and fall discounts are offered. With all that open space, let the young ones try their hand (supervised, of course) at the wheel.

INSIDE ELY

Getaway families don't need to spend their entire vacation in the woods around the campfire. The city of Ely offers loads of ideas for things to do when it rains or the mosquitoes become a problem. Expanding one's craft-making abilities is a good enough reason to visit Ely, where there are workshops, lec-tures, and how-to sessions on building wood or canvas canoes, knitting, or log cabin construction, skills that everyone in your own Swiss Family Robinson can call into play after returning home.

Weekend, weeklong, or customized outdoor and field courses for all ages are available at **Vermilion Community College**, 1900 East Camp, (800) 657-

3609; ENVS@mail.vcc.mnscu.edu. While at the college, take the gang to the **Ely-Winton History Museum**, which is on the college grounds. A visit provides a deeper sense of Ely's Native American, logging, and mining heritages. Call the museum at (218) 365-3226.

The **Dorothy Molter Museum** offers a historical perspective on the area, presented through the eyes of the famous nurse known as the "Root Beer Lady." Molter lived on Knife Lake from the 1930s until her death in 1986, pulling out thousands of fishhooks, tending broken bones and sprains, and serving up homemade root beer to her guests. When she died, her homestead was taken apart and reassembled in Ely where it now contains many artifacts from her life: her first snowmobile, a wind-powered paddle plane, and other odds and ends. The museum is located at 2002 East Sheridan Street, (218) 365-4451; www.canoecountry.com/dorothy or dmolter@canoecountry.com.

Ely Community Education also presents a wide spectrum of activities and courses in computers, foreign languages, cooking, and other classes to help fill the time. The organization has a number of programs aimed at children, including American Red Cross–sanctioned swimming classes. Call the chamber of commerce for details, (218) 365-6123 or (800) 777-7281.

The **Northern Lakes Arts Association** holds concerts and theater performances throughout the year. Call (218) 365-5070. As the summer drags on and the kids hunger for a good book, the Ely Public Library, (218) 365-5140, can accommodate them. Its summer reading programs kick off in June.

Just because this is the North Woods doesn't mean that you have to give up that daily physical workout. **Studio North** has a weight room that stays open 24 hours, seven days a week. Swing in, sign up, and jerk a few hundred pounds of metal up into the air. It gets you in shape for chasing the two-year-old who is just learning to gallop. Contact the facility, 2030 East Sheridan Street, at (218) 365-2493.

Even though Ely is a family place, sometimes it's a good idea to get some alone time for a few hours or share communal time with others outside the paterfamilias spectrum. Drumming circles are one option, held every Thursday evening at Semer's Park. Sessions run from around seven in the evening until everyone tires of rhythm making. Instruments are provided by **Music Outfitters**, which holds sessions in the park pavilion when it rains.

Lots of Water

Ely is surrounded by the Superior National Forest, which encompasses 2,021 lakes of more than 10 acres in size, with a total of 314,545 acres of water. There are also 1,975 miles of streams and rivers in the region. An additional 1,000 lakes of 10 or more acres lie within the Boundary Waters Canoe Area Wilderness.

TWO KID-FRIENDLY ATTRACTIONS

There are two attractions near Ely that the whole family, but especially the kids, will dig and howl about. Twenty-two miles west of Ely on Highway 169 is the **Soudan Underground Mine**, where grimy workers toiled a half mile below the surface of the earth. The complex of tunnels is one of the best-preserved mines in Minnesota, appearing just as it was when it closed in 1963 as the mining industry declined. Mine-themed artwork fills the gift shop where discerning shoppers can find beautiful purple quartz geode pieces for their living rooms back home. The temperature becomes quite cold down in the nether regions of the mine, so bring warm clothes and thick-soled shoes. The mine is open from Memorial Day through Labor Day. There is a small fee, and a state park vehicle permit is required. Contact the Soudan Underground Mine, 1379 Stuntz Bay Road, (218) 753-2245.

The **International Wolf Center**, 1396 Highway 169 just east of Ely, is another must-stop for wolf enthusiasts and anyone else interested in wildlife. This multimillion-dollar facility was built to examine one of the most elusive animals in the world. Tour the "Wolves and Humans" exhibit and observe the resident pack of Great Plains and Arctic yearling wolves. There are even nighttime howling expeditions and daytime tracking trips available for program participants. The center is open daily from May through October and Friday, Saturday, and Sunday from November through April. Call (218) 365-4695 or log onto the center's Web site at www.wolf.org. No one, regardless of age, dozes off while the critters are howling and yowling.

Yep, a getaway to Ely can be a "howlin' good time." The family pack will have a great expedition.

Getting the lowdown at the Soudan Underground Mine near Ely.
Minnesota Office of Tourism photograph.

SCADS OF OTHER ACTIVITIES

The town and the surrounding area also host a rainbow of family-oriented activities throughout the year. The **Finnish-American Festival** is held each June, calling to mind the ethnic background of many of the local residents. On the Fourth of July, a true-blue (and red and white) parade meanders through town and ends at Whiteside Park in the middle of town on Sheridan Street; look for crowds milling around the band shell. The park also hosts Independence Day kids' games and features plenty of space for picnics, mouthwatering grilling, summertime loafing, or frenetic ball playing and Frisbee chasing. Around 10 p.m., the town sets off fireworks over Miner's Lake, their reflections dazzling the broad band of black water that stretches into the deep night.

Looney Days Sidewalk Sales are held in August; young and old shoppers can search for last minute bargains before heading home. The **Embarrass Regional Fair** is also held in August in nearby Embarrass, and a **Harvest Moon Festival** marks the turn of seasons with outdoor fun at Whiteside Park.

After all the healthy outdoor activity you've been exposed to, it's time to throw caution away playing bingo, slots, blackjack, and other games of chance at Fortune Bay Casino in Tower, 23 miles west of Ely. You may get lucky, but don't bet on it. But since youngsters are not allowed in the casino, it might be a better idea to save some of that excess cash for souvenirs.

Subsequently, take home some log furniture or a chainsaw-carved bear from Ely's **Timber Ridge Trading Company**, 228 East Sheridan Street, (218) 365-5397 or (800) 342-0338. The store boasts of having a "unique collection of lesser important things." Or outfit the family with moose-hide mukluks, those snugly warm booties worn when temperatures plummet and the wind howls outside. You can find the footwear—in sizes for the smallest family member to the largest—at **Steger Mukluks**, along with moccasins and other outdoor and indoor apparel. The shop is located at 6 East Sheridan Street, (218) 365-6553 or (800) 685-5857.

Just before coming home, mom and dad can get a massage at one of Ely's licensed therapists to relieve the body strain after all the paddling. For suggested names, check with the **Northwoods Whole Foods Co-op** on Central Avenue. Call (218) 365-4039. Then its time to head home . . . and relax.

PLACES TO STAY

Blue Heron Bed and Breakfast, 827 Kawishiwi Trail, (218) 365-4720

Boundary Waters Motel, 1323 East Sheridan Street, (218) 365-3201 or (800) 544-7736

North Country Campground, 5865 Moose Lake Road, (218) 365-4976 or (800) 777-4431

Northern Lights Lodge and Resort, 9089 County Highway 21, North Babbitt, (218) 827-2501 or (800) 777-4406; info@northern-lights-lodge.com

Paddle Inn, 1314 East Sheridan Street, (218) 365-6036 or (888) 270-2245

Silver Rapids Lodge, 450 Kawishiwi Trail, (800) 950-9425; www.silverrapidslodge.com

Smitty's on Snowbank, 5943 Snowbank Lake Road, (218) 365-6032 or (800) 950-8310

Super 8 Motel, 1605 East Sheridan Street, (218) 365-2873 or (800) 800-8000; www.super8.com

Timber Wolf Lodge, 9130 Escape Road, (218) 827-3512 or (800) 777-8457

Trezona House, 315 East Washington Street, (888) 683-3055 or (218) 365-4809

PLACES FOR FOOD

Blue Heron Dining Room, 827 Kawishiwi Trail, (218) 365-4720

Britton's Cafe, 5 East Chapman Street, (218) 365-3195

Ely Steak House, 216 East Sheridan Street, (218) 365-7412

Evergreen Restaurant, Grand Ely Lodge on Shagawa Lake, 400 North Pioneer Road, (218) 365-6565

Mingelwood Cafe, 528 East Sheridan Street, (218) 365-3398

Stony River Cafe, 9375 State Highway 1, (218) 323-9375

PLACES TO SHOP

Brandenburg Gallery, 11 East Sheridan Street, (218) 365-6563 or (877) 493-8017

Canadian Border Outfitters, 14635 Canadian Border Road, (218) 365-5847

Chapman Street Books, 130 East Chapman Street, (218) 365-2212

Classic Photos, 126 East Washington Street, (800) 881-1570

Country Simple Pleasures, 16 West Sheridan Street, (218) 365-3696

Kess Gallery, 130 East Sheridan Street, (218) 365-5066

FOR MORE INFORMATION

Ely Area Chamber of Commerce Information Center, 1600 East Sheridan Street, Ely 55731, (218) 365-6123 or (800) 777-7281

Kawishiwi Ranger District offices, Superior National Forest, 118 South Fourth Avenue East, Ely 55731, (218) 365-7600; www.fs.fed.us/r9/superior

Northern Lakes Arts Association, (218) 365-5070; www.elyarts.org

IRON TRAIL COUNTRY

When the children in the family hear that the whole gang is headed out to Minnesota's Iron Trail for the weekend, they may react with those quizzical stares reserved just for parents. But their eyes should widen a bit when they learn that they'll be viewing gigantic open-pit mines—still operating—that have yielded billions of tons of iron ore for over 100 years. And they'll be positively ecstatic when they hear about the mines' gargantuan earthmoving machines, whose size, power, and noise dwarf the tiny things they've seen at those monster truck rallies.

And that's not all. The Iron Trail gives families a fascinating glimpse into the colorful past of the Mesabi Range. The area boasts no fewer than 35 sites listed on the National Register of Historic Places. Everyone can learn not only about the mines that made the area world famous but also about the railroad and timber operations that helped turn the region into an economic bonanza. The area also boasts abundant forestland, along with at least 500 lakes and a spiderweb of rivers that would make any angler smile. Easily accessible via a three-hour, 194-mile drive north from the Twin Cities, the Iron Trail lures vacationers into a region of the state that was settled by more than 40 different ethnic groups.

The Iron Trail generally extends eastward along Highway 169 from Hibbing, through Chisholm, Mountain Iron, and Virginia to Highway 53 and the town of Eveleth. It continues east on Highway 135 to Gilbert and Biwabik and then on to Highway 110 to Aurora and Hoyt Lakes.

SOME OUTDOOR FAMILY FUN

Before heading out to the Iron Trail's mining attractions, be sure to stop the car occasionally and use your feet to explore some of the area's natural beauty. This is Minnesota, after all. Some of the state's best hiking opportunities can be found hereabouts, with paths tailor-made for families wanting to see what the wilds have to offer. Dedicated ramblers say there are about 175 miles of trails to discover. Feel free to pick a few jumbo blueberries while meandering along. Exceptional hikes include the nine-mile trek around Bird Lake near Hoyt Lakes; the 10-mile walk around Carey Lake at Hibbing; 15 miles of trekking on Lookout Mountain near the town of Virginia; the 20-mile Sturgeon River walkway in Chisholm; and the extensive network of trails at Giants Ridge Golf and Ski Resort in Biwabik. Giants Ridge alone has almost 65 miles of up-and-down rambling available for the hardcore hikers in your group.

One of the nicest ways to see the countryside in this part of Minnesota is to climb aboard a bike. The **Mesabi Trail** stretches more than 132 miles from Ely to Grand Rapids, with excellent cycling through the Iron Trail region. The Mesabi Trail includes logging roads and abandoned railways along with paved, handicapped-accessible sections. A pass is necessary for using the pathways. Information, maps, and access points can be found at www.mesabitrail.com or by calling (877) 637-2241.

Canoeing is another great way to see this neck of the Minnesota North Woods, especially along the old French-Canadian voyageur route of the St. Louis River. You can put your canoe into the flowage at numerous sites along the way, such as where County Highway 7 crosses the river just south of County Highway 16 about 10 miles south of Virginia. Check with any local bait shop or refer to a good map for other places to drop into the water. This is a great way for the kids to see deer at the waters' edge or to spot bald eagles.

For a more formal expedition, **Vermilion Wildlife Tours** can get the gang out in the forest to observe great blue herons, loons, moose, and, sometimes, black bears. The company provides binoculars, guidebooks, and even cameras. Travel is by boat along various area waterways, past pine-shrouded bluffs, and around great glacial rock formations. This gets the kids up close and almost-personal with the wilderness. Contact the firm at Box 376, Tower 55790, (218) 753-2673; www.vermilionwildlifetours.com.

For other bird-watching opportunities, visit the **Sax-Sim Bog** just south of Eveleth. The bog sprawls over three management zones of public and private lands where the dedicated birder can spot sandpipers, jays, owls, sedge wrens, and dozens of other species. Brochures and maps are available by calling (800) 777-8497. The **Great Scott Wildlife Area**, two miles south of Buhl on County Highway 453 (Morse Road), is a wetland noted for its loons and osprey. Buhl is located between Chisholm and Mountain Iron on Highway 169.

For a much less sedate time in the woods, the state's first designated Department of Natural Resources recreation area for off-road vehicles is located in Gilbert, with more than 1,200 acres of hill-climbing and trail-riding opportunities for dirt bikes, ATVs, and trucks. The facility opened in 2002 to great fanfare among the motorized set of family vacationers, who know they need mufflers and all the related safety gear on their equipment before being allowed to use the area. Kids who like muscle machinery should love watching the national and state races and other events that are regularly held on the dirt tracks here.

GIANT TRUCKS AND OPEN PITS

Talking about machinery and dirt, kids (and some old-timers, too) love playing with gear that shoves the earth around. For almost a century, grownups in this area certainly had plenty of opportunities for that sort of indulging. Think trucks. Big ones. And earthmovers, power shovels, and bulldozers, too. They're all necessary for pushing, digging up, and hauling rock. The machines are so pervasive around here that parts of Iron Trail Country resemble the contents of a giant's toy box.

Get the scoop on the local mining scene at Chisholm's **Minnesota Museum of Mining**, open from Memorial Day to Labor Day. Start a tour for your family's budding geologists by looking over an extensive exhibit to learn to distinguish rock types. Rookie engineers can climb aboard ol' locomotive No. 347, which was built in 1937 to haul ore from the pits. The huge engine was retired in 1953. After checking out the train, the kids can scramble into the cab of a 125-ton dump truck, a monster vehicle used to ferry earth and iron ore from the open-pit mines to the railheads.

Wandering the streets of the museum's re-created mining town and exploring a replica of an underground mine bring to life the how-did-they-do-it aspects of the job. In the "town" are several shops where kids can experience frontier ways: blacksmithing, shoemaking, broom-making, and printing. There is even a small schoolhouse that the gang can explore, reflecting on all those other kids who went before them and who learned so much in such a small space. The museum is located at 900 Lake Street West, (218) 254-5543.

You'll know you've arrived in mining country by spotting the 85-foot-tall bronze-and-steel statue of a miner on Highway 169 leading into the west side

Checking out the gigantic earthmoving machines at the Minnesota Museum of Mining in Chisholm. —Courtesy of the Museum of Mining

of Chisholm. The memorial is a tribute to the past and present workers of the Mesabi Range, who have labored for years digging and carrying out the ore. The statue is across the highway from **Ironworld Discovery Center**, a theme park dedicated to the mining industry. Kids like to ride the trolley that takes them along the rim of the Glen Mine and then play a round of miniature golf at Pellet Pete's. While here, you may run into numerous school groups and youth tours taking part in the center's Beyond School Walls programs. The sessions are geared toward kids from kindergarten through sixth grade who want to learn about the history, culture, and lifestyles of the folks who live nearby. During the summer season, Ironworld also hosts numerous festivals and musical events, including an arts and culture program that runs from May through September and features major entertainers from around the world.

For additional background on the area, take in the **Hibbing Historical Museum**, at 23rd Street and Fifth Avenue in Hibbing, about five miles from Chisholm, (218) 263-8522. The museum is open between mid-May and late September. Displays including logging and mining equipment, with excellent photographic exhibits showing how the tools were used in the "good old days." Youngsters can get an historical bird's-eye view of 1893 Hibbing by looking down at a five-foot-by-eight-foot model of the early town, founded by German-British immigrant Frank Hibbing.

The model is even more interesting when you tell the gang that after the mines began to encroach on the original town limits in the early 1900s, the city of 20,000 had to be moved two miles south. The citizens of Hibbing hauled some 200 buildings down the highway to the new site, where the Hibbing High School, village hall, and other structures were under construction. The move started in 1919 and wasn't fully completed until the 1930s. Family members with a theatrical bent will appreciate the fact that the high school, built with mining-company money, has an 1,800-seat theater modeled after the old Capitol Theater in New York City. Its chandeliers are made of Czech crystal and the

Ironworld's Festivals

Chisholm's Ironworld Discover Center hosts a plethora of music and ethnic festivals. These include the annual National Polkafest in late June, followed in mid-August by the Button Box Music Festival, which celebrates accordion music The center also sponsors a Slavic celebration in July honoring the Czechs, Poles, Hungarians, Romanians, and other Slavic nationalities that emigrated to the region. Festival Finlandia marks the region's Finnish heritage. From the 1920s to 1930s, Minnesota was home to more Finns than anywhere else in the United States except Michigan. Call (218) 254-7959 or (800) 372-6437.

The 1920s-era electric trolley at the Ironworld Discovery Center.
—Courtesy of the Ironworld Discovery Center

Barton pipe organ is only one of two left in the country. Talk about staging school musicals!

If everyone is still in a mining mood (and they should be), it's a convenient jump to Hibbing's **Hull Rust Mahoning Mine,** the world's largest open-pit iron ore excavation site. Now a National Historic Site, the mine was created by moving 1.4 billion tons of earth. The site has yielded more than 800 million gross tons of ore in the years since it opened. The Mahoning Mine was the first "strip mine" or open-pit mine on the Mesabi Iron Range, and the mine shipped its initial train of ore in 1895 over the Duluth, Mississippi River and Northern Logging Railroad, a connection with the Duluth and Winnipeg rail line. The latter led to ore-shipping docks in Superior, Wisconsin. From that Great Lakes port, the ore went worldwide. The current pit system is more than three miles long, two miles wide, and 600 feet deep, incorporating more than 30 individual mines. The Hibbing Taconite Company still quarries the area, so don't be startled by the occasional dynamite blasts that are clearing away the bedrock.

Before rushing out to the overlooks to see the pits, take the kids into the observation building at Hull Rust Mahoning Mine to view a slide show about the mine's history. The mine is located at 401 Penobscot Road. For more information, call (218) 262-4900.

Bob Dylan Remembered

Folksinger Bob Dylan grew up in Hibbing, where he was known as Robert Zimmerman as a young man before changing his name. In May, Hibbing celebrates its native son with a car show, tours, musical programs featuring his songs, writing competitions, and dancing.

Dylan was born on May 24, 1941, in Duluth, and his family moved to Hibbing before the singer started first grade. He taught himself to play the guitar, harmonica, and piano. In 1959, Dylan packed up and left Hibbing to attend the University of Minnesota, then moved on to enormous fame and fortune as the troubadour of a generation.

TWO INDOOR ATTRACTIONS

Getting workers around the mines was a transportation problem until Andrew B. "Bus Andy" Anderson and his buddy Carl Wickman pooled their cash and purchased an old vehicle in 1914. Instead of selling it as they originally planned, the two began hauling miners to and from their job sites and folks from town to town. The company the pair started eventually expanded into the nationally recognized Greyhound Motor Coach Company. While few kids these days have traveled on an interstate bus, they may find the **Greyhound Bus Museum** of interest for its step-into-the-past presentation. The center, located at 1201 Third Avenue in Hibbing, is packed with artifacts and photographs, along with displays of antique and contemporary coaches. Settle the kids into their seats for a short audiovisual presentation that relates the firm's background. Call (218) 263-5814 or (218) 263-6485; www.greyhoundbusmuseum.org.

"Hockey" is the magic word in Iron Trail Country, where it seems that everyone plays the game—and plays hard. So, there is no better place than the town of Eveleth for displaying the "world's largest hockey stick," a sight not easily missed on Grant Avenue in the downtown area. The stick measures 107 feet long and weighs more than three tons. Naturally, a giant rubber puck is there as well, ready to be slapped into space.

Eveleth is also home to the **United States Hockey Hall of Fame**, 801 Hat Trick Avenue, a three-story hall built in 1973 with lots of exhibits celebrating the sport, including its history and notable players and coaches. Pictures and biographies of the hall's 100-plus inductees are on display, as well as memorabilia honoring all levels of competitive hockey in this country. You'll also view videos and movies of great games, and one of the first Zamboni machines, the contraption that applies a new coat of ice to playing surfaces in just a few minutes. The facility is open year-round. In 2002, the Hall of Fame hosted the first-

Several buses from bygone eras, along with other memorabilia, on display at Hibbing's Greyhound Bus Museum. —Courtesy of the Greyhound Bus Museum

ever Cane Hockey Games, featuring area senior citizens who used to play regularly and who still have a mean slap shot. Officials promise that these lighthearted games will become an annual event, just the thing for the whole family. Call the Hall of Fame for details, (218) 744-5167 or (800) 443-7825.

WINTER FUN

A winter getaway is also fun for a family seeking adventure along the Iron Trail. There are more than 2,000 miles of groomed snowmobile trails crisscrossing the forestlands, linking lodges and restaurants for food and fuel stops. A number of resorts even offer a free night's stay with some seasonal vacation packages. Ice fishing is always popular for tough fisher folk seeking walleye, trout, and crappies. Almost 300 miles of cross-country ski trails are always waiting for outdoors lovers of any age, with a challenging range of flatlands and slopes in some of the country's most scenic forestland. Some sites, such as **Giants Ridge** resort in Biwabik, offer lighted nighttime trails. A few exceptional ski paths include a 15-kilometer run at Carey Lake near Hibbing, a meandering 25-kilometer rush at Virginia's Lookout Mountain, and a nicely done five-kilometer stretch at Hoyt Lakes.

It's obvious that a getaway to the Iron Trail certainly "ain't the pits."

PLACES TO STAY

AURORA

Aurora Pines Motel, 310 West First Avenue, (218) 229-3377

BIWABIK
Biwabik Lodge, 100 Vermilion Trail, (218) 865-4588 or (800) 383-3183

EVELETH
Koke's Motel, 714 Fayal Road, (218) 744-4500 or (800) 892-5107

HIBBING
Arrowhead Motel, 3701 West Second Avenue, (218) 262-3477 or (800) 890-3477

Hibbing Park Hotel, 1402 East Howard Street, (218) 262-3481 or (800) 262-3481; www.hibbingparkhotel.com

Star Motel, 3901 First Avenue, (218) 262-5728

Super 8 Motel, 1411 40th Street, (218) 263-8982 or (800) 800-8000; www.super8.com

VIRGINIA
AmericInn Lodge & Suites, 5480 Mountain Iron Drive, (218) 741-7839 or (800) 634-3444; www.americinn.com

Lakeshore Motor Inn, 404 North Sixth Avenue, (218) 741-3360 or (800) 569-8131

Northern Motel, 1705 North Ninth Avenue, (218) 741-8687

PLACES FOR FOOD

AURORA
Tacora, 320 North Main Street, (218) 229-2670

EVELETH
Poor Gary's Pizza, 420 Fayal Road, (218) 744-5508

GILBERT
Whistling Bird Bar & Café, 101 Broadway Street North, (218) 741-7544

HIBBING
Grandma's in the Park, Hibbing Park Hotel, 1402 East Howard Street, (218) 262-3481

TOWER

Bay View Restaurant, 2001 Bayview Drive, (218) 753-4825

VIRGINIA

De De's Rainy Lake Saloon and Deli, 209 Chestnut Avenue, (218) 741-6247

Natural Harvest Food Cooperative, 505 North Third Street, (218) 741-4663

PLACES TO SHOP

BIWABIK

Bonita's Nordic Imports, 206 South Main Street, (218) 865-7100 or (866) 865-7100; www.bonitasnordicimports.com

HIBBING

Sunrise Bakery, 1813 Third Avenue East, (800) 782-6736; www.sunrisegourmet.com

MOUNTAIN IRON

Spring Creek Outfitters, 8873 Main Street, (218) 735-8719; www.canoegear.com

VIRGINIA

Mesabi Recreation, 720 Ninth Street North, (218) 749-6719

FOR MORE INFORMATION

Aurora Chamber of Commerce, Box 53, Aurora 55705, (218) 229-2614; www.ci.aurora.mn.us

Biwabik City Hall, Box 529, Biwabik 55708, (218) 865-4183; www.cityofbiwabik.com

Chisholm Area Chamber of Commerce, 10 N.W. Second Avenue, Chisholm 55719, (218) 254-7930 or (800) 422-0806; www.chisholmmnchamber.com

Eveleth Area Chamber of Commerce, 122 Grant Avenue, Eveleth 55734, (218) 744-1940; ww.evelethmn.com

Gilbert City Hall, 16 Broadway Street South, Gilbert 55741, (218) 741-9443; www.gilberthminn.org

Hibbing Chamber of Commerce, 211 East Howard Street, Hibbing 55746, (800) 4-HIBBING; www.hibbingminn.com

Iron Trail Convention and Visitors Bureau, 403 North First Avenue, Virginia 55777, (218) 749-8161 or (800) 777-8497; www.irontrail.org

LAKE OF THE WOODS

The Lake of the Woods could almost be called the sixth Great Lake: It's that big. With 65,000 miles of shoreline, a length of 90 miles, and a 55-mile width, it covers 317,000 acres. This makes it the 45th-largest lake in the world and the largest in the United States after the five Great Lakes. The lake, which extends north from Minnesota into Canada, varies in depth from 4 to 35 feet in the south to more than 150 feet on its northern side. It's dappled with 14,582 islands. And this watery expanse is filled with fish, lots of fish. This abundance of finny fun means that the little kids can usually do well with their rods and reels.

Speaking of natural wonders, one of the region's prime draws for the whole family is the aurora borealis, the **Northern Lights**, that dazzle the nighttime sky almost any time of the year over the Lake of the Woods. Far from urban sprawl (the Twin Cities are 310 miles to the south), these lights make a marvelous, chin-dropping show even for the teenager who lives and breathes video games. This is about as far north as anyone can get in the continental United States to see the red, green, blue, and violet neonlike vapors glowing above the horizon.

Of course, any of the gang who's taken science can explain to the rest of the family that these are electrified particles shot out from the sun during great flurries of sunspots. Supposedly, the particles strike the upper regions of the atmosphere where gas is rarefied, which results in the arcs and pulsating lights seen from the ground. One of the best places to observe Ma Nature's version of a Hollywood lighting frenzy is along Highway 11 just south of Lake of the Woods. This parcel of Minnesota has subsequently earned the nickname "Waters of the Dancing Sky."

Another wonder in the area—although not quite as natural—is Willie Walleye, the biggest walleye in the world. For the family memory book, snap a photo of your children under this 2.5-ton, 40-foot-long statue in Bay Front Park on International Drive in Baudette. Allegedly, Willie is the most photographed walleye in the world, and judging from the crowds around him on hot summer days, the claim is hard to dispute. The annual Willie Walleye Day each June celebrates Baudette's colorful icon. Street vendors peddle goodies from flavored crushed ice to a hearty walleye shore lunch with such trimmings as fried spuds, coleslaw, and baked beans.

BAUDETTE ACTIVITIES

A string of villages hang like pearls on a necklace along the south shore of Lake of the Woods. Rainy River, Baudette, Pitt, Graceton, Williams, and Roosevelt are

Willie Walleye on display in Bay Front Park in Baudette. Minnesota Office of Tourism photograph.

among them. They are typical resort towns, offering plenty to see and do whatever the time of year. Chief among them is Baudette, the gateway to the big lake.

Baudette's **Lake of the Woods County Fair** in August is free, a bonus for getaway families on a budget. With big-name entertainment, church ladies serving down-home food, and animal exhibits, the fair presents plenty of innocent entertainment. The year's festivities along Lake of the Woods begin to wind down with Baudette's **Oktoberfest** on the last weekend in September—where churchgoers can attend a polka mass and then hop and leap German-style around the dance floor.

While poking around Baudette, take a break at the wayside rest near the toll-free **International Bridge** that has linked this part of Minnesota to Canada since 1960. The small parcel of land is called Peace Park, with plaques telling of historic events happening in the region, including a 1910 fire and a massacre of a party of Frenchmen on a nearby island in 1736. Peace Park is a good place to picnic with the backseat gang, with its stunning view of Canada across the Rainy River. This is definitely a photo opportunity.

And if family picnicking is in the plan for a Lake of the Woods vacation, be sure to pull out the hot dogs and mustard at **Clementson Rapids**, about eight miles east of Baudette on Highway 11. With great drama and over-the-top splashing, the Rainy River here flows over a series of boulders in a swirl of dark-brown water. Sometimes, if the light is just right, rainbows explode over the rushing waterway as glistening droplets are tossed into the fresh, cool air. There are picnic tables and grilling sites in the little park, just as Lake of the Woods County rubs shoulders with Koochiching County to the east. Setting out the plates and cutlery is a great task for the smaller set.

As the weather warms, the town of Williams, about 15 miles west of Baudette, hosts a Wildflower Route Celebration on the third Saturday of June. Locals celebrate the state's flower, the showy pink-and-white lady's slipper, which grows abundantly along Highway 11. This certainly is *the* place in the area for stopping and getting the children to smell the flowers.

In addition, Williams, site of a national seed potato quarantine area, celebrates the exalted spud on the second Sunday in October. The township of Williams in Koochiching County is one of only several small areas left in the potato-growing regions of the United States now known to be free of bacterial ring rot (Corynebacterium sepedonicum), an infectious disease. In addition, certain other highly destructive diseases, such as golden nematode (Heterodera rostochiensis) and potato rot nematode (Ditylenchus destructor) exist in other areas of the country, but not around Williams.

Subsequently, this area has been protected by quarantine under Minnesota state law. The law restricts or prohibits the importation of such potatoes or of other materials capable of carrying plant pests into or through the region. As such, the potato growers in the Williams area are isolated, which provides an ideal condition for growing foundation seed potatoes. Potato growers from all over the United States depend on the Williams farms as a source of seed potatoes free from the various diseases.

Hustle the kids down to the parade, watch the potato queen coronation, attend a dance and eat, eat, eat loads of potatoes in every conceivable form.

Farther west, near Roosevelt, vacationing families can bring their own picnic goodies to **Norris Camp**, a restored 1930s-era Civilian Conservation Corps facility, for a day of CCC reunions and meeting new friends on the last Sunday of June. There are loads of kids' games and plenty of time for adults to chat.

The Rainy River emptying into the Lake of the Woods. Minnesota Office of Tourism photograph.

The Elusive Gray Owl

To find the elusive gray owl in northern Minnesota, visit the Roseau River Wildlife Area on County Highway 10 and the bogs in the Lost River State Forest along Highway 310 from Roseau to the Canadian border. For their hunting grounds, the owls love the alder thickets, black-ash swamps, and open bogs.

Roosevelt holds a Steam and Gas Show, plus an old-fashioned threshing bee on the first weekend in August, with musicians providing some foot-tapping country music to enjoy along with the long-ago farm machinery on display.

ZIPPEL BAY STATE PARK

Located 10 miles northeast of Williams and named after an early pioneer, Zippel Bay State Park is another place to take the kids for an outdoor experience, a picnic, and a leg-stretching hike. The park entrance is on County Highway 8. The 3,000-acre park has a two-mile-long sand beach, the edge of which is 80 miles from the northern rim of the lake. Waves sometimes reach a height of three feet here, and there are no lifeguards, so keep an eye on the smaller fry. There is also a swimming beach and picnic area on County Highway 34, which extends due north from the park entrance and information booth to a dead-end at lakeside. The black, heavy sand here, formed from pulverized iron-ore flakes, is unlike anything the youngsters may have seen before. Take some back for show-and-tell when school kicks back into gear. For details on what the park has to offer, contact the manager, Zippel Bay State Park, HC2, Box 25, Williams 56686, (218) 783-6252.

In June and July, many varieties of lady's slippers and orchids can be found while hiking through Zippel Bay, along with cranberries, pin cherries, and blueberries as the growing season lengthens. There are also plenty of edible mushrooms throughout the park, but don't think about munching unless an experienced picker is along for the trek. Alert the kids that deer will probably be watching them as they in turn are watching the wildflowers. That done, neither child nor animal will be startled.

Birding is one of the most popular activities in the park. Dozens of interesting species call the woods, marshes, and lakeshore home. Give a prize to the first of the backseat gang to spot a sandhill crane or a bald eagle. Advanced bird lovers might be lucky enough to identify the nearly extinct piping plover. Lake of the Woods is the Great Lakes area's largest breeding ground of these elusive little birds, but they remain rare and protected. Tell the youngsters to slowly back away from any nesting birds they find along the beach, to be sure that they aren't disturbed.

Occasionally, park rangers take tour groups out to Pine and Curry Islands, where there are plover preserves under the care of the Nature Conservancy and the state's Scientific and Natural Areas Program. The latter conducts research on how best to preserve the species. Encourage the kids to feel part of that movement by inspiring respect for all the denizens of the forestland and lake.

You can also tour the lake aboard vessels run by Angle Inlet Island Passenger Service, Box 133, Angle Island. On the mainland, call (218) 223-8261.

Another state preserve, **Beltrami Island State Forest**, south of Highway 11, is not really an island but a sprawling sea of green spreading across Lake of the Woods, Roseau, and Beltrami Counties. Several excellent campgrounds can be found inside the park, including Bemis Hill, Blueberry Hill, Faunce Campground, and Hayes Lake State Park. Berry picking in season is one of the best adventures for a summertime holiday. Be sure to have the kids wear long-sleeved shirts and hats to ward off biting insects and to prevent some of the bramble scratches. This is a patience-proving business, but the final reward of nibbling on the fresh fruit makes it worth the effort. For information, call the state forest at (888) 666-6367.

THE TOP OF THE NATION

For a geography lesson with an historical twist, show the kids a map of Minnesota. Point out the Northwest Angle, a peninsula jutting out from Canada on the far northwest side of Lake of the Woods. This area is still part of the United States—consisting of the Northwest Angle State Forest and the Red Lake Indian Reservation—yet separated from the rest of Minnesota by a chunk of Canada's Manitoba Province and Lake of the Woods. In fact, the Angle is the northernmost point in the Lower 48, giving rise to the claim that the area is "the top of the nation."

The geographical anomaly came about because the Treaty of Paris in 1783 established United States authority here. In 1823, members of the Joint Boundary Commission arrived to figure out the true border. There was still a lot of argument over its exact location because the lake's odd-shaped coastline was ragged enough to drive surveyors nuts. It wasn't until years later that the issue was finally resolved. It's okay if the kids don't remember all this. They should remember, however, that a visit to the Angle will take them into a section of the U.S. that is completely separated from the rest of the country.

To get there, you'll cross the Canadian border so be sure to have a photo identification with you. A passport is best but an original birth certificate will do also. Children under the age of 16 should bring identification showing who they are. Bring a letter from the parent of a minor child you are traveling with, if you are not the child's parent or guardian. If you are coming with your child and are the only guardian, bring documentation showing the child has no other guardians. For example: a birth certificate that does not identify the father.

If stopped by an officer from Citizenship and Immigration Canada (CIC) he will speak to you about your visit. It will usually be a quick interview. You will not be allowed into Canada if you give false or incomplete information,

Land of the Sturgeon

Minnesota's largest sturgeon populations are found in the Lake of the Woods, Rainy Lake, and Rainy River, along the northern rim of the state. The huge fish can often live for more than a century. An angler caught a 152-year old, 215-pound, 81-inch long sturgeon on the Lake of the Woods in 1953. In the 1880s, a fisherman brought ashore a 276-pound, eight-foot-long sturgeon from the lake. You can trace the sturgeon's lineage—the fish is regarded as a living fossil—back at least 100 million years, to around the time the dinosaurs disappeared.

or if you do not satisfy the officer you are suitable for entry into Canada. You will also have to satisfy the officer that you will leave Canada at the end of the temporary period authorized for your stay.

A CIC officer may ask you for a cash deposit for security if he or she believes you need extra motivation to respect the conditions of your temporary stay in Canada. The deposit will be returned after you leave Canada if you have not broken the conditions imposed on you.

Take Highway 313 just north of Warroad for the drive into Manitoba and the bus-stop hamlet of Sprague. Then turn north on Highway 308 on the way to the Northwest Angle, which is about 50 miles to the northeast of Sprague. The road off Highway 308 is unsigned, so ask directions in Sprague to be on the safe side. When reaching the border with the United States at the Angle, look for the blue sign with immigration directions.

After spotting the marker, drive about another eight miles to Jim's Corners and stop at the U.S./Canada videophone. Call the U.S. immigration officials by pushing the U.S. button and tell the official that you have just "returned" to the United States. Everyone in the family then needs to stand in front of the security camera and be photographed. The reverse is true on the way back when the head of the family group needs to speak with a Canadian immigrant officer via the Canada button on the phone. However, a photo is not required by the Canadians. Your party will receive a clearance number that must be presented if stopped on the highway by a Canadian official. Check with the United States Immigration and Naturalization Service with any more specific questions.

Unfortunately, in the days following the terrorist attack on September 11, 2001, the rules about border crossings are even more rigidly enforced. They are nothing to take lightly, so follow the appropriate instructions.

Yet don't let the regulations interfere with an interesting visit to a little-known part of the United States. Such a trip will make a great school report for the kids, especially if staying at a resort like **Jake's Northwest Angle**. The six cottages and the campgrounds here are managed by the Colson family, three generations of whom have been residents of the Angle since 1917. They know every fishing trick in the book. Write them at P.O. Box 38, Angle Inlet 56711, (800) 729-0864; www.jakesnorthwestangle.com.

While on the Angle, tour the restored **Fort St. Charles** on Magnuson Island, which occupies the site of a log stockade and trading post erected in 1732 by Pierre La Verendrye and his party of tough voyageurs. At the time, Fort St. Charles was the most northwesterly white settlement in North America, and the outpost remained active until 1794. The rebuilt fort is now on the National Register of Historic Places.

FISHING DAYS

The fur-trading days in the Lake of the Woods region are long gone now, with tourism one of the main industries since the 1920s. Many visitors come for the fishing opportunities on the lake, with most practicing catch and release of smaller fish and when a limit is reached. This environmentally sound process allows the walleye, pike, and other species to continue growing to keeper size.

Even with the cold air and snow from Canada sweeping down over the lake in the wintertime, die-hard vacationers still take a few days' office or school break to drop in a line. Sometimes the ice is three feet thick, which entails a lot of effort to auger the appropriate hole for angling. The older teens can lend their muscle.

But that doesn't stop the dedicated fisher folk of all ages. There are about 45 resorts open year-round in the vicinity of the lake, so the getaway gang doesn't have to do a Jack London routine and live under a snowy pine bough. You can travel to icehouses out on the lake via airboat, hovercraft, or tundra buggies outfitted with wheels taller than a string-bean teen. Snowmobiling is another winter adventure for families taking advantage of a few days in the North Country. A far-flung web of trails crisscrosses the Lake of the Woods area. Winter is rough around here but it doesn't stop the locals—or visiting families—from enjoying what nature has to offer in this part of Minnesota.

PLACES TO STAY

BAUDETTE
Country Bunk-Ins, 1222 Main Street East, (218) 634-2869

Lake of the Woods Campground, 2769 28th Street N.W., (218) 634-1694, (800) 344-1976 or (701) 335-2866 in the winter

Royal Dutchman Resort Motel, 3583 State Highway 11 S.E., (218) 634-1024 or (800) 908-1024

Sportsman's Lodge, 3244 Bur Oak Road N.W., (218) 634-1342 or (800) 862-8602

NORTHWEST ANGLE
Bay Store Camp, P.O. Box 21, Oak Island, (800) 214-2533; www.baystorecamp.com

Sunset Lodge, 42 Main Street, Oak Island, (800) 634-1863 or
(218) 223- 8211; www. sunsetlodgeresort.com

WILLIAMS
Long Point Resort, 7046 Resort Lane N.W., (218) 783-3365

Zippel Bay Resort, 6080 39th Street N.W., (800) 222-2537 or
(218) 783-6235; www.zippelbay.com

PLACES FOR FOOD
BAUDETTE
Cyrus Resort, 3298 Cyrus Road N.W., (218) 634-2548 or (800) 932-2924

North Lake Cafe, 813 N.W. Second Street, (218) 634-9807

Veterans of Foreign Wars, 204 International Drive, (218) 634-9977

WILLIAMS
Too Tall's Grocery, at the intersection of County Road 2 and Highway 11
(218) 783-6335

PLACES TO SHOP
BAUDETTE
Johnson Auto and Machine, 802 Second Street, (218) 634-1636

Northern Sports and Machine, 651 County Road 1 S.W., (218) 634-1089

FOR MORE INFORMATION
International Falls Chamber of Commerce and Visitors Bureau, 301
Second Avenue, International Falls 56649; (800) 325-5766 or
(218) 283-9400; www.intlfalls.org

Lake of the Woods Tourism, 930 West Main, Baudette 56623, (800) 382-
3474; www.lakeofthewoodsmn.com

Northwest Angle and Islands Chamber of Commerce, Box 11, Oak Island
56741, (800) 434-8531 or (866) 692-6453

U.S. Immigration and Naturalization Service, 41781 State Highway 313,
Warroad 56649, (218) 386-1676

MOORHEAD AND FARGO

The mere suggestion of a trip to Moorhead and Fargo might be met with raised eyebrows from even your youngest skeptics, along with some of the older ones too. Tell them not to worry. There's plenty to see and do in this, the largest metropolitan area between Minneapolis and Spokane, Washington. Because Moorhead is in far-western Minnesota and Fargo is just across the Red River in North Dakota, the trip may at first seem like one to Timbuktu. Fact is, the area is only 234 miles west of the Twin Cities, a drive that will reveal the rich variety of the Minnesota countryside

You can astound the kids by telling them that an ancient lake once covered the Moorhead-Fargo region with 200 feet of water. Created by glacial runoff, it was formed as the last of the towering ice sheets retreated to Canada 10,000 years ago. In geological terms, a few thousand years here or there don't make much difference.

But it's what the lake left behind that made the area what it is today. The resulting soil—once the lake bed—is among the most fertile in North America. That means that life is pretty good out here on the prairie. The rich black earth is called chernozem, a Russian word meaning "black earth." In some places, this wonderful soil is more than five feet deep, giving rise to a marketer's motto that western Minnesota is the "Bread Basket to the World." It seems you can put a twig into the ground and grow an oak almost overnight. There is apparently no end to the abundant crops. Fat potatoes, horizon-to-horizon fields of luxurious wheat. You name it, it sprouts here.

The Red River Valley, where Moorhead and Fargo sprang up, has a wonderful history. French-Canadian fur traders from Winnipeg were the first whites to move through the vicinity. They did a booming business with Native Americans in the region who were eager for cloth, hatchets, and beads. The traders' heavily loaded ox carts trundled along through mucky swamps, forded rivers, and blazed trails amid grass as tall as a man on a horse. Many Canadians married Native Americans in those early days on the frontier. Their offspring were called métis, many of whom became teamsters. They were a colorful lot as they traveled between the native and the settlers' worlds wearing with brightly colored sashes around their waists, stocking caps, and heavy boots or even moccasins.

Best Hotel in the West

In 1882, the Grand Pacific Hotel in Moorhead was considered one of the best hotels on the frontier. The 140-room building cost $165,000 to build. During this time, when Moorhead was becoming a major trading center, the town had 13 other hotels as well.

In 1859, settlers established the first permanent dwellings where Moorhead now sprawls. The Red River became a major transportation route, with steamboats plying its rushing waters. The arrival of the Northern Pacific Railroad in 1878 opened the West to more trade and extended farming possibilities. More than 200,000 people flocked to the area between 1879 and 1886 to set down deep family roots that could be nurtured by the rich earth.

MORE TO DO IN MOORHEAD

Today, Moorhead boasts a rich variety of indoor and outdoor fun. To get a feel for the area's ethnic heritage, check out the **Hjemkomst Center**, which captures western Minnesota's Scandinavian past. One of the features of the center is a hand-built Viking long ship on display. High school teacher Robert Asp constructed the vessel, one typical of the sturdy craft that carried early explorers to the New World well before Christopher Columbus. This ship actu-

A hand-built Viking ship on display at the Hjemkomst Center in Moorhead. Minnesota Office of Tourism photograph.

ally sailed a 6,100-mile route from Duluth, Minnesota, across the Atlantic to Bergen, Norway, in 1982. Photos and a documentary record the construction of the boat and the exciting excursion. The center also houses other exhibits that tell about the early pioneers who settled in the region. The interpretive center is located at 202 First Avenue North, (218) 299-5511. Let the kids roam at will through the facility. It'll be their own journey of discovery.

For a surprisingly eclectic art experience, the **Rourke Art Museum**, 521 Main Avenue, (218) 236-8861, has a wide range of artifacts from the Pre-Columbian era, as well as Hispanic, African, and Native American artwork. The gift shop in the museum has plenty of small, interesting—and afford-able—items that can be purchased for souvenirs by the younger set. The **Rourke Art Galley**, in the historic 1880s Martinsen House, houses more ex-hibits. It is open for tours Friday through Sunday afternoons; it's located at 523 South Fourth Street, (218) 236-8861.

The Moorhead art scene has a niche for young thespians with its Goose-berry Park Players, based at Concordia College. The company, sponsored by the Moorhead Parks and Recreation Department, gives kids an opportunity to try their acting skills. The resulting plays, which are directed toward a family audience, are presented each July at the college's Francis Frazier Comstock The-atre—just the thing for a rainy-day visit.

Now that you've shown the kids some of the area's cultural sites, it's time for them to let loose. The FARM Skate Park was constructed for kids who like to skateboard on the edge (literally!) and make their parents nervous. Ramps and jumps challenge the most dexterous among the brave and intrepid. This is the kind of place you'll probably never see anybody over 35 attempting to meet a tough half-pipe challenge. Encourage the kids to act like the pros, suit-ing up in knee and elbow pads, wrist guards, and helmets. The park is open only during the summer months, and it's located at 707 Main Avenue S.E., (218) 299-5340.

Other outdoor activities abound in Moorhead. The city's six municipal golf courses spread their lush greenery where the prairie once stretched to the far horizon. There are also theaters, ice rinks, swimming pools, athletic fields, and a host of other recreational and cultural activities for families seeking a quick vacation escape. High-tech industries and computer businesses now rival agri-culture as the dual communities' economic pillars.

Ferry Boat

In the 1880s, the cost of a license to run a ferry across the Red River be-tween Fargo and Moorhead was $15. There was a toll of 25 cents per horse-drawn wagon. Additional animals cost five cents a head.

Reminding Minnesotans of their "natural" past, more than 5,000 acres of tallgrass prairie are preserved at the nearby **Buffalo River State Park**, the **Blue Stem Prairie Scientific and Natural Area**, and the **University of Minnesota-Moorhead Regional Science Center**. These preserves are havens for wildlife and hundreds of species of plants. Most of the parkland is open for hiking. Have everyone wear comfortable and durable shoes.

Then there is the Red River. Where heavily laded steamboats once sailed, comfortable pontoon and sleek pleasure boats now ply the waterway. Fishing piers line the banks. Canoe races and concerts highlight a **River Splash** Festival in early June.

FARGO FROLICS

Fargo, the seat of North Dakota's farm-rich Cass County, was founded in 1826 and incorporated in 1872. It became a center for railroads carrying freight and passengers to and fro along the vast prairie land, not unlike many other frontier communities.

In one regard, however, Fargo was unlike other towns. At the end of the 1880s, the city became known as the Divorce Capital of the World. A proliferation of lawyers, plus a relaxed view of the "ties that bind," attracted unhappily married couples from around the country seeking to sever that knot. Yet, on the other hand, Fargo was also a hub for Episcopal missionary endeavors during the same era.

You may want to start off your tour of the west side of the Red River at the **Fargo-Moorhead Convention and Visitors Bureau**, 2001 44th Street Southwest, (701) 282-3653 or (800) 235-7634, which promotes attractions and activities for both cities. The offices are easy to find, just look for the Celebrity Walk of Fame on the sidewalk outside. While new personalities are added regularly, wander along the walk and identify as many as you can. Country music star Garth Brooks, the rock group KISS, actress Debbie Reynolds, and former Minnesota governor Jesse Ventura are among the celebrities.

Zoos are great places to kick off a city tour for kids and the **Red River Zoo** is no exception. The zoo emphasizes natural settings, with 30 acres harboring more than 60 animal species, with the hungry carnivores well separated from the potential prey. The petting zoo is good fun for the toddlers, but be sure that everyone washes their hands after feeding the animals. One of the funnest aspects at the zoo is a spin on the restored 1928 carousel. The zoo is at 4220 21st Avenue S.W., (701) 277-9240.

The **Children's Museum at Yunker Farm** also has an old carousel, in addition to a miniature railroad for rides around the grounds. The museum, called one of the top 25 in the country by *Child* magazine, is geared toward the toddler-to-12 age range. Many of the exhibits are showcased in the old farmhouse, the first brick building in the Dakota Territories. A miniature golf course in the shape of North Dakota, with all the proper elevations, opened in 2002. The

The award-winning Children's Museum at Yunker Farm in Fargo, North Dakota.
—Courtesy of the Children's Museum at Yunker Farm

complex is at 1201 28th Avenue North, (701) 232-6102; www.childrensmuseum-yunker.org.

Sports-minded vacationers to Fargo-Moorhead have loads of opportunities for cheering on their favorite sports teams. The Fargo-Moorhead Beez professional basketball team, part of the International Basketball Association, play at the **Fargo Civic Memorial Auditorium** during the winter season, 207 N. 4th Street, (701) 232-4242; www.fmbeez.com.

The Fargo-Moorhead Redhawks professional baseball team does its stuff at the Newman Outdoor Field. Fans call the $4 million park "The Nest." It has a playground in right field and a beer garden and hot tub in left field. The stadium is located at 1515 15th Avenue North, (800) 303-6161; www.fmredhawks.com.

For additional hands-on excitement and extra vacation value, visitors to the area can sharpen their mini-golf skills at the **Thunder Road Family Fun Park**, 2902 Thunder Road, and see how well they can do for distance at the indoor driving range at the Fargo Sports Bubble. Skateland, 3302 Interstate Boulevard Southwest, is an all-around getaway for the gang with its in-line skate rink, arcade games, and snack bar. Call (701) 282-5151.

If all that's not enough, tykes to teens can go nuts at the **I-29 Amusement Park**, 1625 35th Street South, (701) 235-5236, with its 440-foot-long water slide, plus go-carts, batting cages, kiddie rides, and the ever-present arcade. Then there's **Driverz**, with even more go-carts, plus golf and baseball simulators, a food court, a climbing wall, and laser tag. Adults and children sign up for a Driverz license and can play all day. The place even has North Dakota's largest selection of video games.

Eat Your Vegetables . . . or Else

At first, no one thought the Red River Valley would be worth anything. It was hot, dusty, and far from any city. One military officer wrote that the land "is fit only of the Indians and the devil." However, farmers soon discovered that the area's rich soil could grow almost anything.

In the 1870s, one homesteader entered the barroom of a local hotel and showed off the huge vegetables he said he had grown. No one in the tavern believed him. So the farmer pulled out a gun from the middle of his monster peas and massive carrots and shot up the place. Everyone dove for cover. After this display of frontier persuasion, the man quickly sold out his crop.

If art is your family thing, Fargo will fulfill your artistic needs. The city's summertime street fairs that take place on Broadway are an exciting cross between a medieval street market and a Casbah bazaar. Fargo's **Gallery 4 Ltd.**, owned by area artists for more than 30 years, displays artwork from a variety of media. Kids seem to like the photography, stained glass, and dolls. One artist specializes in handmade paper and is always willing to tell a child about the process. The gallery is open Thursday through Sunday, from late morning through the afternoon, 11 Eighth Street South, (701) 237-6867.

Most kids also love movies. And eating. So Fargo has put the two together at the **Fargo Cinema Grill**, where families can plunk down in the theater for a contemporary movie and supper. Pizza is a top seller, but salads, sandwiches, appetizers, and, of course, desserts are also offered. Vacationing doesn't get much better than this. The theater is located at 630 First Avenue North, (701) 239-4716.

And for a complementary film experience, gather the gang in the glittering, glamorous **Fargo Theater**, 314 Broadway, (701) 239-8385. The combination movie palace and vaudeville hall was built in 1926. Today, the refurbished theater is a registered historical landmark, one that still shows films and hosts touring plays and concerts. Youngsters are always amazed when the restored theater's pipe organ, the Mighty Wurlitzer, is played.

IN THE AREA

Usher the kids out to **Bonanzaville,** 1351 West Main Avenue, West Fargo, where they step back a century or so to see how butter was churned, wheat threshed, and rugs made. The park has several historical buildings reminiscent of an old-time village, complete with blacksmith shop, church, sod house, and country store. By looking over all the old-time farm equipment, kids get a chance to learn how their great-grandparents might have worked in another era. During Bonanzaville's Pioneer Days in August, the family can bounce along in a stagecoach to see what transportation was like in the good old days. Bumpy, that's what. Pony rides, ethnic food, and a vintage-car parade are also part of the festivities. Call (800) 700-5317.

Visiting families flock to the region to spend a few days enjoying the wide-open spaces and the multitudinous attractions offered by the two cities. The area's tourism marketers chuckle with their slogan, "There's Far-Moor Fun" in Fargo-Moorhead. When you visit, be sure to take advantage of this bi-state two-for-one deal.

PLACES TO STAY

FARGO

Airport Dome Days Inn and Suites, 1507 19th Avenue North, (701) 232-0000 or (800) 329-7466

Best Western Doublewood Inn, 3333 13th Avenue South, (701) 235-3333 or (800) 433-3235

Red Roof Inn, 901 38th Street, (701) 282-9100 or (800) THE-ROOF

Rodeway Inn, 2202 South University Drive, (701) 239-8022 or (800) 228-2000

MOORHEAD

Moorhead Motel 75, 810 Belsly Boulevard, (218) 233-7501 or (800) 628-4171

Red River Inn, 600 30th Avenue, (218) 233-6171 or (800) 328-6173

Super 8 Motel, 3621 Eighth Street South, (218) 233-8880 or (800) 800-8000; www.super8.com

Travelodge and Suites, 3027 South Frontage Road, Highway 10 East, (218) 233-5333 or (800) 578-7878

PLACES FOR FOOD

FARGO

The Bowler, 2630 South University Drive, (701) 293-0200

Broadway Junction, 2828 North Broadway, (701) 280-1231

Buffalo Wild Wings, 1515 19th Avenue North, (701) 280-9464

Cafe Muse at the Plains Art Museum, 704 First Avenue North, (701) 232-3821

The Cookery, 3150 39th Street S.W., (701) 282-5585

CourtYard Cafe, 3105 Broadway, (701) 237-6593

Cynthia's Custom Cakes, Soup and Sandwich Bar, 524 Broadway, (701) 234-0664

Dakota Grill Rotisserie (in Best Western), 3333 13th Avenue S.W., (701) 235-3333

The Fargo Cork and Cleaver, 3315 South University Drive, (701) 237-6790

Gallery Terrace and Café, 3803 13th Avenue South, (701) 282-2700

Kroll's Diner, 2901 Main Avenue, (701) 476-3090, and 1570 32nd Avenue South, (701) 297-5936

Lone Star Steakhouse, 4328 13th Avenue S.W., (701) 282-6642

Mom's Kitchen, 1322 Main Avenue, (701) 235-4460

Outback Steakhouse, 401 38th Street S.W., (701) 277-5698

Pepper's American Cafe, 2510 South University Drive, (701) 232-2366

Space Aliens Grill and Bar, 1840 45th Street S.W., (701) 281-2033

MOORHEAD
Bogie's, 401 34th Street South, (218) 299-5247

Fry'n Pan, 2920 Highway 10 East, (218) 236-0292

Grand Junction Grilled Steaks, Subs, Wings, 435 Main Avenue, (218) 287-5651

Perkin's Family Restaurant, 3005 Highway 10 East, (218) 299-6454

Red River Inn, 600 30th Avenue South, (218) 233-6171

Trucker's Inn Restaurant, 7025 County Road 11, Exit 6, (218) 287-2272

Village Inn, 625 30th Avenue South, (218) 233-1329

PLACES TO SHOP
FARGO
Crafter's Mall, 4101 13th Avenue S.W., (701) 281-8326

MOORHEAD
Moorhead Antique Mall, 2811 S.E. Main Avenue, (218) 287-1313

FOR MORE INFORMATION
Fargo-Moorhead Convention and Visitors Bureau, 2001 44th Street S.W., Fargo 58103, (701) 282-3653 or (800) 235-7634; www.fargomoorhead.org

OTTER TAIL COUNTRY

Minnesota may be the Gopher State, but Otter Tail Country (OTC) claims another wild critter as its mascot. OTC, which consists primarily of Otter Tail County, is located in west-central Minnesota southeast of Fargo-Moorhead. The region has at least 1,000 named lakes, where kids can splish-splash away their long vacation weekends, mom and pop can fish to their hearts' content, and any teens in the family can check out the swimming beaches and boat docks.

The range of lake sizes allows a variety of getaway experiences, from the small, quiet backwaters to the larger lakes perfect for more active water sports, such as waterskiing and tubing. Rivers and streams meander through the countryside, offering more fishing opportunities.

The folks in Otter Tail Country proudly proclaim that every season is unique in their neighborhood and that every season offers something great to do. These affirmations are not just a bit o' blowin' in the wind, because whether a spring, summer, fall, or winter adventure is in the cards, a family is assured of boatloads of fun. You can do a short weekender or spend a bit more time exploring. It's your call.

Tired of paddling around the water during the summer? Hit one of the many fairs or festivals. Autumn? Roast hot dogs and marshmallows over an open campfire. Don't forget the ghost stories! Winter brings out the skis and snowmobiles, the ice-fishing houses, and romantic weekends at a bed-and-breakfast (okay, that would be the one time to leave the backseat gang at home!). In spring, the countryside becomes a junior botanist's delight, with the perfume of apple blossoms and the fragrance of lilacs washing over the days and nights.

A TALE OF TWO TRAILS

One of the best ways for the family to see much of what there is to see in OTC is via the **Otter Trail Scenic Byway**. You can pick up the 150-mile roadway just about anywhere along the route, which is well-marked by signage depicting a happy otter splashing and peeking out of water. The kids can entertain themselves by counting the number of promotional otters along the way and seeing who counts the most. A good place to start the drive, however, is in Fergus Falls. Then follow the signs north to Maine, edge over to Pelican Falls, head back east to Dent, jog north to Perham, zoom down to Ottertail, move farther south to Battle Lake, then east again to Clitherall and Vining. (One undeniable fact is the plentitude of colorful town names around here, but what else would you expect in an area named after a mammal's posterior appendage?) From here, drive west to Dalton where you can then travel northwest to Fergus Falls and your starting point.

There are more than 20 designated historical and culturally significant locales along the way, with seven offering informational kiosks that describe the flora and fauna in the area. Among the best stops are the roadside sculptures in Vining, one of which is a 1,200-pound depiction of a foot and another is a large square knot made of metal. Have the kids look for other oversize statues on the drive along the trail, such as an otter tail (of course) and a goose in Fergus Falls.

The more-or-less circular route is one of nine roads officially designated as a Minnesota Scenic Byway. Maps of the route are available from Minnesota Information Centers at key points around the state. Travel information can be secured at these locales: the Explore Minnesota USA Store, Mall of America, N129 North Garden, Bloomington; Albert Lea TIC, Northbound Lane of Interstate 35 at the Iowa border; Anchor Lake, 10 Miles south of Eveleth; Beaver Creek TIC, East Interstate 90 at the South Dakota border; Dresbach TIC, West Interstate 90/U.S. Highway 61 at the Wisconsin border; Fisher's Landing TIC, U.S. Highway 2, 10 miles east of North Dakota border; and Grand Portage Bay TIC, U.S. Highway 61, five miles south of Canadian border, (open May-Oct only).

Others are located at International Falls TIC, U.S. Highway 53, downtown International Falls; Moorhead TIC, eastbound Interstate-94, one Mile east of U.S. Highway 75; St. Cloud TIC, Highway 10, one mile southeast of St. Cloud; St. Croix TIC, westbound Interstate 94, three miles west of the Wisconsin border; Thompson Hill TIC, Interstate 35 at U.S. Highway 2-West Duluth; Worthington TIC, US Highways 59/60, five miles north of the Iowa border.

If you have a question, you can also write to http://www.exploreminnesota.com/index.asp?section=TRAVEL. In addition to the state's tourism Web site at www.exploreminnesota.com, the Minnesota Office of Tourism operates a travel information center staffed by travel counselors weekdays from 8 a.m. to 4:30 p.m. They provide personalized travel assistance as well as a variety of materials to make travel planning easier. Call 800-657-3700; 651/296-5029 in the Twin Cities area or mail a question to the Minnesota Office of Tourism 100 Metro Square, 121 7th Place East, St. Paul, MN 55101.

On the drive, be sure to stop in the towns to check out their history, restaurants, and attractions. There's something for everyone. The kids will want grub, mom might want to visit a museum, grandpa might go for a bit of fishing, grandma might desire an antique store, and dad—well—he'll probably hunt for a parking space for the van.

You can also explore Otter Tail Country along the **Pine to Prairie Birding Trail**, which runs more than 200 miles from Warroad near the Canadian border to Fergus Falls. The trail moves southward along Highways 11 and 32 to

Why Is It Called Otter Tail?

The name Otter Tail dates back to the time when the Ojibwe fished from a spit of sand that looked like an otter tail. When white lumbermen arrived in the 19th century, however, they seized control of the area and destroyed the sand spit so that they could more easily maneuver their logs downstream. The name, however, endured.

Highway 59 at Thief River Falls taking travelers through thick forests and to tallgrass prairie, along bogs, past lakes, and over rivers. This is a fantastic drive, one of the best to show the kids the splendid variety and abundance of wildlife in Minnesota. Some of the 275 species of birds that can be spotted along the way include three-toed woodpeckers, the greater prairie chicken, grosbeaks, chickadees, and gray owls. Be sure everyone in the car has a pair of binoculars, a bird-identification book, and a notebook for taking down observations, which can be the basis for school reports back home.

Among the trail sponsors are the U.S. Fish and Wildlife Service, the Minnesota Department of Natural Resources, the Lakes Area Birding Club, the Minnesota Ornithologists Union, and numerous tourist organizations along the way. The jaunt passes near Hayes Lake, Lake Bronson, Old Mill, and other state parks, along with state forests and wildlife management areas. Don't just zoom through. Get the gang out of the SUV, minivan, or whatever you are driving and do some hiking, loafing, photographing, or picnicking. For more information contact the Detroit Lakes Regional Chamber of Commerce, (800) 433-1888; www.mnbirdtrail.com.

Otter Tail Country has more than 100 resorts, plus motels, campgrounds, and plenty of snug bed-and-breakfasts for getaway lolling about. Bring books, games, and puzzles for those quiet days and nights along the shoreline or on a cabin porch.

FERGUS FALLS HISTORY

In 1854, land developer (read "speculator") James B. Fergus contracted with a surveyor named Joseph Whitford to stake some claims in western Minnesota. Following the advice of a band of Native Americans, Whitford eventually made his way to a large waterfall on the Otter Tail River, and he named the beautiful site after Fergus. However, neither Fergus nor Whitford stayed around to watch the crossroads become one of western Minnesota's most important cities. Fergus followed the era's gold fever to Montana, where he struck it rich and died in 1902 as a wealthy man. Poor Whitford wasn't as lucky. He was killed in Minnesota's Dakota Uprising of 1862.

As the frontier finally settled down, Fergus Falls built lumber mills along the river to ensure economic stability. The arrival of the railroad in 1879 solidified its position.

Today, Fergus Falls is a city of festivals, including SummerFest and a Blues and Brews Festival in June, the West Otter Tail County Fair in July, the Lincoln Avenue Fine Arts Festival over Labor Day weekend, and a Frostbite Festival in February. The Fergus Falls Classic Car Club holds an annual car show and swap meet in August, with parades and exhibits of vintage automobiles.

BATTLE LAKE AND GLENDALOUGH STATE PARK

One of Minnesota's newest state parks, **Glendalough**, has a long history as a private game farm and retreat to such notables as Dwight Eisenhower and Richard Nixon. Established as a state park in 1992, Glendalough is located two miles north of Battle Lake, which is about 20 miles east of Fergus Falls. The park entrance is on County Highway 16, east of Highway 78. The site remains one of the largest tracts of undeveloped forestland in the western part of the state. Hikers with long legs (and those with short ones, as well) enjoy the flower-dappled prairie and the extensive oak forests that make up the undulating landscape. West Battle Lake located across from the park, covers 5,624 acres and bottoms out at 113 feet.

The park itself is 1,931 acres, with 9.1 miles of shoreline. As such, the park provides plenty of opportunities for long weekends of fishing for elusive muskies or delicious northerns, as well as for lazy, hazy days of boating and

A typical scene at unspoiled Glendalough State Park. Copyright State of Minnesota, Department of Natural Resources.

swimming. There are several resorts on West Battle Lake, with Sunset Beach Resort and Campground on the east side of the lake, and The First Resort and Sand Bay Resort on the west. For details, contact the park manager, Glendalough State Park, Box 358, Battle Lake 56515, (218) 864-0110.

NEW YORK MILLS

Continuing in a northeasterly direction, be sure to take the family members to New York Mills. Not surprisingly, lumbermen and mill owners from New York State in the 1870s founded the town. After the timber was cleared, settlers—many from Finland—arrived, seeking farmland to cultivate. As such, New York Mills is now the hub of a major agricultural region. The whole clan can enjoy reminders of the area's rugged pioneer past at **Finn Creek**, a refurbished farm and open-air museum about three miles southeast of New York Mills. Dating from the early 1900s, the complex includes farm buildings, a general store, schoolhouse, town hall, blacksmith shop, and other structures. Kids enjoy looking at the antique farm equipment and poking around the school. Contact P.O. Box 134, New York Mills 56567, (218) 385-2233 or (218) 285-2230.

Over the years, other businesses sprang up in town, with Lund Boats being one of the most noteworthy. Howard Lund built his first fishing boats in his garage in 1947, and today the company's line of quality metal fishing boats are popular with fishing fans all over the country.

Mythical Stones

Ten miles south of Lake Park, on the north shore of Big Cormorant Lake, are three large boulders called the "anchor stones." Because holes have been drilled through them, legend has it that they were used by Vikings in 1362 to tie up their ships. According to the stories, they could have been the same Norsemen who inscribed a tale of adventure onto the Kensington Runestone, which was found in a field 70 miles to the south, in Douglas County. Historians have pooh-poohed the tales, but the story refuses to die.

You can't miss the **Continental Divide Monument** in downtown New York Mills; it is marked by flags of the nations that once controlled this territory. The memorial marks the watershed between Hudson Bay and the Gulf of Mexico.

Although the **New York Mills Regional Cultural Center** may not be every kid's cup of tea, it's still an enlightening departure from the area's outdoorsy ambience. The facility has classrooms for art programs, plus a gallery and open area for cultural events. The cultural center hosts the annual Great American Think-Off in June, which spotlights writings, readings, and reports on a current issue prepared by hundreds of people from around the globe. Finalists are invited to New York Mills to debate the pros and cons of the issue. Media from all over the world have covered the event. The 2002 discussion was "Is the Pen Mightier than the Sword?" It was won by Paul Higday, an information technology manager from Richmond, Virginia. The 2001 topic was "Should assisted suicide be legal?" and the 2000 competition focused on "Is Democracy Fair?" In 1999, participants wrestled with "Which is more Dangerous -- Science or Religion?" The subject for the particular year is announced in January and contestants have until April to submit their responses. Four finalists are announced in May, with a debate in June. The facility is located at 24 North Main Avenue, (218) 385-3339.

Some last-minute words of encouragement at the Perham turtle races.

TURTLES AND TIME IN PERHAM

Be sure to hit Perham with the kids in tow on a Wednesday morning during the summer. That's when the town's famous **turtle races** are held at City Hall Park. Youngsters jump and yell to get their slowpoke partners to burn rubber, peel out, make a mad dash, charge ahead—or just plain move! Eventually, the tiny competitors do find their way to the finish line. Another reason to visit Perham, 10 miles northeast of New York Mills via Highway 10 is **Travel Through Time**, 230 First Avenue North, (218) 346-7676. This regional-history museum brings the life and lore of the good old days into sharp focus for today's Internet generation. Besides, when it's raining, this is a swell place to haul the kids for the railroad exhibit and other displays. **The Perham Area Community Center**, 620 Third Avenue S.E., (218) 346-7222, is open year-round, with swimming pools, water slides, gyms, and fitness rooms—because staying in shape is important, even when on vacation.

WALLEYE IN PELICAN RAPIDS

Finally, head over to Pelican Rapids, about 25 miles west of New York Mills, a pleasant community smack in the middle of several marvelous fishing lakes, including Pelican Lake, of course. It's hard to miss, since it covers 3,986 acres to a maximum depth of 55 feet. Claims of wondrous walleye and marvelous muskie are heard around the resort bars after every Saturday of good fishing. Most of the stories are true. If the truth is sometimes stretched, well, that's okay too. Boat docks are on the western and eastern shores. On the east side of the lake is Fair Hills Resort, while on the southwest you can find Bayview Shores Resort.

Although Pelican Rapids was settled by northern European immigrants, it is now a multinational city with residents from Central America, Asia, and Africa. Every June the city celebrates newcomers by hosting an **International Friendship Festival** in E. L. Peterson Memorial Park, with a variety of ethnic food booths, dancing, and entertainment. Watch performances by dance troops from such faraway places as Mexico, Bosnia, Sweden, and Japan. Kids' games and arts and crafts from the various countries are part of the festivities and always offer something different and exciting.

Maplewood State Park, six miles east of Pelican Rapids on Highway 108, presents 9,000 acres, more than 20 lakes and a scenic drive, taking sightseers through 6,000 years of geologic history. It's believed that the first human inhabitants of Maplewood roamed the land almost 1,200 years ago. Kids love exploring the park and sleeping in tents under the stars at the park's campground, but make sure you remind them not to feed the wild critters. The visitor information center at the park has loads of information on the early inhabitants, hunter artifacts, and archaeological sites in the vicinity. One of the more unusual sights, sure to appeal to the little ones, is a series of "gnome

A few of the "gnome houses" hidden away in Maplewood State Park.
Copyright State of Minnesota, Department of Natural Resources

houses," whimsical miniature structures hidden away in the park. Created by local artist Jim Fletcher, they are meant to spark the imagination and get children of all ages drawn into their fantasy world. The park is located at 39721 Park Entrance Road, or call (218) 863-8383 for more information.

PLACES TO STAY

BATTLE LAKE

The First Resort, 715 Lakeshore Drive, (218) 864-9961

Sand Bay Resort, 405 Washington North, (218) 864-5244 or (800) 546-9316

Sunset Beach Resort and Campground, 42502 240th Street, (888) 583-2750; www.sunsetbeachresort.net

FERGUS FALLS

AmericInn Lodge and Suites of Fergus Falls, 526 Western Avenue North, (218) 739-3900 or (800) 634-3444; www.americinn.com

Comfort Inn, 425 Western Avenue, (218) 736-5787 or (800) 228-5150

Swan Lake Resort and Campground, 17463 County Highway 29, (800) 697-4626; www.swanlkresort.com

PELICAN RAPIDS

Bayview Shores Resort, RV and Trailer Park, 20393 South Pelican Drive, (218) 737-4689

Cross Point Resort, 39870 Cross Point Lane, (218) 863-8593 or (877) 646-6994

Fair Hills Resort, 24270 County Road 20, (218) 847-7638 or (800) 323-2849

Oak Lodge Resort, 41524 Dawn Road, (800) 982-5432; www.oaklodgeresort.com

PLACES FOR FOOD

BATTLE LAKE

Old Brick Inn, 123 Lake Avenue South, (218) 864-5395

Shoreline Restaurant and Lanes, 505 Lake Avenue North, (218) 864-5265

FERGUS FALLS

Barringer's Coffee House, 127 East Lincoln Avenue, (218) 736-2090

Viking Cafe, 203 West Lincoln Avenue, (218) 736-6660

Tomacelli's Pizza and Pasta, City Center Mall, 120-1/2 West Cavour Street, (218) 739-6373

Thomas Kao Chinese Restaurant, 419 West Lincoln Avenue, (218) 739-3800

PELICAN RAPIDS

P. J.'s at Bayview Restaurant, 20393 South Pelican Drive, (218) 731-4689

PLACES TO SHOP

FERGUS FALLS

Ann's Hallmark Shop, WestRidge Mall, 2001 Lincoln Avenue at the junction of Interstate 94 and Highway 210, (218) 739-3031 or (800) 706-9865

The Prairie Sportsman, 106 West Lincoln Avenue, (218) 739-9655

Riverfront Square Mall, 221 West Lincoln Avenue, (218) 739-2757

PELICAN RAPIDS

Karen's Korner Gift Shop, Highways 59 and 34, (218) 863-5585

Peco Collectibles, 900 North Broadway, (281) 863-3281

FOR MORE INFORMATION

Battle Lake Civic and Commerce Association, Box 75, Battle Lake 56515, (215) 864-5889 or 888-933-5253; www.battlelake-mn.com

Fergus Falls Area Chamber of Commerce, 202 South Court, Fergus Falls 56537, (218) 736-6951 or (800) 726-8959; www.visitfergusfalls.com

New York Mills Civic and Commerce, Box 176, New York Mills 56567, (218) 385-2213; www.newyorkmills.com

Otter Tail Country Tourism Association, Box 110, Ottertail 56571, (800) 423-4571; www.ottertailcountry.com

Pelican Rapids Area Chamber of Commerce, Box 206, City Hall, Dept. T, Pelican Rapids 56572, (218) 863-1221; www.pelicanrapids.com

Perham Chamber of Commerce, Box 234, Perham 56573, (800) 634-6112

Pine to Prairie Birding Trail, Detroit Lakes City Hall, 1025 Roosevelt Avenue, Detroit Lakes 56502, (218) 847-5658 or (800) 433-1888; www.mnbirdtrail.com

BEMIDJI AND ENVIRONS

When in the Bemidji area, it's easy for kids to see how Minnesota got its famous motto. The state is indeed "the land of 10,000 lakes," and they all seem to be located around Bemidji. There is water everywhere, with large and small, named and unnamed bodies of water of all shapes and sizes. Ten thousand years ago, the last glacier retreated from this land, leaving behind bogs, potholes—and lakes. Even Lake Bemidji is the result of melting ice left behind by the towering ice pack.

For generations, the forerunners of today's Native Americans fished and hunted this food-rich region and fished the choppy waters of the lake. Around 1750, the Ojibwe arrived in the area, calling the lake *Bemiji-gua-maug*, meaning "cut sideways." They settled in the area and constructed compact, comfortable villages. It wasn't long before the Europeans arrived. The first French traders in the region called the lake "Lac Traverse," using the French word for "diagonal" because of the direction the Mississippi River takes as it cuts through the 6,420-acre lake.

The woods remained relatively peaceful until the late 1800s, with only the peeping of tree frogs, howl of wolves, and cry of the jays to disturb the calm. As the 19th century drew to a close, thousands of young European immigrants were drawn to the area as loggers, setting out to harvest what seemed to be never-ending acres of white and Norway pine. The busy sawmills on the south side of the lake meant bucketloads of money. Entrepreneurs too numerous to mention became tycoons as board feet after quality board feet headed south to help build the Midwest's booming urban areas. Today, the only remaining sign of those halcyon days is the foundation of an old Crookston Lumber Company building on the south shore of Lake Bemidji, still on the spot where it burned to the ground in 1924, drawing the timber business around here to a close.

RELIVING THE LUMBERING PAST

To get a feel for what it must have been like to work the local forests, take the crew out to **Camp Rabideau**, one of only three preserved Civilian Conservation Corps (CCC) camps in the country. The facilities were used in the 1930s to house workers laboring in the forests to build campgrounds, fire towers, dams, and recreation facilities. Until the end of 1941 when the government phased out the CCC, the teams of young men in the Bemidji area were also kept busy by constructing the Blackduck Ranger Station, counting deer, and searching for lost berry pickers. The U.S. government placed the camp on the National Register of Historic Places in 1976. Fifteen of the original 25 buildings remain on the site that once sprawled over 112 acres. Tours are conducted between 10 a.m. and 5 p.m. on Wednesdays during the summer. Call (218) 835-4291 for details. The complex is six miles south of Blackduck on County Highway 39; Blackduck is about 23 miles northeast of Bemidji on Highway 71. For another look into the old days, stroll through the old **Soo Line Depot** in the town of Cass Lake, about 20 miles southeast of Bemidji on Highway 2. The depot includes a replica of a lumber camp bunkhouse and cook shack.

Yet to really understand what the logging years were all about, be sure to escort the family out to the **Lost Forty**, a 144-acre parcel of white pine that was saved from the loggers axes and saws due to a map error. The virgin trees that remain are up to 350 years old and are between 22 and 48 inches in diameter. From Blackduck, drive east on Highway 30/13 for 12 miles to Alvwood. Then go north on Highway 46 for one-half mile to County Highway 29. Turn right, and then follow this road to Dora Lake, where you pick up County Road 26. Travel north on 26 to Forest Road 2240. About 1.5 miles west of this intersection is a sign directing visitors to the Lost Forty.

Park at the sign and then walk along the quarter-mile trail through this natural shrine. Self-guided-tour pamphlets can be picked up at a kiosk at the trailhead. The road is unplowed in the winter. For more information on this tract of trees, contact the U.S. Forest Service Blackduck Ranger District, 417 Forestry Drive, Blackduck 56630, (218) 835-4291.

MORE NEARBY RECREATION

After the lumber barons depleted the woodlands near Bemidji, the government bought up thousands of raw acres and turned them into **Lake Bemidji State Park** in 1923. Today, the replanted trees have matured, and more than 150,000 guests each year take advantage of the hiking trails, the swimming holes, the campsites, and the walleye-fishing opportunities within the park's 1,688 acres.

The park, on the northeast shore of the lake, is a playground par excellence whatever the season. True to the rugged spirit of Minnesotans—and anyone else wanting a winter weekend away—the park's campgrounds are open year-round. Shake up the kids, load extra woolies, pack another blanket, and head to the snow for a couple of days in the drifts. Be sure to empty out the closet and bring skis, snowboards, inner tubes, or whatever other recreational equipment is needed for frosty frivolity.

One drive-in site in the park is maintained, but other campsites are available only on a walk-in or ski-in basis. Subsequently, put the kids on snowshoes, load 'em up with grub and other camping gear, and tramp out into the forest

Native Presence

Native Americans lived in the vicinity of Leech Lake as early as A.D. 1000. The Dakota were among the first residents. In the 18th and 19th centuries, they were forced out of the area by the Ojibwe, who had been driven westward from their ancestral lands by white settlers. There were many battles between the two Native American nations, as they fought over ownership of land and lakes. Soon after the Dakota were chased out of the woods and onto the prairies, the Ojibwe were decimated by smallpox brought to their camps by white traders. It took several generations before the Ojibwe population was able to rebound.

for the adventure of their young lives. Leave the television and the popcorn popper at home. Why? Well, there's no electricity out here in the winter. (Though if the camping clan comes in the nonfrosty season, 43 of the park's sites are wired for action.) For the active types who like wrestling with Old Man Winter, Lake Bemidji has 11 miles of fantastic, groomed cross-country ski trails and three miles set aside for rip-roaring snowmobiles. For details on what else the park has in store for the short-term visitor, contact its headquarters at 3401 State Park Road N.E., Bemidji 56601, (218) 755-3843.

The vast **Chippewa National Forest** lies a short distance east of Bemidji. A beautiful log building, made of native red pine, was built in 1935 to house the forest headquarters. Kids, as well as adults, feel mighty small standing next to the building lobby's 50-foot-high fireplace, made from 265 tons of split glacial rocks that were dug up in the area. Arranging the kids in front of this massive build-out makes a good photo. For the history books, in 1908, the forest became the first national forest designated east of the Mississippi River. And it would take a Paul Bunyan and his seven-league boots to stride across this expanse of woodland and lakes, which encompasses almost 1.2 million acres.

For fishing and canoeing fans, there are more than 700 lakes, 920 miles of rivers and streams, and 150,000 acres of wetlands within the forest borders. Bass, muskie, panfish, and other watery game goodies are plentiful throughout the region. With this wonderful mix of woods and water, it's like an all-you-can-eat brunch table for the bald eagles who live here in the largest gathering of the majestic birds in the Lower 48.

Another 243 species of birds live in the forest, ranging from rat-tat-tatting woodpeckers to squawking blue jays. A good way for the kids to spot them is to utilize the 280 miles of trails that spiderweb through the Chippewa. Cross-country skiers also use the trails in the winter. Much of the system is multi-use, such as the *Mi-gi-zi* ("Eagle") Trail with its two paths—one paved for joggers, skaters, and cyclists; and an adjoining path for wintertime snowmobile use. To find out more about the forest's recreational opportunities for young people, contact the Chippewa National Forest, Route 3, Box 244, Cass Lake 56633, (218) 335-8600.

INSIDE BEMIDJI

Many of the lumber barons of years gone by built mansions along an eight-block section of Bemidji's **Lake Boulevard**, nicknamed the Gold Coast. Take the family for a drive down the street today to give the group a sense of the past. Despite the grand homes, not everyone who lived in the neighborhood was a mogul. For instance, the fellow who installed the city's electric-light plant built the Warfield House in 1912. A judge had a log cabin on the boulevard, albeit a very fancy one, where he partied with the rich and famous of his day, including author F. Scott Fitzgerald, who would ride up on the train to Bemidji from his home in St. Paul.

Family vacationers have a large menu of in-town activities with which to while away the hours. Spend time strolling the sidewalks of Bemidji and other towns in the area while eating ice-cream cones, peeking into the souvenir shops, and visiting historic attractions. Bemidji's **Great Northern Depot** is a nice stop, especially if the weather turns sour. Built in 1912, the building was the last such one constructed by James J. Hill, the St. Paul railroad mogul known as the "empire builder." On the National Register of Historic Places since 1988, the venerable old depot downtown now houses the Beltrami County History Center and a gift shop.

The kiddies will especially love meeting Bemidji's version of the legendary lumberman Paul Bunyan. It's all part and parcel of a vacation here. The muscular lad and his friendly blue ox, Babe, have been on the local scene since their statues were built in 1937 overlooking Lake Bemidji. Earl Bucklen, then town mayor, was used as the model for the brawny boy of legend. Footings for the 18-foot-tall lumberjack consist of 5.5 tons of poured concrete, with the character himself weighing in at 2.5 tons.

An early Babe was built from a wooden skeleton covered with wire, a padding of fiber, and a canvas covering. Automobile headlights served as Babe's eyes, gleaming whenever the battery was cranked up. The beast's tin horns measured 14 feet tip to tip. Early in its career, Babe was placed on a truck bed and used in parades throughout Minnesota to promote holiday festivities in Bemidji. Yet all this travel meant the ox took a beating, so the big blue critter was returned to Bemidji where the deteriorating canvas was removed and replaced by concrete.

This stronger, more-durable Babe was subsequently placed next to Bunyan, and the couple has become Bemidji's tourist icon. Everyone in town knows when the vacation season opens: When Paul and Babe are washed off and their paint touched up, merchants and townspeople know the crowds will soon fill their town again.

Paul Bunyan and his trusty companion Babe standing guard in downtown Bemidji.
Minnesota Office of Tourism photograph.

After snapping shots of the family with guy-'n-ox, arrange the kids around the statue of Chief Bemidji, who peers into the future from his place of honor in the city's Library Park. Bemidji's hand shades his face as he looks outward into a new world, one far removed from the days when Native Americans called this land home.

A NATIVE AMERICAN EXPERIENCE

To give the family a glimpse of Native American traditions, take them to the vast **Red Lake Indian Reservation**, an historic area where the Ojibwe originally settled in the mid-1700s after driving away the Dakota; it's about 30 miles northwest of Bemidji via Highway 89. A Northwest Fur Company trading post was set up here in the 1800s and a mission school established in 1843. Located in the village of Redby, known as the Chief's Village after an early tribal leader Chief May-dway-fwon-no-nind, are the reservation's fisheries and a stand of maple trees used for sugaring. Another old village on the reservation is Ponemah, home of an early boarding school. Indian burial grounds are on nearby Ponemah Point.

The Final Indian Battle

Leech Lake was the scene of the "last deadly engagement between Native Americans and the American military in the United States." In 1898, a federal force was sent to Sugar Point, in the northeastern corner of the lake, to arrest Chief Bug-Oh-Nay-Geshig (whose nickname was "Old Bug"), an Ojibwe leader accused of possessing and selling alcohol on the Leech Lake Reservation. Many believe the charge was trumped up by lumber interests to get rid of Old Bug, who staunchly opposed timber operations in the area. On an earlier occasion, he was forced to walk more than 100 miles from Duluth, where he had to defend himself against similar charges, back to Leech Lake in the middle of winter.

In response to the new threat, Old Bug fled into the woods where he was joined by a band of Ojibwe. No one knows exactly what happened next, but a battle ensued with the hundred or so troops, followed by daylong skirmishes all along the eastern shore of the lake. In all, six soldiers and a federal marshal were killed. There were no estimates of the Ojibwe losses.

Eventually, the government arrested 12 Ojibwe; many Americans called for their execution. President William McKinley, however, after reviewing accounts of the attack, pardoned all of them.

A WOODSY WALK

Before leaving the area, get the backseat gang's legs stretched and hearts pumped on a woodsy stroll (or bike ride) along the **Heartland State Trail**. The pathway covers 49 miles on an old railway bed between Park Rapids and Cass Lake south and southeast of Bemidji. Except for a four-mile span north of Walker where there is rolling terrain, the trail is relatively flat. Therefore, just about anyone in the family can "go take a hike."

The trail edges through some magnificent stands of hardwood forest and pine. Once in awhile a lonesome white pine stands in solitary splendor near the path, a reminder that these forests were once made up of hundreds of thousands of these majestic trees before the loggers got them. Keep the kids on alert for deer, raccoons, porcupines, red fox, and other denizens of the forest. Be aware that there are black bears around here, as well as coyotes, weasels, bobcats, and related fang types. But remember that these animals are usually more frightened around people than vice versa, and attack only when they feel threatened. When hiking, make noise. This alerts some of the bigger animals to your presence, and it gives them a chance to make their escape. What you don't want to do is startle a bear, which can result in a nasty confrontation. Besides, kids like to make noise anyway.

The 27 miles of the trail between Park Rapids and Walker is paved, with a second grassy path for horseback riding and mountain bikes. The last long 22-mile section to Cass Lake is compacted gravel and railroad ballast with occasional sandy areas. In the winter, the trail is used for snowmobiles and links with an extensive system in the surrounding counties.

The entry points for the paved section of the Heartland State Trail are located in Park Rapids and Walker. Parking is available in Park Rapids at Heartland County Park, Dorset, Nevis, Akeley, Walker, and at Erickson's Landing north of Walker. Remind the kids not to leave any valuables in the family vehicle, because sometimes there are bad guys 'n gals, even in the woods, who don't respect other folks' property. Maps of the trail can be secured from the Minnesota Department of Transportation, 395 John Ireland Boulevard, Room B-2, St. Paul 55155, (651) 296-2216.

While in the Cass Lake area, check out 1,163-acre Star Island, an oddity in the heart of the lake. The island has its own 195-acre Lake Windigo, featured by the old *Ripley's Believe It or Not* newspaper column as "the lake in the island in the lake." Star Island is accessible only by powerboat or canoe.

For a completely different type of North Woods walk, the Bemidji area is rife with splendid golf courses. Cass Lake alone has eight courses within 30 minutes of its downtown. Nobody minds the occasional deer wandering across a green. After all, the creatures were here first. The courses range from professional-level to par-3 facilities, which makes it great for entire families of golf aficionados regardless of skill level. Among the links are **Sandtrap Golf Course**, one mile south of Highway 2 on Highway 371, (218) 335-6531; **Tianna Country Club**, about two miles south of Walker on Highway 34, (218) 547-1712; and **LongBow Golf Club**, located off Highway 371, fourteen miles south of Cass Lake or six miles north of Walker. Call (218) 547-4121 or (877) 881-4653.

PLACES TO STAY

BEMIDJI

A Place in the Woods, 11380 Turtle River Lake Road N.E., (218) 586-2345 or (800) 676-4547; www.aplaceinthewoodsresort.com

Bemidji KOA Kampground, 5707 U.S. Highway 2 West, (218) 751-1792 or (800) 562-1742

Best Western Bemidji Inn, 2420 Paul Bunyan Drive, (218) 751-0390 or (877) 857-8599

Big Wolf Lake Resort and Campground, 12150 Walleye Lane S.E., (218) 751-5749 or (800) 322-0281; www.bigwolfresort.org

Holiday Inn Express, 2422 Ridgeway Avenue N.W., (218) 751-2487 or (800) 617-4379

Oak Haven Resort, 14333 Roosevelt Road S.E., (218) 335-2092 or (877) 860-9948

Super 8 Motel, 1815 Paul Bunyan Drive N.W., (218) 751-8481 or (800) 800-8000; www.super8.com

BLACKDUCK

Tepee-Tonka, P.O. Box 360, Blackduck Lake, (800) 346-5674 or (218) 835-4862; www.mn-resort.com

Tomahawk Lodge, P.O. Box 177, Blackduck Lake, (218) 835-4510 or (800) 452-8023; www.tomahawklodge.com

White Birch Resort, P.O. Box 186, Blackduck Lake, (218) 835-4552; www.resortwebonline.com/whitebirch

CASS LAKE

Cass Lake Lodge and Campground, 16293 60th Avenue N.W., (218) 335-6658; www.casslakelodge.com

Ojibway Resort, 15191 Pike Bay Loop N.W., (218) 335-6695

Platzer's River/Lake Resort, 3333 Morningside Lane S.E., (218) 335-8822 or (800) 301-8822; www.sahtay.com

Whispering Pines Motel, 6318 U.S. Highway 2 N.W., (218) 335-8852 or (800) 371-8852

PLACES FOR FOOD

BEMIDJI

Back Yard, 2450 Paul Bunyan Drive, (218) 751-7853

Coachman Cafe, 509 Beltrami Avenue, (218) 751-0436

Dave's Pizza, 422 West 15th Street, (218) 751-3225

Family Countryside Restaurant, 7052 U.S. Highway 2 West, (218) 751-8248

Harmony Food Co-op, 117 Third Street N.W., (218) 751-2009

Peppercorn Restaurant and Lounge, 1813 Paul Bunyan Drive, (218) 759-2794

Raphael's Bakery and Restaurant, 319 Minnesota Avenue, (218) 759-2015

Ruttger's Birchmont Lodge, 530 Birchmont Beach Road, (218) 444-3463 or 888-RUTTGERS; www.ruttgers.com

Southside Restaurant, 3417 Washington Avenue S.E., (218) 751-5110

Stats Sports Bar, 102 First Street, Union Square, (218) 751-0441

Tutto Bene, 300 Beltrami Avenue N.W., (218) 751-1100

Union Station, 128 First Street, (218) 751-9261

BLACKDUCK
Countryside Restaurant, 240 Summit Avenue Northwest, (218) 835-3333

PLACES TO SHOP
BEMIDJI
Bemidji Locker and Fish Company, 3001 Bemidji Avenue, (218) 751-2244

Bemidji Snowmobile Rental and Sales, 2015 Highway Avenue N.W., (218) 751-6268

Bemidji Woolen Mills, 301 Irvine Avenue N.W., (218) 751-5166 or (888) 751-5166; www.bemidjiwoolenmills.com

Emily's Country Cottage, 705 Washington Avenue S.E., (218) 751-6387

Julie's Hallmark Shop, 423 Beltrami Avenue, (218) 751-9425

McKenzie Place, 802 Paul Bunyan Drive South, (218) 755-8009

Morell's Chippewa Trading Post, 7040 U.S. Highway 2, (888) 667-3557; www.morellstradingpost.com

Willow Wood Market, Route 8, Box 581, (218) 759-2310

CASS LAKE
Forest Trail Gifts, 7246 U.S. Highway 2 N.W., (218) 335-8312

Reimer's Marine, 113 First Avenue, (218) 335-8835

FOR MORE INFORMATION
Bemidji Area Chamber of Commerce, 300 Bemidji Avenue, Bemidji 56601, (218) 444-3541 or (800) 458-2223; www.visitbemidji.com

Bemidji Visitors and Convention Bureau, P.O. Box 66, Bemidji 56601, (800) 458-2223, ext. 105, or (218) 759-0164; www.visitbemidji.com

Minnesota Northwoods Tourism Bureau, (866) 866-1866; www.minnesotanorthwoods.com

Pennington Triangle Resort Association, Blackduck 56630; www.penningtonvacation.com

U.S. Forest Service, Blackduck Ranger District, 417 Forestry Drive, Blackduck 56630, (218) 835-4291

MISSISSIPPI HEADWATERS COUNTRY

Ever dream of leaping across the Mississippi River? Well, in this region, the whole family can scamper across the tiny creek that eventually becomes one of the world's most formidable flowages. The Mississippi begins its 2,552-mile trek to the Gulf of Mexico in northwestern Minnesota at Itasca State Park, located southeast of Bemidji on Highway 71 and spread over Clearwater, Hubbard, and Becker Counties. Among the largest communities closest to the park are Bagley, 25 miles to the northwest, and Park Rapids, some 25 miles south.

PARK ORIGINS

The state established the park in 1891 to save the remnants of virgin white pine that once spread for miles across northern Minnesota. The park now contains about 20 percent of the state's remaining old-growth forest. Subsequently, the park is an important environmental buffer for this part of Minnesota, protecting the basin surrounding the origins of the Mississippi River in what is called the Pine Moraine Region.

The area is a girdle of sharp slopes and deep ravines left after the passing of the glaciers more than 10,000 years ago. The highest hills in the park reach 1,700 feet above sea level, making for excellent vistas. Lake Itasca, where the Mississippi begins, was formed when glacial ice melted in a valley.

People have lived here for more than 8,000 years. When archaeologists were poking around the area in 1937, they found dozens of human artifacts mixed with bison bones. In the early 1960s, researchers from the University of Minnesota discovered camp and garbage sites in the vicinity, attesting to the vibrant life that was prevalent here ages ago. Apparently, these early people were the first to visit the Mississippi headwaters. They were migrating hunters who followed the moose, deer, and bison.

Over the centuries, these early Minnesotans were followed by other ancestors of the Native Americans who eventually settled here. Burial mounds from the Woodland Culture can still be seen next to the river headwaters. Their permanent settlements were models of efficiency and organization. A later Native

A rock-strewn shoreline at Itasca State Park. Minnesota Office of Tourism photograph.

American cemetery, with some graves estimated to be several hundred years old, is found within the park grounds. Signs tells about the customs of the people buried here. After the Woodland Culture came the Ojibwe and other nations whose imprint is still on the land here, many living on reservations scattered throughout northern Minnesota.

Explorer Henry Rowe Schoolcraft was the first white to describe Lake Itasca as the birthplace of the mighty Mississippi. He was guided there in the steamy, mosquito-filled summer of 1832 by Ojibwe chief Ozawindib. Schoolcraft made up the name of the lake by combining parts of the two Latin words *veriITAS CAput*, which means "truth's head."

By the late 1800s, the logging industry was clear-cutting the state to feed the nation's appetite for cheap lumber. Subsequently, the timber barons had their eye on the headwaters district. Conservationist Jacob Brower fought them off until he died in 1905. The gauntlet was picked up by such friends as local game warden Theodore Wegmann; a replica of Wegmann's cabin home can be toured in the park.

The Forest and Biological Station set up by the University of Minnesota in 1909 has been working ever since to limit development in the Itasca woods. The first of its kind in the United States, the station continues to host wildlife and environmental classes.

Bugged Out in the Woods

Don't go buggy when you're in the deep woods. Insects do serve a purpose by providing food for birds and by pollinating flowers. However, they aren't fun to have around a campsite. Carry a bug repellant such as Muskol or one containing DEET. Bug nets are also helpful, especially in midsummer. Wear long-sleeved, tightly woven shirts so bugs can't bite. Avoid dark colors, especially blue, which attract insects. Green is the best bug-neutral color to wear. Dedicated hikers are not embarrassed to wear gloves and headnets, and they make sure their pants are tucked into their socks so the biting black flies can't get at them.

NAVIGATING THE PARK

Begin a visit to the park at the **Forest Inn**, a huge timber-and-stone structure built by the Civilian Conservation Corps in the 1930s. The kids will go wild in the souvenir shop there and have a grand learning experience in the interpretive center. At least they'll know what to look for when they're out and about the park. The inn is located at the end of East Entrance Road (County Highway 48). It also hosts ranger programs and is a warming center for frost-nipped cross-country skiers in the winter. Have the kids check the bulletin boards for times of the educational get-togethers.

Youngsters can also take part in the **Junior Park Naturalist** program managed through the Minnesota State Park system. Itasca is one of several participating sites where kids 7 to 14 can earn certificates and a patch by working on a number of activities in the park, such as identifying plants and looking for birds. In a special booklet secured at the interpretive center, youngsters can write down what they discover.

The historic **Douglas Lodge** is one of the neatest places to stay on the park grounds. The timber structure, built between 1903 and 1905, was the first building to serve the park's guests. Lodge suites and guestrooms are available, along with a public dining room. A nearby clubhouse has 10 rooms that are great for family groups on a getaway. A central lobby with a fireplace is a cozy spot for chats, games, and rainy-day book reading. Call (800) 765-2267.

A short, self-guided trail winds away from the back of the lodge, a walkway perfect for orienting the kids to the woods. Part of the trail follows the East

Arm of Lake Itasca and then turns inland to tiny Lyendecker Lake. Have the youngsters look for the fragile pink-and-white lady's slipper, Minnesota's state flower, which grows in abundance along this pathway. Pictures of the blossom can be found at the interpretive center.

Another perfect woodsy hideaway is the **Squaw Lake Wilderness Cabin**, located off Wilderness Drive on Squaw Lake. The cabin, which can sleep up to four persons, is about 1.5 miles from the Mississippi River headwaters. Other housekeeping cabins are also available in the park.

Camping is special here, due to the value-added aspect of the river's headwaters. Campgrounds are scattered around the park, with Pine Ridge and Bear Paw being the two major sites. Tent pads are located in the southern section of the park, where determined overnighters need to trek from one to five miles to their reserved clearing.

Don't worry too much about the gang getting lost. The park's excellent road system makes for easy driving to campsites, historical attractions, and the headwaters themselves. Kids can act as navigators, using maps provided at the park's information centers.

Highlights of a park visit include the bison kill site along the 11-mile-long **Wilderness Drive**, just after passing the **Itasca Wilderness Sanctuary Scientific and Natural Area**. The drive is one-way starting at the North Entrance and ending near the South Entrance, so motorists can't miss the location of the kill site that was excavated in 1963. Evidence showed that long-ago Native American hunters drove herds of the massive animals over the cliff face to their deaths. The natives then skinned and carved the beasts for clothing and food, a sobering thought for the backseat gang more used to a trip to the mall and fast-food drive-up than actually having to catch their britches or chase down lunch.

Minnesota's record white and red pines are located in the park, found on **Wilderness Road** not far from the bison kill site. The 120-foot red pine is first, a scarred old veteran of at least six forest fires. Scientists estimate the tree to be 300 years old, with a circumference of 115 inches necessitating the arms of several skinny kids to encircle the trunk—another perfect photo opportunity for moms and dads. Also called a Norway pine, the red pine is Minnesota's state tree. A giant white pine is further along the drive, with a circumference of 173 inches and a height of 112 feet. A short trail from the road leads to this tree.

Take the gang along the trail through a forestry demonstration area, also found on Wilderness Drive. Tree varieties such as red and Scotch pine and white spruce are showcased with numbered signposts keyed to an informational flier picked up at one of the information centers. Children can learn why tree plantations are thinned to allow stronger growth and how a tree naturally prunes itself.

Preacher's Grove, on County Highway 38 north of the Forest Inn, is a favorite place to pause for a look-around. Scientists estimate the seeds of the red pines now standing in the grove sprouted in the early 1700s after a tumultuous forest fire decimated this area of Minnesota. The grove is named after a religious gathering that camped here years ago.

Of course, the big thing at the park is leaping from stone to stone across the shallow, narrow creek at the north end of Lake Itasca. This area is the headwaters of the Mississippi, the official beginning of this magnificent symbol of America's restless spirit. For a time, the river actually flows north, then northeast toward Lake Bemidji, where it picks up steam. According to tradition, if jumpers get wet feet, they'll have bad luck that day. Just in case, keep a towel handy in the car, which can be parked nearby. You can easily reach the headwaters via the park's north entrance at the intersection of Highway 200 and County Highway 2. The Mississippi Headwaters State Forest is on the north side of Highway 200, and the state park is on the south side. Coming from the south, use County Highway 38, which runs along the east side of Lake Itasca. Native American burial mounds, an amphitheater, and picnic grounds are along the highway, waiting to be explored. For more information, contact Itasca State Park, HC05, Lake Itasca 56360, (218) 266-2114.

BAGLEY

The old logging town of Bagley is about 25 miles north of the park, via Highway 200 and Highway 92. The town's 25-acre municipal tourist park on the shore of Lake Lamond offers campsites, showers, electric hookups, and picnic shelters—everything the traveling family needs to make a home away from home for a few days. Lifeguards keep watch at a nearby swimming beach. The park also has a lighted softball field, tennis courts, fishing dock, and a place to pitch horseshoes. So get out the athletic stuff and issue a family challenge to see who can hit the first home run, play the best set, catch the biggest fish, and toss the most ringers.

Bagley, as seat of Clearwater County, is host to the **Clearwater County Fair** on the second week of August. Kids can admire the plethora of farm animals and twirl around in a Ferris wheel on the glittering midway. The whole clan can enjoy the grandstand shows. After sampling the butter-dipped corn-on-the-cob, the sticky cotton candy, and crunchy caramel corn, parents would be wise to provide finger wipes for the kids.

The **Bagley Wildlife Museum** has more than 780 stuffed creatures in a natural habitat milieu. The organizers laugh that they have mice to mouse and minnows to muskies on display. It's rather spooky to be that close to an eagle or look eyeball-to-eyeball with a hummingbird. The museum is located on Highway 2 West, (218) 694-2491.

PARK RAPIDS

Park Rapids is about 25 miles south of Itasca State Park on Highway 70. In 1879, the first white settlers struggled through thick Minnesota forests to establish the city, a hub for the lumber industry. The founders named the town after the lovely parklike groves in the area and the roaring rapids of the Fishhook River.

Over the years, Park Rapids has become a tourist jumping-off place for the **Paul Bunyan State Forest**, just north of town, where alert bird-watchers can see bald eagles and osprey. In the quiet of the woods, have the kids pause and listen for the eerie call of common loons echoing over the nearby lakes. The common loon, as any true-blue Minnesotan knows, is the state bird. The **Tamarac National Wildlife Refuge** and the **Chippewa National Forest** are also within a short drive of downtown Park Rapids. So if trees are a family fixation, Park Rapids is the place for a few day's retreat.

If you brought bicycles, the group can try out the 27-mile **Heartland Trail**, which begins in town at Heartland Park, east of Highway 34 and Highway 71. The paved trail meanders though the villages of Dorset, Nevis, Akeley, and Walker, with a parallel trail open for horseback riding from spring to autumn and for snowmobiling in the winter. Canoe lovers can break out the paddles, life jackets, snacks, and beverages for a good day of paddling along tributaries of the Mississippi such as the Straight and Crow Wing Rivers. One effective paddling strategy is to put the smallest kid in the middle of the canoe and have the strongest teen in the front to provide the power; mom or dad can just sit back and steer from the stern.

With all the lakes and waterways nearby, fishing is serious business. Once walleye season opens in mid-May, it's hard for bait shops to keep up with the demand. But there always seems to be enough worms for any kid's first-time hook. Each year in early June, Park Rapids holds a Take a Kid Fishing Weekend where the children can learn the fun of casting and trolling.

Campers looking for a day in town find fun at the **Founder's Day Social**, usually held one of the first few days of July, with ice cream sold along Main Street. Then there's the Fourth of July parade and fireworks for an old-time, small-town feel. St. Peter's Parish holds a Halloween Carnival on October 31, for a bit of scare and prayer. Young winter visitors find Santa's Secret Shop at the Park Rapids Public Library to be just the place for their pre-holiday purchases.

Animal lovers in the family will get their fill of creatures large and small in the Park Rapids region. Kids can even watch bison calves being nursed at the **Northland Bison Ranch**, 22376 Glacial Ridge Trail (877) 453-9499. For a modest fee, a small school bus on the grounds takes travelers out into the pastureland or forest to see a mighty bison up close, wherever they are grazing. Check out the granddaddy of the herd: Big Thunder. He's the bull who runs the show here. The ranch sells bison leather products, gifts that the kids certainly can't purchase in their local mall. Bring back some frozen bison meat for a heart-healthy cookout at home. Northland is closed on Monday. The **Heart of Minnesota Emu Ranch**, 24200 Fairwood Lane, (218) 652-3790, at nearby Nevis will also fascinate the kids. More than 450 birds roam the ranch grounds. Try to hug an emu and let the kids take a photo. A store on the grounds carries emu feathers and painted eggs—just the things for show-and-tell.

Also in Nevis, budding cow-kids can ride horses at **BK Ranch Trail Riding**, 30880 County Highway 91, (218) 652-3540. The ranch offers three-day "day camps" for kids in June. Riding is by reservation, so there is no waiting in line to get a horse. The rides meander through the Paul Bunyan State Forest.

The village of Two Inlets, noted for its grotto, is 14 miles north of Park Rapids. The grotto is a replica of the shrine to Our Lady of Lourdes in southern France, which was built on the site where a young Frenchwoman saw a vision of the Blessed Mother in 1856. Today, Lourdes is a shrine visited by pilgrims from around the world seeking miraculous cures. Local folks built the Two Inlets grotto to re-create the image of the original site.

PLACES TO STAY

BAGLEY
Dutch Mill Motel, State Highway 2 West, (218) 694-2050
The Farm by the Lake, Box 329, Route 1, (218) 694-2084

PARK RAPIDS
Cedar Shores Lodge, 17915 Dayspring Drive, (218) 732-4626 or (888) 732-4625

Vagabond Village Campground, 23801 Green Pines Road, (218) 732-5234; www.vagabondvillage.com

Wilderness Bay Resort, 36701 Wilderness Bay Drive, (218) 732-5608; www.wildernessbay.com

PLACES FOR FOOD

BAGLEY
Coaches Corner, State Highway 2 West, (218) 694-2220

DaRoo's Pizza, 107 Central Street East, (218) 694-6936

D&R Cafe, 27 Central Street West, (218) 694-3747

PARK RAPIDS
3rd Street Market, 120 West Third Street, (218) 732-9063

Duran's Italian Eatery, 600 Park Avenue, (218) 732-9377

Gilbert's Uptown Cafe, 309 Third Street East, (218) 732-6190

Great Northern Café, 218 First Street Northeast, State Highway 34 East, (218) 732-9565

PLACES TO SHOP

PARK RAPIDS

Ament's Heartland Bakery, 203 South Main Avenue, (218) 731-4275

Aunt Belle's Confectionery, 110 South Main Avenue, (218) 732-7019

Bears on Main, 403 South Main Avenue, (218) 732-8930

Candles, 19974 129th Avenue, (218) 732-9368

Forestedge Winery, 35295 State Highway 64, (218) 224-3535

Wildwood Gifts, 316 South Main Avenue, (218) 732-5914

FOR MORE INFORMATION

Bagley Chamber of Commerce/City Clerk, 18 Main Avenue, Bagley 56621, (218) 694-2865

Minnesota Department of Natural Resources, Division of Parks and Recreation, Information Center, Box 40, 500 Lafayette Road, St. Paul 55155, (651) 296-6157; www.dnr.state.mn.us

Park Rapids Area Chamber of Commerce, State Highway 72 South, Park Rapids 56470, (218) 732-4111 or (800) 247-0054; www.parkrapids.com

BRAINERD AND THE MILLE LACS AREA

In north-central Minnesota, it would be foolhardy for vacationing families to limit themselves to having fun in just one community. There are simply too many places that know how to show visitors a great time, regardless of the length of stay. The Brainerd–Mille Lacs area is certainly one of these. Located within an easy hour-and-one-half drive of the Twin Cities, the region abounds in lapping lakes, marvelous maples, great golf, and wild walleyes, to say nothing of hammocks, steakhouses, hiking trails, and history. There are several dozen villages and towns scattered amid the lakes here that cater to the getaway family in search of . . . well, you name it.

As if anyone was counting, there are at least 465 lakes scattered around this chunk of Gopherland real estate, along with rivers and streams to explore. Lake Mille Lacs, by the way, is the second largest freshwater lake within Minnesota's borders. At about 14 miles long and some 12 miles wide, it is no wonder the tourism marketers call this "Big Lake Country."

Father Louis Hennepin, a French Jesuit, wandered through this area in 1679 searching for souls, as well as for land to claim for his home country. **Father Hennepin State Park**, on the south end of Lake Mille Lacs, is a reminder of that era, although it wasn't the site where Hennepin had been actually held. The 316-acre park has two drive-in boat launches on Lake Mille Lacs, a swimming beach, as well as hiking and cross-country ski trails. The park office is on Highway 27, one mile west of the town of Isle, (320) 676-8763.

BRAINERD'S FAMILY FUN

Was that who we think it is? Look again. And again. It's hard to miss seeing Paul Bunyan, the legendary lumberjack, and Babe, his giant blue ox, around these parts. One place where you can spot him saying hello and waving his hand to greet guests is the **Paul Bunyan Amusement Center**, (218) 829-6342 or (877) 728-6926, a well-known family amusement park at the intersection of Highways 210 and 371. After saying howdy to the big guy and his bovine companion, turn the kids loose on the theme park's 40 rides. Trains, bumper cars, Ferris wheels—all the best rides are here, with new rides added every year.

Youngsters awaiting a photo opportunity with the 27-foot-tall Paul Bunyan at Brainerd's Paul Bunyan Amusement Center. —Courtesy of the Paul Bunyan Amusement Center

Rides are unlimited once you pay the admission fee. The **Paul Bunyan Miniature Golf Course** is just outside the park.

All this frantic activity is a great way to tire out the gang, all of whom can then easily be hauled next door for a nap at—what else?—the rustic **Paul Bunyan Inn**, 1800 Fairview Drive North, (218) 829-3571 or (877) 728-6926; www.paulbunyancenter.com/motel.

If the kiddies haven't yet had their fill of fiberglass fun, head north about 10 miles from the inn on Highway 371 to the **Nisswa Family Fun Center**, (218) 963-

The Road to Prosperity

In the 19th century, the railroad surveyor was influential in establishing frontier towns, and Minnesota was no exception. Wherever he set the tracks, economic prosperity was sure to follow. But with no tracks, little or no business was the result. Such was the case with Crow Wing Village, which died out when railroad tracks were run a few miles away through another settlement on the Mississippi called the Crossings. With the train traffic, that little community eventually grew into the city of Brainerd, renamed in honor of the railroad president's wife, whose maiden name was Brainerd.

3645. It has a 400-foot water slide, hot tubs, and a monster wading pool for the kiddies. There are even Rollerblade rentals that can be used off-site for a cruise around the neighborhood. The town of Nisswa is also the home of the original turtle races, now a staple of summer fun in many towns around Minnesota, where kids see whose little critter can make it first across a finish line. The races are held at 2 p.m., every Wednesday, during the summer in downtown Nisswa. Kids can bring their own turtle or rent one. Call (218) 963-2620 for details.

If indoor fun is in order, due to rain or snow, sign in at the **Comfort Suites** in Baxter (five miles west of Brainerd on Highway 210) with its 11,000-square-foot indoor water park and a video arcade that has enough winking, blinking machines to rival the Vegas strip. While the kids splash and the teens talk around the giant lobby fireplace, the adults can soak in the whirlpool. For the fitness-minded who also want to stay inside, there is even an exercise room and sauna. The hotel is at 1221 Edgewood Drive, (877) 4GET-WET; www.comfortinn.com/Hotel/MN060.

For those in the family seeking more heart-pounding action, the **Colonel's Brainerd International Raceway** is considered one of the state's top motor sports facilities. The complex has a three-mile, ten-turn track and a drag strip, and the raceway hosts events sanctioned by the National Hotel Rod Association, the Sports Car Club of America, and the American Motorcycle Association. There's no lack of seats, even during the peak of the season. More than 26,000 persons can be accommodated at the raceway, which also offers 525 acres of camping for fans who can't tear themselves away from the track. For weekenders, there are street-rod and muscle-car events, which attract auto fans from around the country. The site is on Highway 371 North. Call (810) 249-5530.

Continuing in the spectator sports vein, the **Mighty Gulls** baseball team runs the bases at Mills Field in Brainerd. Made up of collegiate stars wanting to retain their out-of-the-ballpark-hitting skills, the Gulls play 32 home games every summer against other Northwoods League competitors. When the players come out of the dugout ready for action, join in the cheering. It's a chance for everyone in the family to let loose a vocal blast. Call (218) 828-8901 for the schedule and ticket prices.

A Bitter Strike

In 1922, a lengthy strike of railroad workers split Brainerd into factions favoring the strikers and those opposing them, a division which deteriorated into street battles. The Northern Pacific Railroad brought in strikebreakers to work the line, and it took years before the community fully recovered from the trauma.

Far from the roar of engines and the crack of bats, golfers can tee off on some of the Upper Midwest's best courses. More than 20 of them grace the Brainerd area, making this a mecca for players who crave challenging holes and enjoy lush scenery. Robert Trent Jones, Arnold Palmer, and other top course designers have created some dandy layouts for die-hard golfers in the family. For details on the area's golfing scene, call (800) 450-2838 or visit www.golfbrainerdlakes.com.

Families can scamper around the area's other attractions while dads, moms, or older teens take their turn swinging the clubs. Among the best-known courses are **Breezy Point Resort**, (218) 562-7811 or (800) 432-3777, www.breezypoint.com; and **Grand View Lodge**, (800) 432-3788, www.grandviewlodge.com. **Cragun's Conference and Golf Resort** is Minnesota's largest four-season golf facility with its 27 holes along the shores of Gull Lake. Call (218) 825-2700 or (800) 272-4867; or tap into Cragun's Web site at www.craguns.com/chs01.

All the golf facilities offer packages, many of which are reasonable, comprehensive, and worth every ball that flips into the rough. In addition, they have restaurants, pool areas, and other amenities to enjoy after the spikes are put away. It's not necessary to be registered at the resorts to take advantage of the top-quality dining opportunities. Most of the eateries are open to all.

OUT ON THE TRAILS

For those who prefer their activity a bit more on the strenuous side, bicyclists who know Minnesota have high praise for the **Paul Bunyan Trail**, a 100-mile route from just west of Brainerd north to Bemidji. The paved trail runs along an abandoned right-of-way once used by the Burlington Northern Railroad. The path extends through Crow Wing, Cass, Hubbard, and Beltrami Counties before ending at Lake Bemidji State Park. Along the way, cyclists will whir through Merrifield, Nisswa, Pequot Lakes, Jenkins, Pine River, Backus, Hackensack, Walker, Benedict, LaPorte, Guthrie, and Nary. There are plenty of restaurants, shops, and hostelries to accommodate bikers, who range in age from children on bikes with training wheels to old-timers using three-wheelers.

Each leg of the trail is an easy distance, but plan ahead to be sure that all those in the family are up for the various sections. For instance, the run from Brainerd to Merrifield is only nine miles, while the Hackensack to Walker link is 16.8 miles. Perhaps a short run, such as the Pequot Lakes to Jenkins connection—at three miles—is a better choice if little kids are along for the ride. Information on the route can be found from the chambers of commerce of each community along the way or from the Mille Lacs Area Tourism Council, Box 758, Onamia 56359, (888) 350-2692; vacation@millelacs.com.

This midsection of Minnesota has several state timberlands open for hiking and snowmobiling opportunities in their respective seasons. Subsequently, a vacationer has a pick of traveling hot or cold during a jaunt here. **Foothills**, **Paul Bunyan**, **Land 'o Lakes**, **Crow Wing**, and **Pillsbury State Forests** are just a few of the region's nature areas to explore. Once heavily logged by 19th-century lumberjacks, the land is covered anew by second-growth trees, which provide a wonderful, shady canopy of leaves. The forests are managed by the state's Department of Natural Resources. There are many resorts, cabins, campgrounds, and recreation areas scattered throughout these forests, with amenities ranging from plush to rustic and simple.

LAKE MILLE LACS

Twenty miles east of Brainerd you'll find the vast freshwater expanse of Lake Mille Lacs. One of the largest bodies of water in Minnesota, the lake has been drawing visitors not only with its abundant recreational activities, and the numerous landlocked attractions that surround it. One special place is the **Mille Lacs Indian Museum**, where your brood can learn more about the Ojibwe language and the tribe's art, culture, and music. A special Four Seasons Room takes vacationers through a typical year of Native American life, from spring

Learning about Ojibwe culture at the Mille Lacs Indian Museum.
—Courtesy of the Minnesota Historical Society

First Native Americans

The Dakota who lived in the Mille Lacs area when the first whites arrived belonged to the Mdewakanton tribe. The name meant "people by the spirit lake," and the lake was considered the spiritual hub of the Dakota. The lake was later renamed by the French as Mille Lacs.

to summer, to autumn to winter, in a series of dioramas. A 1930s-era trading post is the place to purchase crafts and other souvenirs to show the pals back home. The museum, 43411 Oodena Drive, is on Highway 169 on the south shore of Lake Mille Lacs, 12 miles north of Onamia and eight miles south of Garrison. Call (320) 532-3632; www.millelacs.com/whattodo/attractions.html. The museum is administered by the Minnesota Historical Society.

To capture a sense of what Native Americans might have seen when they held sway over this region, take the family to **Mille Lacs Kathio State Park** on the southwestern corner of the lake. At 10,000 acres, the state park is the fourth largest in Minnesota. The main park entry is one mile off Highway 169 on County Highway 26, about 100 miles from the Twin Cities.

The kids will appreciate the rolling woodlands of the park where they can hike or bike. By visiting the park's interpretive center, the youngsters will learn that the hills are actually a terminal moraine, a low ridge of debris marking the farthest reach of a melting glacier. About 10,000 years ago, refuse originally blocked the earth's natural drainage, creating a prehistoric lake even larger than Mille Lacs. Over the centuries, that lake shrank to the current size.

In the mid-1800s, the sprawling forest of red and white pine naturally attracted loggers, who clear-cut the woods, with only a few isolated stands of the original trees surviving. Mille Lacs Kathio State Park is now carpeted with aspen, maple, oak, and other northern hardwood cousins. For an excellent view of all this greenery, climb the observation tower in the middle of the park. One of the many sights the kids will see is Lake Ogechie, a long, narrow lake near the park campground, once a primary source of wild rice for the Native American tribes in the area. Archaeologists believe that humans have inhabited this region for at least 4,000 years, with the Dakota and the Ojibwe in turn making it one of their primary settlements. For information on Mille Lacs Kathio, contact the park manager at Star Route, Box 85, Onamia 56359, (320) 532-3523.

Lake Mille Lacs is the source of the Rum River, another of the area's big draws. This flowage edges through the state park and ultimately links with the Mississippi River, about 80 miles downstream at Anoka. The canoeing opportunities on the Rum River attracts vacationers from around the Upper Midwest, drawn to the scenery and the chance to run some interesting rapids. Don't take the kids out on the river, however, without the proper safety gear such as life jackets. And don't act the voyageur role if canoeing is not a strong

An idyllic scene on Lake Mille Lacs. Minnesota Office of Tourism photo.

suit, as parts of the Rum River can be quite challenging. After traversing Lake Ogechie and Shakopee Lake, the river flows through Lake Onamia. Depending on the time of year, usually in dry seasons between spring and autumn, the latter lake can be more of a cattail covered wetland in which it is easy to get lost. However, below Princeton, there is a long stretch of slow, shallow water where beginners can get a good taste of how much fun this sport really is. Some die-hards even make it all the way to Anoka, just north of the Twin Cities.

To top off your area tour, make one last stop at the 33,180-acre **Rum River State Forest**, about 10 miles south of Mille Lacs Kathio State Park. The largest part of the forest can be reached by taking County Highway 20 east from Highway 169. Hiking and horseback riding are favored activities within the forest, with the 14-mile-long Hoot Owl Ridge Trail also designated and groomed for winter snowmobiling. Southeast of the Rum River State Forest in Kanabec County, the 5.3-mile Kanabec Trail is earmarked for winter snowmobiling as well, but hiking and horseback riding hold sway in the summer. The Kanabec Trail can be entered along Kanabec county roads 10, 26, 55, and 56. A picnic area with tables, toilets, and a 1 1/2 mile nature trail perfect for little kids is located on a forest road just off County Road 56. For more information contact the Moose Lake area forester at the DNR field office, Route 2, 701 South Kenwood Street, Moose Lake, MN 55767 (218) 485-4474.

PLACES TO STAY

BRAINERD AREA

Madden's on Gull Lake, 11266 Pine Beach Peninsula, Brainerd 56401, (218) 829-2811 or (800) 233-2934; www.maddens.com

Ramada Inn, 2115 South Sixth Street, Brainerd 56401, (218) 829-1441 or (888) 562-2944

Rice Lake Campground, 1619 N.E. Washington Street, Brainerd, (218) 828-2320

Shady Hollow Resort, Hardy Lake, 2115 Shady Hollow Road, Brainerd 56401, (218) 628-9308 or (800) 450-9308; www.ShadyHollowResort.com

Sullivan's Resort and Campground, 7685 County Highway 127, North Long Lake, (888) 829-5697; www.sullivansresort.com

Twin Oaks Resort, 1777 Nokay Lake Road N.E., Nokay Lake, (218) 764-2965 or (888) 244-9399; www.twinoaksresort.com

LAKE MILLE LACS AREA
Liberty Beach Resort, 5452 Waterway Road, Isle, (320) 676-3646

McQuoid's Inn, 1325 County Highway 47 North, Isle, (320) 320-692-4325 or (800) 435-8720

Nitti's Hunter Point Resort, 5436 47th Street, Isle, (320) 676-3227

Severson's Resort, 510 West Lake Street, Isle, (320) 676-3148

PLACES TO EAT

BRAINERD
Choppers Bar and Grill, 723 Mill Avenue, (218) 825-8782

Coco Moon, 601 Laurel Street, (218) 825-7955

Front Street Cafe, 616 Front Street, (218) 828-1102

Giovanni's Pizza, 625 Oak Street, (218) 828-4978

Kavanaugh's Resort and Restaurant, 2300 Kavanaugh Drive S.W., (218) 824-5226

Northwind Grille, 603 Laurel Street, (218) 829-1551

Ron's Steak House, 1549 Squaw Point Road N.W., Gull Lake, (218) 829-3918

LAKE MILLE LACS AREA
Bayview Bar and Grill, 39497 92nd Avenue, Onamia, (320) 532-3936

Eddy's Lake Mille Lacs Resort, 41334 Shakopee Lake Road, Onamia, (320) 532-3657 or (800) 657-4704

Happy's Family Restaurant, 11373 Stevens Road, Onamia, (320) 532-3336

Isle Bowl and Pizza, Third Street South (1 block south of Highway 27), Isle, (320) 676-8880

Izatys Golf and Yacht Club, 4005 85th Avenue, Onamia, (320) 532-3101 or (800) 533-1728

Little Whitefish Resort and Cafe, 18087 463rd Street, Garrison, (320) 692-4531 or (888) 692-4531

Mille Lacs Golf Resort, 18517 Captive Lake Road, Garrison, (320) 692-4325 or (800) 435-8720

Westerlund's Sunrise Cafe, 22167 State Highway 47, Malmo, (320) 684-2664

PLACES TO SHOP

BRAINERD
Adirondack Coffee Specialties, Inc., 538 Main Street, (218) 963-3421

Bargains on Seventh, 211 South Seventh Street, (218) 829-8822

CatTale's Book Exchange and Gifts, 609 Laurel Street, (218) 825-8611

Christmas Point Wild Rice Company, Westgate Mall, (218) 828-1909

Country Fresh Bakery, 1924 South 10th Street, (218) 828-0804

Easy Riders Bicycle and Sportshop, 415 Washington Street, (218) 829-5516

Finders Keepers, 309 State Highway 371 North, (218) 829-1611

Nesheim Bait and Tackle, 722 South Sixth Street, (218) 829-4600

Tykes Antiques, 522 Northeast 11th Avenue, (218) 829-3878

LAKE MILLE LACS AREA
Black Bear Pottery, 10797 Black Bear Road (State Highway 18 between Brainerd and Garrison, Aitkin), (218) 764-3296

Country Caboose, 135 First Avenue, Wahkon 56386, (320) 495-3658

Culture Thru Art Company, 9696 Winona Way, Onamia 56359, (320) 532-3135

Johnson's Portside, 42099 Highway 47, Isle 56342, (320) 676-3811

Kathy's Quilts and Crafts, 1595 395th Street, Isle, (320) 676-3359

North Forty Creations, 2016 State Highway 27, Isle, (320) 676-3137

North Star Outback, 38765 U.S. Highway 169, Onamia, (320) 532-4558

Northern Inn Gifts and Crafts, 125 North Main Street, Wahkon, (320) 495-3332

Pepperberry's Gifts, 105 North Main Street, Wahkon, (320) 495-3528

FOR MORE INFORMATION

Brainerd Lakes Area Chamber of Commerce, Box 356, Brainerd 56401, (800) 450-2838; www.explorebrainerdlakes.com

Mille Lacs Area Tourism Council, Box 363, Isle 56342, (888) 350-2692

Mille Lacs Area Tourism Council, Box 758, Onamia 56359, (888) 350.2692; vacation@millelacs.com

ST. CLOUD AND LITTLE FALLS

Radio personality Garrison Keillor allegedly drew inspiration for his popular *Prairie Home Companion* radio show from life in central Minnesota, where St. Cloud and Little Falls are anchor communities. Even though the kids may regard radio—and especially a program that features people who actually . . . well . . . like . . . *tell stories*—as out of touch with their MTV view of the world, they may be interested in knowing that Keillor got his start more than three decades ago at the first Minnesota Public Radio outlet at St. John's University in Collegeville, just outside St. Cloud. His tales of a fictional small town called Lake Wobegon have enchanted listeners for years.

There is a lot of Minnesota in the stories, however, and the folks here are proud to have been the inspiration for Keillor's sometimes poignant, sometimes serious, sometimes sad, sometimes silly stories. This part of the state is a crossroads of woods and prairies, with a vibrant urbanity amid the pasture and cropland, the mix serving as nourishment for entertaining narratives.

SOARING IN ST. CLOUD

Originally, St. Cloud consisted of three settlements along the Mississippi River. A former slave owner founded one, and he attracted other advocates of slavery to the area. An antislavery entrepreneur founded the second village, and the third village was a sawmill company town that drew in hundreds of German Catholics as workers. After a great deal of discussion, the communities settled their differences and merged in 1856. They chose the St. Cloud name to honor central Minnesota's French heritage. The name comes from that of St. Clodoald, grandson of an ancient French king Clovis. St. Clodoald founded a monastery where the current Paris suburb of St. Cloud is now in the department of Seine-et Oise, adjoining the city to the southwest. Over the generations, many French nobles built mansions in St. Cloud, France. One, erected in 1572, was the site where Henry III was assassinated in 1572 while seeking refuge from a rebellion in Paris. During the Franco-Prussian War, St. Cloud was the center of the final effort to defend Paris against the Prussians who burned many of the great homes there. The discovery of quality granite deposits led to the founding of many quarries around St. Cloud. St. Cloud granite helped build the Twin Cities, 65 miles to the southeast via Highway 10.

Four major colleges make their homes in the St. Cloud area and thus afford plenty of opportunities for family fun. With St. John's University, the College of St. Benedict, St. Cloud State University, and St. Cloud Technical College, there is a youthful feel to the city, from the vibrant cultural life to the pubs to the stores to the general street scene.

Each of the schools offers campus tours. If visiting St. John's, be sure to take the university's nature trail along the east side of Lake Sagatagan. A prairie wetland trail also makes for a pleasant walk. Call (320) 363-2610 for permits.

A VIBRANT ARTS SCENE

The schools also welcome vacationing guests to their arts programs. For instance, the Minnesota Orchestra performs regularly at the **Benedicta Arts Center** at the College of St. Benedict, taking advantage of the building's excellent acoustics. Call (320) 363-5777. The College of St. Benedict and St. John's University have joint arts programs, with a diverse range of entertainment options consisting of more than 400 events open to the public each year.

All ages can enjoy the dance programs, theater, and music at the Benedicta Arts Center and at St. John's **Steven B. Humphrey Theater**. For reservations, call (320) 363-5777. The **St. John's Boys' Choir**, (320) 363-2558, is internationally known, with a regular series of productions that the kids will find enthralling. The **Performing Arts Center** at St. Cloud State University offers student productions, touring shows, poetry readings, and one-person shows. Contact the university's box office, (320) 255-2455, or check the Web site at www.stcloudstate.edu/~bulletin/thfs.

St. Cloud's **Paramount Arts District** provides presentation and office space for 10 of the city's major arts groups. The district is anchored by the dazzling **Paramount Theatre**, 913 West St. Germain Street, which has been refurbished to its original splendor. For ticket information, call (320) 259-5463 or visit www.paramountarts.org. Among the theater's residents, the **Central Minnesota Children's Theater** has a full season of shows aimed at the younger set, with such wonderful presentations as *The Witch of Blackbird Pond* and *Peter Pan*. For

Sinclair Lewis

Sinclair Lewis (1885–1951) was one of Minnesota's most famous and influential writers. One of his novels, *Main Street*, published in 1920, cast a satirical eye on small-town Midwestern life. Folks in his hometown of Sauk Centre, approximately 40 miles northwest of St. Cloud, thought he was writing about them and became most upset. Today, however, Minnesotans are proud of their native son, and the town now calls itself "the original Main Street."

additional details on the shows, call (320) 259-0250. The **Multicultural Children's Art Connection** is also housed in the theater building. Youngsters can take advantage of all sorts of programs and projects here. Call (320) 257-3118.

There are many other top-notch performance spaces around St. Cloud, helping solidify its position as a major Minnesota arts hub. **Pioneer Place on Fifth**, 22 Fifth Avenue South, is one such space. The renovated, historic building stages an eight-show series, ranging from comedy to dinner theater, creating a cultural package that central Minnesota theatergoers love. Many of the shows are appropriate for children, as well. Call (320) 203-0331, or visit their Web site at www.pioneerplaceonfifth.com. The **St. Cloud Municipal Band** presents concerts throughout the year, capitalizing on its more-than-a-century-old history. Each year, 20 or more shows are presented around the community, with highlights being the summer series in Barden Park.

GETTING ACTIVE

Speaking of summer, loads of splish-splash fun can be had at **Summerland Water Park**, two miles east of St. Cloud on Highway 23, (320) 251-0940. The theme park has miniature golf, go-karts, batting cages, bumper boats, and an arcade to capture any loose quarters.

For more adventure, bring the kids' mountain bikes to try the trails at **Pineview Park** on the city's west side, just off West Division and Ridgewood Road (County Highway 134). Many families come here for Monday night racing (weather permitting), allowing them to spend a long weekend in St. Cloud. Call the track phone at (320) 251-7540 for details or check in with Granite City Schwinn, (320) 251-7540. Any racers must belong to the American Bicycle Association (ABA). In addition to the trails at Pineview Park, mountain bikers will find well-marked trails along Clearwater Road and in Whitney Park. The young mountain-bike set will enjoy these adventures. Helmets are important safety gear, even for teen hotdoggers.

County roads west of St. Cloud are also popular with the biking set. They will also enjoy pedaling the 2.5-mile long **Beaver Island Trail** along the west side of the Mississippi River, from the 10th Street Dam south to Sportsman Island Road. St. Cloud also sponsors its Wheels Wings Water Festival in June, where participants take part in the Tour of the Saints bike jaunt around the area. Call (320) 255-7216 for details on numerous other biking opportunities in the community. A bit farther out of town, the new **Lake Wobegon Trail** stretches for 28 miles between Avon and Sauk Centre. It's a hiking and biking path set on a rail corridor, and plans are afoot to lengthen it.

Winter doesn't slow down anyone in St. Cloud. Weekend cross-country skiers of all ages and agility brackets swoosh along the **Greystone Trail**, a half-mile west of Highway 10 on County Highway 30 (Minnesota Boulevard). The trail is across from the Minnesota Correctional Facility's main entrance. Locals point out that parking is allowed only in the area behind the large white barn.

Cruising the Lake Wobegon Trail northwest of Saint Cloud.
Minnesota Office of Tourism photograph.

The trail is only used in the winter because the surrounding landscape is a rifle range in the spring, summer, and fall. Other recommended cross-country routes around St. Cloud include Quarry Park, Warner Lake, the Wildwood Trail, and several tracks along the Mississippi River. Call the Nordic Ski Club of Central Minnesota, (320) 252-1177, for additional tips on area ski routes.

LOTS TO SEE IN LITTLE FALLS

The Mississippi begins to pick up power by the time it gets to Little Falls, 35 miles north of St. Cloud on Highway 10. The Ojibwe lived here a dozen generations ago, sometimes feuding with their Dakota and Ho-Chunk neighbors. The Ojibwe settled here because a slab of granite in the river slowed down the rushing waters, creating a small waterfall. They called the drop *Ka Ka Bikans*, which loosely translates to "small square rock" or "cutoff rock." The earliest French explorers were well acquainted with the *petite chutes*, or "little falls." American adventurer Lieutenant Zebulon Pike mapped out the territory, writing admiringly of the region in 1805.

The first white frontier folk arrived in the 1840s to clear the land for their farms and to establish homes. A dam was built at the falls in 1849, whose water power was used to turn the mill wheels linked to grindstones for milling flour for the bustling little community that was growing on both banks of the river. During the logging era, lumber firms such as Weyerhauser and Hennepin Paper Company utilized the force of the waterway for their mills and plants. It was a boom time for the town that took the name Little Falls after its most

Military Road

Highway 371 follows the route taken by the military road between Point Douglas and Little Falls. The military roadway was completed in 1858, following what had been an ox-cart track north from Crow Wing Village to trading posts in Canada. Cart tracks can still be spotted along the edges of the Mississippi and Crow Wing Rivers near Crow Wing State Park.

notable geographic feature. Even when farming replaced the timbering, Little Falls remained an economic powerhouse in central Minnesota.

Vacationers today readily pick up on that get-down-and-do-it spirit, regardless if their stay is a day, a week, or longer. The old homes and refurbished storefronts downtown show a community pride, even if local folks are reluctant to brag about it. And that, indeed, is a Prairie Home Companion way of doing things.

No matter the season, families can experience a busy weekend in Little Falls. For animal lovers in the family, take in the **Morrison County Fair**. Held each August on the grounds just east of Little Falls on Highway 27, 4-H kids show the fruits of the past season's farm labors. Championship sheep, steers, pigs, chickens, rabbits—you name the critter, and it is probably exhibited there. Call (320) 632-9432.

No matter where you go in Little Falls, you can't avoid the legacy of Charles A. Lindbergh, who spent boyhood summers here only to grow up to complete the first nonstop transatlantic airplane flight in 1927. "Lucky Lindy" was the son of a noted Minnesota political figure who drew his political base from this part of the state. Lead the family on a tour of yesteryear through the **Charles A. Lindbergh House State Historic Site**, 1620 Lindbergh Drive South. Check out the snug kitchen and peer through the windows to observe the thick stands of sighing pine surrounding the trim white house. The building is on the National Register of Historic Places and operated by the Minnesota Historical Society, open from Memorial Day to Labor Day.

A nearby visitor center relates the Lindbergh family history, including details on Lindbergh's solo flight across the Atlantic Ocean that earned him the admiration of the world. It's then just a short stroll to the house where one of Minnesota's favorite sons dreamed of flying. Call (320) 632-3154 for hours and other details.

Lindbergh enjoyed his younger years fishing in the Mississippi River, which flows just east of the house. He hunted the woods and fields with his father, Charles A. Lindbergh, Sr. In 1931, his family donated their 110-acre family holdings to the state for a park, which was then named in honor of the elder Lindbergh. For further details, contact the facility's manager at **Charles A. Lindbergh State Park**, 1600 Lindbergh Drive South, (320) 616-2525.

The Charles A. Lindbergh House in Little Falls. —Courtesy of the Minnesota Historical Society

Just down the road from the state park and the Lindbergh house is the **Charles A. Weyerhauser Memorial Museum**, 2151 South Lindbergh Drive, (320) 632-4007. The site, owned by the Morrison Country Historical Society, overlooks the Mississippi River. Get out of the car and stroll through the prairie gardens, check out the Victorian fountain, and plunk down for a rest in the old gazebo near the river. The free museum, which is packed with artifacts and documents featuring the Weyerhauser family, the Minnesota lumber industry, and local history, is open Tuesday through Sunday. This makes it simple to visit when in the Little Falls area for a short family getaway.

Camp Ripley

Camp Ripley, a Minnesota National Guard training site, originated in 1849 as a military outpost on the west bank of the Mississippi River. The first fort was built to separate the Ojibwe and Dakota, who were fighting over the surrounding land. Soldiers based here also served to prevent the Winnebago (now called the Ho-Chunk) from leaving their reservation in the nearby Long Prairie region. Only 30 soldiers were stationed at the fort at the time.

During the Dakota Uprising of 1862, numerous settlers sought refuge in the fort. The facility was abandoned in 1878 but was reconstituted as a national-guard training site after World War II. The grounds now encompass around 20,000 acres, which are used in the summer for military exercises.

The original fort was called Fort Marcey and then became Fort Gaines. It was then named after General Eleazar W. Ripley.

For something a bit different, take the troops to Camp Ripley, north of Little Falls. It's home to the **Minnesota Military Museum**, which showcases the experiences of the state's servicemen and women. Visitors who call in advance can join a group tour of historic Fort Ripley, which is on the National Register of Historic Places; those just dropping by can drive around the central cantonment area. The kids will appreciate the valor demonstrated by the Minnesota military over the years when looking at the trucks, tanks, helicopters, and other museum displays from the frontier days through the nation's most recent wars. Admission is free but a donation is suggested. The entrance to the base is located at the intersection of Highways 371 and 115, seven miles north of Little Falls. Call (320) 632-7374.

PLACES TO STAY

LITTLE FALLS
AmericInn, 306 LeMieur Street, (320) 632-1964 or (800) 632-3444; www.americinn.com

Cliffwood Motel, 1201 Haven Road, (320) 632-5488

Super 8 Motel, 300 12th Street N.E., (320) 632-2351 or (800) 800-8000; www.super8.com

ST. CLOUD
Comfort Inn, 4040 Second Street South, (320) 251-1500 or (800) 228-5150

St. Cloud Campground and R.V. Park, 2491 Second Street S.E., (320) 251-4463

Super 8 Motel, 50 Park Avenue South, (320) 253-5530 or (800) 800-8000; www.super8.com

NEARBY
Shady River Campground, 21353 County Highway 5, Big Lake, (763) 263-3705

Timberwoods Resort and Campground, 10255 Nevens Avenue N.W., South Haven, (320) 274-5140

Your Haven Campground, 18337 State Highway 22, Richmond, (320) 453-2148

PLACES FOR FOOD

LITTLE FALLS
Black and White Hamburger Shop, 114 First Street S.E., (320) 632-5374

Coborn's Deli, 1101 Second Avenue N.E., (320) 632-2367

Green Mill Restaurant, Kelly Inn, 100 Fourth Avenue North, (320) 259-6455

Pete and Joy's Bakery, 121 East Broadway, (320) 632-6388

Royal Cafe, 120 West Broadway, (320) 632-6401

ST. CLOUD

Grizzly's Grill n' Saloon, 4201 West Division Street, (320) 253-4092

Old Country Buffet, 3333 West Division Street, (320) 259-5422

Park Diner, 1531 Division Street, (320) 252-0080

Perkins Family Restaurant, Crossroads Shopping Center, 30 Park Avenue South, (320) 253-0300

Waldo's Pizza, 3360 West Division Street, (320) 253-7170; www.waldo.pizza.com

PLACES TO SHOP

LITTLE FALLS

Bookin' It, 113 First Street S.E., (320) 632-1848 or (800) 809-1848; bookinit@fallsnet.com

Pap's Sport Shop, 64 East Broadway, (320) 632-5171

ST. CLOUD

Art and Heritage Place, St. Benedict's Monastery, 104 Chapel Lane, (320) 363-7100; www.sbm.osb.org

The Bookworm, 25183 21st Avenue, (320) 252-6989 or (800) 535-6260

Crossroads Center, 4101 Division Street, (320) 240-2988

Electric Fetus, 28 South Fifth Avenue, (320) 251-2569

Log Cabin Court Specialty Shoppes, 2005 West Frontage Road, North Waite Park, (320) 230-0412

Once Upon a Child, 3419 West Division Street, (320) 253-7193

FOR MORE INFORMATION

Little Falls Convention and Visitors Bureau, 606 First Street S.E., Little Falls 56345, (320) 616-4959 or (800) 325-5916

St. Cloud Area Convention and Visitors Bureau, 525 Highway 10 South, Suite 1, St. Cloud 56304, (320) 251-4170 or (800) 265-2940; www.visitstcloud.com

THE SOUTHWEST CORNER

Western Minnesota is a glorious swale of grass stretching from horizon to horizon. You can ask the kids to imagine how the region might have looked eons ago when the first inhabitants walked across these plains, when the landscape was dappled with wildflowers. Today, farm fields predominate, yet the immensity of the scene is awe-inspiring and a bit humbling.

Southwestern Minnesota is also a land of rock—lots of rock—with area quarries supplying a lot of the raw material for the Midwest's building boom of the 19th century. Thousands of mansions, train stations, courthouses, and other buildings were constructed of southwestern Minnesota's stone. Notice the towns out here—they are solid. Artisans built them to withstand the wind that constantly ruffles the tree leaves and shakes the reeds along the shallow rivers of the region. It's therefore no surprise that Rock is the name of the county tucked deeply into the state's far southwestern corner. At the **Jasper Quarry Festival** in July, the county seat, Luverne, celebrates the quarrymen and their history, with fire truck rides, a tractor pull, go-cart races, and a street dance.

Reached via I-94, Rock, neighboring Pipestone, and the rest of the counties of this fascinating region offer up a marvelous menu of historical, geological, and recreational fun for a weekend family adventure.

BLUE MOUNDS STATE PARK

Rock isn't the only thing the area is famous for. There are the buffalo (or "bison" to be zoologically accurate), and they roam the prairie within **Blue Mounds State Park**, north of Luverne about five miles. It's probably hard for kids to imagine the size of a bull bison. Just think big: Bison move where and when they want. Being eyeball-to-eyeball with a bison will convince the most questioning child that bulk counts out here on the prairie.

The park is a remnant of what were once endless miles of prairie. While homesteaders made short shrift of much of the surrounding fertile landscape, nonproducing rocky outcrops and shallow soil led to the preservation of most of the land within what is today's park. Subsequently, it is one of the neatest places in Minnesota to experience spring. The post-winter landscape is glorious, a wonderful time for viewing the floral riot of color. By the end of the growing

An expanse of western Minnesota prairie preserved at Blue Mounds State Park.
Minnesota Office of Tourism photograph.

season, some of the plants can reach up to seven feet tall. And the park is one of the few places in Minnesota where prickly pear cacti have found a foothold.

The rock formations found in the park are at least 1.5 billion years old, having developed on the bottom of an ancient sea. Sandstone, undergoing pressure and chemical reactions, eventually turned into the hard quartzite found today in the region. Iron oxide causes the purple-blue coloring.

The former home of noted author Frederick Manfred doubles as the park's visitor and interpretive center. The late author used the house from 1960 to 1975 and wrote many exciting tales about Native Americans, working on his stories in a circular upper room that now serves as an observation deck. Encourage the kids to look out over the rolling hills from Manfred's study, which he called his "tipi," and dream of what the land was like generations ago.

The park has 73 semimodern campsites and 40 with electrical hookups. A dump station is available for trailers. There is also a primitive group camp and picnic grounds with a shelter. The swimming beach is along Lower Mound Lake. There are 13 miles of foot trails and seven miles available for snowmobiling. For all the lowdown on the bison and all the other park attractions, contact the manager, RR1, Box 52, Luverne 56156, (507) 283-1307.

LUVERNE

Luverne is the main entryway to the park. It is also home to the **Tri-State Band Festival**, held on the last Saturday of September. Families plan entire va-

Bringing the Mail

Luverne's first settler was mail carrier Philo Hawkins, who delivered the post between Blue Earth City and Yankton, South Dakota. He eventually settled down where the Yankton Trail crossed the Rock River and built the area's first post office in 1868.

cations around the event, which attracts participants from Canada, Minnesota, Iowa, Nebraska, and the Dakotas. There is plenty of high-spirited parading along Main Street, in addition to the intense competition at the Luverne High School athletic fields.

Celebrating its links to the buffalo scene . . . oops, bison . . . the city's **Buffalo Days** the first weekend in June also means a kids' parade, antique-car exhibits, and concerts. Enter the buffalo-chip–tossing competition in the park along the banks of the slow-moving Rock River. Buffalo burgers are for sale, naturally. If a visitor to these parts needs more bison, and most youngsters will, visit the **Prairie Heights Bison** ranch. Tours are available May through Labor Day, and visitors can visit a pasture and carefully hand-feed the bison. Guests will also learn about the animals' physical characteristics, spring calving, weaning, the rut or mating season, and other facts of life on a bison ranch. Contact the facility at, RR 1, Box 37, Luverne 56156, (507) 283-8136; www.buybison.com.

Working off that meat-fueled energy, athletes flock to Luverne for the kick-off leg of the **Border to Border Triathlon**, starting the second week of August. Participants race—on foot, aboard bikes, and in canoes—from Luverne to Crane Lake on the Minnesota-Canada border. The event, consisting of at least 60 two-person teams, kicks off with a parade. Since most youngsters love a procession of any sort, they'll dig this one for certain.

But if expending all that energy seems a bit much, a leisurely stroll through Luverne's downtown is an eye-opener for vacationers. A suggested tour covers about a mile and takes 30 minutes of easy ambling for everyone in the clan. No need to hurry—just slow down and take in the scene. Start at the Chamber of Commerce office in the ornate **Palace Theatre**, which was built in 1915 and is still used for films and live entertainment. Check out the old pipe organ here, originally used to provide background music for silent movies.

Then lead the pack east on Main Street to peek into the **Brandenburg Gallery**, where works by award-winning nature photographer Jim Brandenburg are showcased. A native of Luverne—his great-great-grandparents broke sod here as early settlers—Brandenburg roamed the globe for *National Geographic* magazine for more than 20 years and opened the gallery in 1999. Families can see the world through his eyes by exploring the nooks and crannies of his spacious space. Profits from sales of books, videos, and photos at the facility support area preservation projects, most notably prairie restoration and protection, which environmentally conscious children will appreciate. The gallery is located at 211 East Main Street, (507) 283-1884; prairieimages@dtgnet.com.

You and the kids will get a kick out of a visit to the **Skinny Building**, actually built as an office in 1890. It is only 10 feet wide and 26 feet long, but three stories tall. After looking at this amazing building, walk over to **Holy Trinity Church.** Placed on the Minnesota State Historical Register in 1975, the church was built in 1891 and is a fine demonstration of the use of locally quarried Sioux quartzite stone. The structure also has amazing stained-glass windows. Bordering the church on the north is the **Rock County Courthouse**, also built of quartzite, in 1888.

The **Hinkly House Museum** on Luverne Street helps kids understand the city and its background. Built in 1892, it was once the home of Mayor R. B. Hinkly and is now on the National Register of Historic Sites. If the kids ask about the two lions at the front entrance, tell them that they were made by Norwegian stonecutter Knute Steine in 1895. Be sure to point out the word *hinkly* in a panel of stained glass in the house and welcome in the oak parquet floor. For another insider's tip, the storage doors reaching to the ceiling in the library allegedly were made by a one-armed artisan, name unknown.

The **Carnegie Cultural Center**, built in 1903 at the corner of Lincoln Street and Freeman Avenue, received its jump start with a $10,000 donation by steel tycoon and philanthropist Andrew Carnegie. The building once housed the city library and became a hub of cultural activities in Luverne when the library shifted to new quarters in 1992. Check at the desk about dates here for kid-oriented storytelling sessions, concerts, and craft demonstrations.

The **Rock County Historical Museum** was once a Unitarian Church and then a Masonic Hall before becoming a receptacle for the county's artifacts. Kids can see old-time school furnishings and marvel that there were once days before computers and television. At the courthouse, youngsters love climbing on the old Civil War cannon displayed on the lawn. On the west side of the courthouse, look over the memorial in honor of pioneers who settled the Luverne area.

PIPESTONE NATIONAL MONUMENT

When the noted American artist George Catlin visited the region in 1863, he found out from local Native Americans how the Great Spirit came to earth in the shape of a bird that landed on a wall of rock. The location of that wall is now one of the quarries of the **Pipestone National Monument**, just outside of the town of Pipestone, 23 miles north of Luverne.

Kids will be fascinated to learn that, according to Catlin, the Great Spirit told the Native American nations to gather around him, as he broke off a chunk of the red stone on which he was perched and formed it into a pipe. As he smoked, the Great Spirit told his "red children that this red stone was their flesh." They were to smoke in homage to him, treating the quarry ground as

Winnewissa Falls amid the rocky formations at the Pipestone National Monument.
Minnesota Office of Tourism photograph.

sacred territory. No weapons were to be used there or brought upon it, the Great Spirit warned.

Whether that was the real reason for the Pipestone quarries or not, Native Americans were digging here as early as the 1600s, when metal tools acquired from Europeans came into use. By 1700, the Dakota nation controlled the quarries and bartered for other goods with the stone. Pipes eventually became an income source for carvers and the Yankton Dakota secured unrestricted access to the quarries in an 1858 treaty. In 1928, the tribe, which had been resettled on a reservation 150 miles away from the quarry, sold its interest in the site to the federal government.

Discovering the Stone

According to legend, Wahegela, a Native American woman, discovered the valuable pipestone of western Minnesota while trailing a sacred white bison whose great hooves dug up the stone as it thundered across the prairie.

But when the area became a national monument in 1937, quarrying was again limited to Native Americans. American Indian carvers still work in the modernistic visitor center. The craft sales area in the same building is operated by the Pipestone Indian Shrine Association, with walls lined with intricately carved pipes. Each bears the name of its maker. The stems are made from native sumac or such exotic material as redwood. Turtle totems, said to ensure fertility and long life, and other special objects are also available for purchase.

After looking at the displays and learning the story of Pipestone, take the family outside and walk along the trails connecting the ancient quarry pits to gain a sense of history. Have everyone listen to the whispering breeze through the tall prairie grasses. Remind the kids "to take nothing but pictures and leave nothing but tracks."

In this region that was a seabed eons ago, pipestone started out as dark clay covered with sand. Pressure and heat, along with a chemical reaction, formed the sand into quartzite, and the clay eventually became pipestone. The youngsters can ask a craft worker in the visitor center if they can hold a piece of the rock. Its smooth, hard surface has an interesting feel. But it can easily be carved into intricate shapes depicting animals and people at work, as well as geometric figures.

Climb along the marked path, and let the kids bring cameras to take photos of such formations as Leaping Rock. Here's a real test. See if the youngsters can find the features of the facelike oracle. It will take a few minutes and then, there it is: A great stone face peering down at the trail. After a look-see, pass Winnewissa Falls and walk alongside the pits quarried by the same Native American families for generations. The chip marks of their tools are clearly defined in the stone embankments.

From Pipestone's downtown, drive north on Hiawatha Avenue, turn west at the Song of Hiawatha pageant grounds, drive past the Three Sisters Stone landmark, and follow the road around a bend to the monument entrance, 36 Reservation Avenue, (507) 825-5464; www.nps.gov/pipe.

PIPESTONE

The town of Pipestone is a fascinating place for a weekend stop. The city's landmark water tower, is in the shape of—what else?—a peace pipe and is visible for miles across the surrounding flat farm country. The 132-foot-tall structure was constructed in 1921, and a park at its base is the focal point of the annual Water Tower Festival.

The **Pipestone County Historical Society**, housed in the old city hall building, is a good place to begin a stroll around the downtown. The society's displays put the town's history into perspective. The attached gift shop is perfect for the pint-sized ones, who can purchase drums, beads, dream catchers, beaded jewelry, and porcupine-quill pouches and purses. Handmade pipes, in a variety of shapes and sizes, are also available. The knowledgeable clerks can explain the different styles and their significance in the cultures of the various Native American tribes. For instance, there are plains pipes, elbow pipes, four winds pipes, effigy pipes, hatchet pipes, and inlay pipes—each beautiful in their distinctive designs. The museum is located at 113 Hiawatha Avenue, (507) 825-2563; www.pipestoneminnesota.com/museum.

National and state preservationists consider numerous buildings in Pipestone excellent examples of 19th-century architectural styles. While the kids might not immediately appreciate the significance of the **Syndicate Block** or the **Ober-Hubbard Building**, they'll probably enjoy pausing for lunch in the grand old **Calumet Hotel**, built in 1888. A performing-arts center and art gallery are major components of the **Ferris Grand Block** of buildings downtown, which attract visiting families and locals to a variety of productions and exhibits.

An outdoor performance of The Song of Hiawatha in Pipestone.
Minnesota Office of Tourism photograph.

Pipestone prides itself on its cultural events. Local amateur actors enjoy performing in *The Song of Hiawatha,* an outdoor pageant taken from Henry Wadsworth Longfellow's famous tale. The show is held on the last two weekends in July and the first weekend in August at a three-acre, open-air site with seating for 2,500. Even the children will enjoy this fast-paced program. The performance area is between Fourth Street N.E. and Reservation Avenue, reached via Hiawatha Avenue from Highway 30. Call (507) 825-4126 or (800) 430-4126.

OTHER AREA ATTRACTIONS

Camden State Park is about 32 miles northeast of Pipestone along Highway 23. Here, early pioneers appreciated the cool valley, arriving sunburned, dusty, and bedraggled after crossing the windswept prairie. There is evidence that even more ancient travelers drank from the sweet-water springs in the region, travelers dating back at least 8,000 years.

Today, the park has a regular series of programs that trace the history of southwestern Minnesota, programs of interest to adults and kids alike. There are also activities highlighting plants, geology, and wildlife. A bulletin board near the information center relates times and dates for the activities, which generally occur between Labor Day and Memorial Day when the park is most visited. For specifics, contact the park manager, 1897 County Highway 68, Lynd, (507) 865-4530; www.marshall-mn.org.

Marshall is the closest large town, about 10 miles northeast of the park on Highway 23. It is home to Southwest State University, which contains several attractions the kids might enjoy. The **Museum of Anthropology** on campus has cultural exhibits from around the world, and the William Whipple Art Gallery on the first floor of the library features internationally known artists, as well as local, regional, and student works. The school's **History Center** has a wide collection of artifacts and regional-history material dating back to the earliest settlers, with a wealth of fascinating oral histories; call (507) 537-7373. You and

Temperance Settlers

Worthington, 30 miles east of Luverne and the county seat of Nobles County, was first settled by a group of temperance advocates called the National Colony Company. They first called their settlement Okabena, which means "nesting place of herons." Although liquor was outlawed there, a determined patron could still find some bootleg booze. The name of the community was changed to Worthington to memorialize one of the founders of the colony.

the kids can stargaze at the school's **Planetarium**, but you'll need to make an appointment. However, the **Museum of Natural History** is open throughout the academic year. Contact these last two facilities through the Department of Biology and Earth/Space Science, Southwest State University, (507) 537-6178.

In town, the **Marshall Fine Arts Center**, 313 West Main Street, also showcases local and touring artists and performances. Art exhibits are free during the center's afternoon hours from Tuesday through Friday, which is a handy notation for the family pocketbook police. Call (507) 532-5463.

Kids especially love Marshall's **Festival of Kites** held each July 4, with plenty of games for the youngsters, including a fishing tournament and kite-flying competition. The **Lyon County Fair** is held in mid-August, with oodles of 4-H exhibits to admire, a professional rodeo to gasp at, and headline acts to applaud. The **International Rolle Bolle Tournament** is on the calendar for every August, drawing competitors trying their hand at this game from Belgium—a cross between horseshoes and bowling. Throughout the summer, city band concerts are held Wednesday evenings at the Liberty Park Band Shell on East College Drive, making a perfect conclusion to a midweek getaway.

BACK INTO TIME WITH LAURA INGALLS WILDER

Minnesota's southwest corner boasts an attraction sure to delight the female side of the family, although the younger ones may not immediately recognize *The Little House on the Prairie* connection (after all, the immensely popular TV series was cancelled in 1983). Laura Ingalls Wilder, author of the book series, lived in Walnut Grove from 1874 to 1876, one of several places in the Midwest she and her family called home. Located about 20 miles southeast of Marshall on Highway 14, the small town now is the site of the **Wilder Museum**, a complex that includes a late-19th-century schoolhouse, depot, and several other restored buildings. The museum also houses a wonderful collection of dolls from the 1870s to the present, as well as Wilder-related memorabilia. The museum is located at 330 Eighth Street, (800) 528-7280. You can visit the original **Ingalls Homestead** a mile and a half north of town. You won't see any original buildings, but a dugout that Laura built and a few natural landmarks described in *On the Banks of Plum Creek* remain intact. During three weekends in mid-July, the **Wilder Pageant** depicts the life of Laura in an outdoor theater set on the banks of Plum Creek. Call (888) 859-1670 for more information.

PLACES TO STAY

LUVERNE

Comfort Inn of Luverne, 801 South Kniss, (507) 283-9488 or (800) 228-5160

Cozy Rest Motel, 116 South Kniss, (507) 283-4461

Hillcrest Motel, 210 West Virginia Street, (507) 283-2363 or (800) 588-3763

Sunrise Motel, 114 Sunshine Avenue, (507) 283-2347 or (877) 641-2345

Super 8 Motel, U.S. Highway 75 and I-90, (507) 283-9541 or (800) 800-8000; www.super8.com

MARSHALL
AmericInn, 1406 East Lyon Street, (507) 537-9424 or (800) 634-3444; www.americinn.com

Arbor Inn Bed and Breakfast, 305 North Fifth Street, (507) 532-2457; kathy@arborinnbb.com

Best Western Marshall Inn, 1500 East College Drive, (507) 532-3221 or (800) 422-0897

Comfort Inn, 1511 East College Drive, (507) 532-3070

DeLux Motel, 516 East Main Street, (507) 337-4441

Super 8 Motel, 1106 East Main Street, (507) 537-1461 or (800) 800-8000; www.super8.com

Traveler's Lodge, 1425 East College Drive, (507) 532-5721 or (800) 532-5721

PIPESTONE
Arrow Motel, 600 Eighth Avenue N.E., (507) 825-3331

Historic Calumet Inn, 104 West Main Street, (507) 825-5871

Pipestone RV Campground, 919 North Hiawatha Avenue, (507) 825-2455; vcmpgrd@rconnect.com

Super 8 Motel, 605 Eighth Avenue S.E., (507) 825-4217 or (800) 800-8000; www.super8.com

PLACES FOR FOOD
LUVERNE
Coffey Haus, 111 East Main Street, (507) 283-8676

Magnolia Steak House, Highway 75 South and I-90, (507) 283-9161

Pizza Ranch, 110 East Main Street, (507) 283-2379

MARSHALL
Chicken Connection, 1407 East College Drive, (507) 537-1988

Daily Grind, 316 East Main Street, (507) 537-9565

Mike's Cafe, 203 East College Drive, (507) 532-5477

Shay's Restaurant, 1500 East College Drive, (507) 532-3221

Wooden Nickel, 448 West Main Street, (507) 532-3875

PIPESTONE

Glass House Restaurant, 102 Waldo Street South, (507) 348-7651

Historic Calumet Restaurant, 104 West Main Street, (507) 825-5871

Lange's Cafe, 110 Eighth Avenue S.E., (507) 825-4488

McDonald's, 609 Eighth Avenue S.E., (507) 825-3222

Pizza Hut, 413 Eighth Avenue S.E., (507) 825-5886

Villager Restaurant, 607 Eighth Avenue N.E., (507) 825-5242

PLACES TO SHOP

LUVERNE

Brown Church Antiques, 202 West Main, (507) 283-2586

Hillside Antiques, Box 22B, RR 3, 121st Street, (507) 283-2985

Laudon Gifts and Collectibles, 121 East Main Street, (507) 283-2137

Playing in the Mud, 106 East Main Street, (507) 283-2679

Rocking Horse Gift Shop, 208 East Main Street, (507) 283-4441

MARSHALL

Market Street Mall, 1420 East College Drive, (507) 532-5417

Seasons Gallery, 1209 East College Drive, (507) 532-9774

PIPESTONE

Keepers Gift Shop and Coffee Gallery, 400 North Hiawatha, (507) 825-3734 or (888) 550-3734; www.pipekeepers.org

Pipestone County Historical Museum, 113 South Hiawatha, (507) 825-2563; www.pipestoneminnesota.com/museum

Where Two Worlds Meet, 317 Fourth Street N.E., (507) 825-3579

FOR MORE INFORMATION

Luverne Chamber of Commerce, 102 East Main Street, Luverne 55156, (507) 283-4061; luvernemn@dtgnet.com

Marshall Area Chamber of Commerce, Box 352B, 317 West Main Street, Marshall 56258, (507) 532-4484

Pipestone Chamber of Commerce/Convention and Visitors Bureau, 117 Eighth Avenue, Pipestone 55164, (507) 825-3316 or (800) 336-6125; pipecham@pipestoneminnesota.com

NEW ULM

It's hard to argue when the good burghers of New Ulm brag that their town is the "City of Charm and Tradition." Tucked into the Minnesota River Valley a mere 90 miles southwest of the Twin Cities, the community has a diverse and colorful history, outstanding food, and diverting attractions. And just about everything here reflects an Old World German influence. A visit provides a great history lesson for the kids, as well as an opportunity for some fun for the whole family.

It's no wonder that New Ulm is full of European charm; founding *vater* Frederick Beinhorn conceived the idea for the town when he still lived in Germany. Beinhorn came to America in 1852, and by 1853 he was in Chicago, where he and a few other German immigrants formed the Chicago Land Society.

The society sent out an advance party of eager pioneers to explore the Upper Midwest in search of the perfect spot for Beinhorn's burg. In 1854, the scouting party selected the site of today's New Ulm. The proximity to the Cottonwood and Minnesota Rivers was a big plus, with visions of a hometown brewery using the rivers' sparkling water already dancing in the heads of the thirsty explorers.

The name New Ulm was selected by the core planning group because many of the original settlers were from the kingdom of Württemberg, today part of Germany, of which Ulm is the principal city. In 1856, Wilhelm Pfaender showed up in New Ulm with members of the Turner Colonization Society of Cincinnati. His group merged with Beinhorn's party, and the combined group incorporated the town in 1857.

The German heritage of New Ulm, now a town of about 14,000 folks, shows up well in the architecture, neat houses and trim yards, ethnic foods and festivals—in short, just about everywhere in town. The town **glockenspiel** (for extra credit, have the kids learn to spell the word), is one of the world's only free-standing carillon clock towers, rising 45 feet into the air. The bells chime in chorus daily at 3 and 5 p.m., and more often during the city's many festivals. Three animated polka bands "perform" most of the year, replaced by a Nativity scene around Christmas. Glockenspiels like New Ulm's are found in town squares all across Germany. The **Hermann Monument**, erected in 1897, is another Teutonic reminder. The monument stands in memory of an ancient warrior who battled the Romans. Take the kids to the monument grounds at

Hermann Heights Park at Center and Monument streets for a photographic overlook of the city and the river valley.

The German-Bohemian Immigrant Monument on German Street, erected in 1991, is another reminder of the city's heritage..The statue atop a granite pedestal depicts a family looking toward a bright future, according to German sculptor Leopold Hafner. At the base of the memorial are 350 surnames of area émigré families. Perhaps the children can find an ancestor.

FESTS, FESTS, AND MORE FESTS

It's the town's abundant Old World festivals, however, that make New Ulm a great place for young and old to sample some "oom-pah-pah" and other German delights. The schedule ensures that *kleine Kinder und Jugendliche, Mutter, Vater, Oma und Opa geder hat viel Spass* ("that the toddlers, teens, mom, dad and grandma and grandpa will have a lot of fun").

One of the year's first events is **Bockfest**, held early in the spring, either in February or March. Activities—mostly munching and brew sampling, as well as a bock treasure hunt in Flandrau State Park—are outdoors. Even the most blustery weather doesn't keep these Minnesotans away from some fun; besides bonfires help ward off the chill. New Ulmites are quick to point out that the "bock" (goat) is an ancient symbol of a stubborn winter. While this is mostly an adult venue, kids can still sled and slide at area slopes on a Bockfest Saturday. The center of all the festivities is the August Schell Brewery (more about that later).

Flandrau State Park, inside the New Ulm city limits along the Cottonwood River, is the site of the annual **FlandrauFest**. The day of activities is usually held on the last Saturday in June, with plenty of music, food, beverages, and snacks. This family-oriented festival features a water-balloon battle, a dunk tank, and a medallion hunt amid the trees. Try the Hula-Hoop–spinning completion or test the family's artistic talent with a sand sculpture. A Frisbee-throwing contest, as well as a tug-of-war, hoop toss, basketball shoot, and rubber-ducky race are among the other events. Depending on the depth of the slow-moving river, families can go tubing and canoeing.

By the way, **Flandrau State Park**, all 1,006 acres, is also a wonderful place to visit during nonfestival times. The area is thick with cedar, sugar maple, basswood, and cottonwoods, as well as brilliant sunflowers, big bluestem, and other

Taxes and Signs

Minnesota was one of the first states to levy a tax on gasoline to help pay for new roads. It was also the first state to number its highways, a numerical system that all states follow today.

The sand-bottom swimming pool at Flandrau State Park. Copyright State of Minnesota, Department of Natural Resources.

prairie flowers. The park has both semimodern and rustic campsites available that the kids will dig, plus a mile-long interpretive trail easily maneuvered by the smaller set. One of the park's unique features is a swimming pool that combines the best of two worlds: it has a sand bottom, just like a lake; but the water is filtered, just like a regular pool. The park is located at 1300 Summit Avenue, a few blocks southwest of Highway 15 and two miles south of Highway 14, (507) 233-9800; www.stayatmnpark.com or www.dnr.state.mn.us.

During the summer, New Ulm's festival binge continues, giving vacationing families a chance to "Discover Germany in Minnesota" at the city's annual **Heritagefest**. It's usually held on two consecutive weekends in mid-July at the Brown County Fairgrounds. Heritagefest trots out European show bands and lots of other Old World entertainment each weekend. A 100-unit parade is held on the last Sunday of the festival. Travel professionals and tour companies who book travel for individuals and organizations consider this one of the top 100 events in North America.

The fest features humorous costumed dancers called the *Narren* and the gnomelike *Heinzelmannchen*, as well as singers and musicians, who roam the grounds performing for the crowds. Visitors can also listen to yodeling and folk tunes at any one of the five large stages. Voluminous tents provide a festive look (as well as shelter when it rains), and they are also the spot to find plenty of hearty, locally-brewed Schell's beer and loads of good German food. A special Kinderfest area is reserved for children's games. Kids also like mean-

Enjoying Oktoberfest in New Ulm, a city famous for its high-spirited public celebrations. Minnesota Office of Tourism photograph.

dering through the arts-and-crafts exhibits, plus poking around a Bavarian gift shop to find those special knickknacks for mementos. For more information, call (507) 534-8850 or visit www.heritagefest.net.

Oktoberfest in early October is a joint program sponsored by the New Ulm Holiday Inn and the New Ulm Chamber of Commerce (1 North Minnesota Street; (888) 463-9856; www.ic.new-ulm.mn.us). The hoopla spotlights still more musical entertainment, including New Ulm's famous Concord Singers, who have performed throughout Europe and the United States. As always there's food: sauerkraut, landjaegers (a style of sausage), German potato salad, and apple strudel. A craft show is held both weekends of the festival at the Marktplatz Mall in downtown New Ulm. Horse-drawn trolley rides given on Saturdays from downtown are fun for the *kinder*.

New Ulm goes nuts over Christmas, capitalizing on the fact that many American holiday traditions originated in Germany, not the least of which are decorated Christmas tree and wreaths. Since 1925, the downtown business district gets into the yule spirit by draping everything that doesn't run away with evergreen boughs. Buildings are outlined with thousands of lights, and dozens of Christmas trees line the streets, decked out in their red bow ties. It can be a jaw-dropper for the tiny tyke set.

The townsfolk also play up the festive spirit. Daytrippers from around the area flock to New Ulm to drive through the residential areas and see the beautifully decorated homes and parks. For more seasonal glow, the **Christmas Parade of Lights** on the Friday evening after Thanksgiving indicates that Santa Claus has officially arrived. A 30-unit parade rolls through downtown.

Early in December, children flock to the New Ulm Middle School auditorium to welcome St. Nicholas. Dressed in traditional costumes, St. Nicholas and his sidekick Krumpus tell the youngsters about the European legend of St. Nicholas. Plenty of entertainment and treats keep up the holiday buzz. Early in January, a thoroughly German Christmas is celebrated under the stars in German Park, featuring jolly old St. Nick and a traditional Christmas bonfire.

Not content to pitch Christmas only at the end of December, the Guten Tag Haus gift shop in New Ulm holds its year-round **Christkindlmarkt**, with an array of loud cuckoo clocks, massive beer steins, wide-mouthed nutcrackers, delicate glass ornaments, lovely dolls, and delicious foods for sale. Kids love coming here to stock up on secret goodies for their family holiday.

As Lent approaches, locals and out-of-towners alike prepare for **Fasching**, the German Mardi Gras, celebrated at New Ulm's Turner Hall. The first hall, built by German immigrants as a social and athletic center, was destroyed by a Dakota war party during the Dakota Uprising of 1862. It's much calmer these days, but the city's party times continue. Choral groups, hearty German food and beverages, plus music, dancing, and a costume contest round out the day and evening. Fasching got its historical start in the Alps, as a way to chase away the winter blues. Turner Hall is at 102 South State Street, (507) 354-8850; www.newulmtel.net/~municipal/concords/fasching.html.

MORE GEMÜTLICHKEIT

New Ulm has even managed to squeeze in a couple of non-German festivals. In mid-August, the Brown County Fair relieves the heat summer heat with a carnival, plus tractor pulls and plenty of exhibits of giant produce, huge rabbits, crowing roosters, and mighty bulls. Among the kid-powered highlights of the fair's four days is the bang 'em, crunch 'em demolition derby. Families can note that there are special children, seniors, and teen days, with a wide range of entertainment throughout the fairgrounds. So haul the grandfolks along for an extended outing.

In July, the free **Auto Fest** on the grounds of Maday Motors features displays of more than 240 antique cars dating back to the early 1900s. New Ulm streets are filled with the beeping, honking, and putt-putting of the old cars as they come into town for the event. Anyone who loves cars will have a blast checking out the refurbished vehicles, which are always in mint condition. **RiverBlast** in September reinforces the locals love of the water, with canoe races, fishing competitions, and music, always music.

If you happen to drop into New Ulm when there isn't a festival in full swing, never fear. You can visit the **August Schell Brewing Company**. Built in 1860, the facility still sits in its original location along the Cottonwood River on a 30-acre site amid formal gardens. The vision of the founders certainly paid off, with a variety of brews such as Doppel Bock, Schell's Pils, Maifest, Schmaltz's Alt available for mom and dad. Plus there's 1919 Rootbeer, Buddy's Orange and Grape for the miniature set. Tours run from Memorial Day through Labor Day, with off-season tours on Saturdays. The kids usually enjoy a brewing museum that is part of the tour, learning about hops, wort, and all that sort of heady stuff. The brewery is located at 18609 Schell Road, (507) 354-5528; www.schellsbrewery.com.

For those who wish to sample something other than beer, Morgan Creek Vineyards offer a stomping good time. Wine tastings are available for the elders, while the backseat gang can pick up details on grapes and fermentation. Having a vineyard in Minnesota isn't that far-fetched; Morgan Creek, established in 1993, produces some hardy varieties. It releases its Black Ice label at the end of September, a St. Wenceslaus in November, a Bacchanal in mid-May and—for the German touch—a Gewürztraminer in July. Morgan Creek is located near the intersection of Highway 68 and County Highway 47 about eight miles east of town. For more information, call (507) 947-3547; or e-mail martiMCV@aol.com.

You may want to remind the kids that New Ulm is not just for fun and festivals. The city has a long and occasionally bloody history, having survived two separate sieges by Native Americans during the Dakota Uprising in August 1862. Several buildings, which still stand along Minnesota Street, were hiding places for refugees. There are stories of kids hiding from the Dakota and making their way to town, leading their little brothers and sisters to safety. If that wasn't enough, New Ulm survived an infestation of grasshoppers in 1870, and a tornado smashed much of the town in 1881.

Ya, things are quieter now in New Ulm. But not too quiet. It's that wonderful mix of the old and the new, making it perfect for a quick weekend getaway. If there is one German word that will sum up your visit to New Ulm, it has to be *gemütlichkeit*.

PLACES TO STAY

Budget Holiday, 1316 North Broadway, (507) 354-4145

Colonial Inn, 1315 North Broadway, (507) 354-3128 or (888) 215-2143

Deutsche Strasse Bed and Breakfast, 404 South German Street, (507) 354-2005

Holiday Inn, 2101 South Broadway, (507) 359-2941 or (877) 359-2941

Microtel Inns and Suites, 424 South 20th Street, (507) 354-9800 or (888) 771-7171

New Ulm Motel, 1427 South Broadway, (507) 359-1414

Super 8, 1901 South Broadway, (507) 359-2400 or (800) 800-8000; www.super8.com

PLACES FOR FOOD

The Backerei and Coffeeshop, 27 South Minnesota Street, (507) 354-6011

China Buffet, 400 North Minnesota Street, (507) 354-6668

Corner Stone Coffee, 213 South Minnesota Street, (507) 354-5552

DJ's, 1200 North Broadway, (507) 354-3843

Happy Joe's, 1700 North Broadway, (507) 359-9811

V's Kitchen (Hy-Vee), 2015 South Broadway, (507) 354-8255

Kaiserhoff, 221 North Minnesota Street, (507) 359-2071

Lamplighter, 214 North Minnesota Street, (507) 354-2185

Main Jiang House, 206 North Minnesota Street, (507) 354-1218 or (507) 354-1228

Ulmer Cafe, 115 North Minnesota Street, (507) 354-8122

PLACES TO SHOP

Antiques Plus, 117 North Broadway, (507) 359-1090

Bookshelves and Coffeecups, 123 North Minnesota Street, (507) 359-4600

Christmas Haus, 203 North Minnesota Street, (507) 359-7017

Country Loft and Doll Haus, 204 North Minnesota Street, (507) 354-8493

Domeier's, 1020 South Minnesota Street, (507) 354-4231

Fudge and Stuff, 210 North Minnesota Street, (507) 359-5272

Guten Tag Haus, 127 North Minnesota Street, (507) 233-4287; gutentag@newulmtel.net

Horizon Gallery, 208 North Minnesota Street, (507) 354-8300

NadelKunst, 212 North Minnesota Street, 507-354-8708

Rieke's Books, 13 North Minnesota Street, (507) 354-7833 or (877) 437-3485; www.riekesbk@newulm.net

Rivervine, 1510 North Broadway, (507) 354-6716

Sandy's Hallmark, 28 North Minnesota Street, (507) 354-1355

Schell's Gift Shop, August Schell Brewery, 18609 Schell Road, (507) 354-5528

The Thimble Box, 526 South Minnesota Street, (507) 354-6721

FOR MORE INFORMATION

New Ulm Convention and Visitors Bureau, 1 North Minnesota Street, New Ulm 56073, (507) 233-4300 or (888) 4NEW-ULM; www.newulm.com

MANKATO

It's hard to believe today, but quiet Mankato used to be a major transportation hub for southern Minnesota. And its major brush with history is tinged with sadness. It's a tale that should enlighten older children—and remind adults—about the treatment Native Americans have received from the federal government over the years.

A POIGNANT PAST

A granite marker downtown indicates the site where 38 Dakota were hanged from a single gallows on December 26, 1862. The incident followed the U.S. Army's quelling of a Native American rebellion that set the prairie land of southern Minnesota and northern Iowa ablaze that year. At the time, the Dakota were living on reservations and were at the mercy of corrupt government agents and traders. There was usually no recourse for a Native American when cheated, a predicament which caused resentment, especially among younger warriors.

Violence eventually broke out between the Dakota and the whites, although many Dakota stayed out of the fighting. Some 200 settlers died in the resulting conflict, as well as numerous Dakota and persons of mixed blood. About 2,000 white refugees fled to Mankato after nearby New Ulm was attacked and destroyed. After finally surrendering or being captured, hundreds of Dakota were put on trial and 307 condemned to death. The lives of most of them were spared, however, through the intervention of President Lincoln. But the group execution of the remaining 38 Dakota, who were not pardoned by the president, became the largest mass execution in U.S. history.

It's not a happy story, but it's one worth telling to the children—and remembering. The remembrance stone is located at the corner of Main Street and Riverfront Drive beside the **Mankato Depot**. Each year, either the second or third weekend in September, Native Americans gather for a memorial pow-wow at Sibley Park. Take Riverfront Drive west to the bend in the river, turn north and go two blocks to the park where the dancing is held.

A photograph of the hanging can be seen at the **Blue Earth County Heritage Center Museum**, 415 Cherry Street. The museum itself, aside from that grim reminder of an unhappy era, is worth a couple of hours of exploration. Kids love meandering through the well-designed exhibits in the place, home

The Birth of Mankato

Daniel Williams, Parson Johnson, and Henry Jackson founded Mankato in 1852. They traveled six days by sled from St. Paul to stake their claims. Their arrival dismayed Native Americans in the region who had yet to be paid for the land they had given up in a treaty the year before. But after giving a barrel of pork to a local chief, the three white men were allowed to continue their journey and to build their first houses.

to the Blue Earth County Historical Society. The site also houses research archives and a museum store packed with books and souvenirs that youngsters can purchase for show-and-tell at school back home. An exhibit gallery presents loads of artifacts from Blue Earth County's good old frontier days, showing off industrial, farming, and household implements.

The "Ghosts from the Past" pageant is held early in October, sponsored by the historical society. This annual family event highlights important Mankato events and personalities from long ago. So be sure to collect the kids and gather 'round the costumed interpreters who are guaranteed to spin a good yarn. Need information? Call the society at (507) 345-5566 for details.

Some of the other things your brood will learn is that Mankato is located at the head of navigation on the Minnesota River, 80 miles southwest of the Twin Cities, and thus early steamboats could reach the town. As such, the community grew quickly after its settlement in 1852. By 1868, railroads made it to Mankato, and the economic future of the city was secured. The growth of the rail lines brought an end to steamboat travel; the last commercial vessel—the *Henrietta*—made its final trip between St. Peter and Mankato on April 17, 1897. By the way, the word mankato is Dakota for "blue earth," a reference to the color of the clay in the area.

MANKATO TODAY

After the history lessons, your kids will want to get out and see what the town offers in the way of present-day excitement. If you're in Mankato during the summer, there's a host of fun things to see and do.

Professional football fans, even those of the Packer or Bear persuasion, will get a kick out of watching the **Minnesota Vikings** football team strain through their training camp. Just be sure to be there sometime between late July to early August. Visitors to town can watch the team train on Blakeslee Field at Minnesota State University–Mankato (MSUM). The team holds workouts twice a day, six days a week during that time. Call The Hub, MSU-Mankato's first point of information contact on anything to do with the university, at (800) 722-

0544 or (507) 389-1866. The crack of a bat means the **Mankato Mashers** baseball club is at it again. The team plays in the Northwoods League, offering loads of family fun at Franklin Rogers Park from June to the middle of August. Most games are played at 7 p.m. For tickets and schedules, call (507) 387-8649.

For golfing enthusiasts, no short vacation is worth its salt without at least one jaunt around the links. Mankato-area duffers suggest several courses. **North Links Golf Club**, at Highway 14 West and County Highway 66, North Mankato, has a regulation 18 holes with a marvelous driving range, plus a golf academy for those who want to sparkle up their game. The club's restaurant and lounge are then perfect après golf. Call (507) 947-3355. For another ball-whacking opportunity, check out the Minneopa Golf Club along Highway 169 South, about a mile and a half out of town. Some golf fans consider this southern Minnesota's "sportiest golf course." The club is open daily to the general public, except Wednesday, which is ladies day, and during any scheduled stag nights. Anyone not having clubs in the car trunk can rent them, along with all-important carts. Of course, there is a lounge and snack bar for the thirsty and hungry. Vacationing families can reach the club at (507) 625-5777.

And if there are budding Tiger Woods–type golfers in the backseat gang, take them to **Grand Champions Mini Golf**, **Driving Range and Batting Cages** on County Highway 3 (across from Menard's). Call (507) 386-0001 to get the details on this three-course range, which also has several batting cages for the power hitters. For more fun, the **Kato Entertainment Center**, 200 Chestnut, (507) 625-7553, is one of Mankato's major entertainment complexes. The center features concerts, a dinner theater, and dancing whenever the getaway gang wants to get down and boogie on a weekend.

During the winter, the **Midwest Wireless Civic Center**, One Civic Center Plaza, is home to the MSUM hockey teams and also caters to concerts, rodeos, and ice shows. Tickets are available at the Civic Center ticket office or Ticketmaster outlets. Charge by phone at (507) 625-7919, or online at www.midwestwirelesscenter.com. For general information, call (507) 389-3000.

No matter what the weather, let the kids work off some steam by knocking down some pins at **Victory Bowl**, 202 South Victory Drive, (507) 387-7991; www.victorybowl.com. This well-appointed bowling center features Frameworx automatic scoring with 3-D color graphics and computer-controlled bumpers for tiny keglers. Take in a Thunder Alley Sound and Light show on Fridays and Saturdays for disco-like blowout bowling. The lanes are smoke-free on Friday, Saturday and Sunday afternoons until 6 p.m. After bowling, the gang can pile into Mickey's Sports Bar, Victory Bowl's adjacent grill for pub grub and soda pop. What more could a bowler want?

Well, for starters, how about checking out **Jerry Dutler's Bowl**, U.S. Highway 169 North, North Mankato. Determined alley fans find 24 Brunswick "Glow Anvilane" synthetic lanes with automatic scoring, saving the math-challenged a lot of embarrassment. Some evenings, try the trendy new color pin or wacky "cosmic bowling," which only die-hard young bowlers seem to understand. This place is great for holiday-going youngsters and oldsters. Pool, video games, and satellite TV round out the bustling entertainment package. Get in touch with the folks at Dutler's by calling (507) 387-3439.

MANKATO ARTS SCENE

Even with all this sports action, the city does not ignore the arts arena, especially with several local colleges to maintain a fresh supply of performance and service talent, as well as to attract a continuous pool of visitors who bring their families for a cultural outing.

The public is welcome to attend events at **Bethany Lutheran College**, 700 Luther Drive, (507) 344-7000, home to fine-arts programming throughout the year. Theater choir, concert band, jazz ensemble, and handbell choir are among the musical groups that both adults and kids enjoy. Bethany's art gallery hosts student art shows in December and May and sponsors guest artists throughout the year. The **MSUM Department of Art**—in 136 Nelson Hall on campus—also hosts an extensive array of exhibitions for both touring and student artists. Named after the school's emeritus professor of art, Effie Conkling, the university's Conkling Gallery is home to most of the shows, which highlight regional, national, and international professionals. Call (507) 389-6412.

Gustavus Adolphus College, 800 West College Avenue in nearby St. Peter, manages more than 200 art shows, recitals, concerts, dance performances, and

A picturesque view from the Gustavus Adolphus College campus in Saint Peter.

Young Drift Plains

The Young Drift Plains of central and western Minnesota are made up of low, rolling farmland. Drift is the name for the thick, rich topsoil left behind by the glaciers tens of thousands of years ago. The few hills in the region are called moraines, mounds of rock left behind by the melting ice packs.

theater presentations a year, ensuring that any family on holiday can find exactly the right artistic event for its enjoyment. The school's productions are directed by Office of Fine Arts instructors who have studied around the world and brought their theatrical and musical skills to the school.For program information, call (507) 933-7363, and for tickets, call (507) 933-7590.

For a broad range of the arts, stop with the kids at Mankato's **Carnegie Art Center**, 120 South Broad Street, (507) 625-2730, to see the monthly gallery exhibitions featuring regional artists, as well as touring shows. The center also sponsors art education programs, some of which are aimed at children. With its **Broad Street Gallery Gift Shop**, anyone with loose change can find plenty of swell mementos or gifts to take home. Call the art center number above and ask for the gallery.

FESTIVAL FUN

Folks in Mankato are willing and eager to celebrate anything, which in itself makes the city a great place to visit any time of the year. Families can always be assured of finding plenty of diversions from day-to-day reality at home. The **International Festival**, usually held in mid-April, means eating, eating, eating, and checking out the costumes and craft demonstrations adorned and performed by international students attending MSUM and folks from other countries now living in the surrounding area. Mankato's **Rockin' in the Quarry** in mid-June is held in the Kasota Quarry, with the Mankato Symphony Orchestra doing the musical honors free of charge. Getaway families who are repeat vacationers in Mankato attend with their lawn chairs in tow and either pack a picnic or buy food at the quarry.

Nearby North Mankato offers **Fun Days** early in July. This community celebration covers four days of frivolity, with a carnival, as well as the requisite food stands, plus bingo and a beer garden. There is dancing for the elders and a kiddy parade for the tykes.

Back in Mankato, the **Hickory Street Ribfest** is held in August. Smeared cheeks and sticky fingers are a small price to pay for enjoying a platter packed with saucy, award-winning ribs. Live bands keep everyone up and dancing.The **Old Town Festival** in mid-September has still more food (of course, this is Minnesota), plus games, entertainment, music, hayrides, and kiddy train rides.

Kids love the minnow racing, an event not quite akin to the Kentucky Derby, but full of laughs anyway. The fest is held in the Old Town parking lot on the 600 block of Riverfront Drive. Nobody forgets the winter holidays, either. The **Celebration of Lights** runs from Thanksgiving through Christmas. During the celebration, thousands of sparkling lights adorn businesses and homes throughout Mankato and North Mankato. There is also a beautiful display of decorated trees dotting the campus of MSUM.

BUILDINGS FROM THE PAST

Mankato's rich history is reflected and exemplified in the city's architectural gems. These are places that the whole family will enjoy. The historic **Our Lady of Good Counsel**, 170 Good Counsel Drive, (507) 389-4200, is the landmark home of the School Sisters of Notre Dame. The good nuns have been on the Mankato scene since 1865 as teachers and caregivers. The towering steeple of their chapel was built in 1924 and stands over the community as a symbol of faith and charity. The kids might not dig the Romanesque church with its brilliant stained-glass windows handcrafted in Munich, Germany. But they'll surely get a kick out of the restored 117-year-old year old William Johnson Organ Opus 499. There's a bit of religious rockin' when that baby cranks up, as the sound bounces off the Italian-marble altars and a ceramic floor that was brought all the way from Mettlach, Germany. Show the youngsters the oil paintings of the Stations of the Cross, also created by Munich artists.

Minnesota's Capital? It Was Almost St. Peter

Early settlers in the village of St. Peter tried to have the territorial capital moved to their community from St. Paul. They had hoped that the northern boundary of Minnesota would be set just above the Twin Cities. If this were the case, St. Peter would have been in the center of the new state, a desirable location for a state capital. Land was donated and a frame capitol building constructed in anticipation of what would follow.

A bill to move the capital passed both the Minnesota House and the Senate. But, in a move that puts modern political skullduggery to shame, the written legislation was spirited out of the Twin Cities by Representative Joseph Rolette before the governor could sign it. Rolette hid out in a hotel room until the constitutional time limit on the bill expired, and St. Peter lost out on its bid.

Poking around an old home can be another visual and historical adventure. Start with the 1871 **R. D. Hubbard House** at 606 South Broad Street, open May through early September. It is the oldest remaining example of a Victorian home in the area, and it is presently being restored to its 1905 look. Tiffany lamps, marble fireplaces (three, count 'em, three), and fabulous woodwork and wall hangings round out the decor. A few original furniture pieces from the Hubbard family and other 19th-century antiques can be viewed. However, the younger kids often appreciate walking through the carriage house more than the actual home. Horse-drawn carts and buggies, antique cars, and fire-fighting gear are displayed here. The house is listed on the National Register of Historic Places. Call (507) 345-5566 for details.

The **Judge Lorin P. Cray** home at 603 South Second Street is also open for tours by calling (507) 345-4629 to confirm times. The Cray house is like an oversized dollhouse. The fancy Queen Anne–style mansion was built in 1898 at a cost of $13,000. It has towers perfect for freeing a young person's imagination, along with a side balcony and loads of stained- and etched-glass windows. Fanciful garlands adorn the porch, with its intricate trim and stately columns. The building is listed on the National Register of Historic Places and has been the home of the Mankato YWCA since 1927.

North Mankato's **Guns of the Pioneers** is another museum kids love. Weaponry of the Old West is displayed so youngsters (and oldsters) can understand the firearms used by the White Hats and the Black Hats. The museum also has a gift shop and sells antique and replica firearms of the frontier era. The museum is housed in the old Stewart Building, 300 Belgrade Avenue, (507) 344-4440. Take readers in the family to the top of Center Street, where there is a plaque celebrating the memory of local author **Maud Hart Lovelace**. Located on a small bench made of Kasota stone, the plaque honors Lovelace as someone "who here began the childhood daydreams that one day would be our windows to the past." To the author's fans, Center Street was Hill Street in the town she called Deep Valley. These were the settings for 13 childrens' books in the Betsy-Tacy series.

Lovelace drew on her memories of growing up in Mankato, as well as extensive historical research, to bring the two little girls and their friends to life for contemporary readers. In 1990, several Mankato-area residents formed the international Betsy-Tacy Society, which hosts an annual convention of folks who love the books. The organization has a Web site with oodles of details about the writer, her characters, and what to see and do in Mankato. Tap in to www.betsy-tacysociety.org for all the latest details.

To get a feel for the pioneer days, pitch a tent and huddle in for the night at the **Land of Memories Campground**. The name of this 47-site campground, operated by the Division of Parks and Forestry, was translated from the Dakota words *wokiksuye makoce*. The park is located where the Minnesota River lazily turns north toward its marriage with the Mississippi. The site has soccer fields, a cross-country ski track, and groomed ski trails in the winter, volleyball courts and open space for a round of leaping and jumping by the kids. Call (507) 387-8649.

PLACES TO STAY

AmericInn, 240 Stadium Road, (507) 345-8011 or (800) 634-3444; www.americinn.com

Budgethost Inn, 1255 Range Street, (507) 388-1644 or (800) 822-2521

Comfort Inn, 131 Apache Place (507) 388-5107

Holiday Inn Downtown, 101 East Main Street, (507) 345-1234

Riverfront Inn, 1727 North Riverfront Drive, (507) 388-1638

PLACES FOR FOOD

Big Dog, 1712 Commerce Drive, North Mankato, (507) 386-8463

Boomtown, 1610 Warren Street, (507) 625-9264

Chevy's, 119 South Front Street, (507) 345-1446

Erberts and Gerberts Subs and Clubs, 501 South Front Street, (507) 386-0708

Jake's Stadium Pizza, 1614 Monks Avenue, (507) 345-3185

The Peddler of Rapidan, 19075 Rapidan Avenue, (507) 278-4808

PLACES TO SHOP

Farmer's Market, Madison East Center parking lot, 1400 Madison Avenue (June through October)

Hilltop Shopping, Madison East Center, 1400 Madison Avenue, (507) 388-9353

River Hills Mall, 1850 Adams Street, (507) 388-1100; www.riverhillsmall.com

FOR MORE INFORMATION

Mankato Area Chamber and Convention Bureau, 112 Riverfront Drive, P. O. Box 999, Mankato 56002, (507) 345-4519 or (800) 657-4733; maccb@mankato.com

ALBERT LEA

Although Albert Lea has a lot of child-friendly things to see and do, this weekend adventure is geared more toward the mommies and daddies. Think of it as a reward for visiting all the attractions that catered to kids and for putting up with their search for the next thrill ride, hamburger joint, or restroom.

Albert Lea is the ideal spot for relaxing and taking in the historic and lovingly preserved architecture of small-town America. To help you do that, the city promotes a self-guided historic walking or driving tour around town, which the kids may or may not enjoy. To ward off any squirming or eye rolling, just hold out the promise of a hand-dipped ice-cream cone at the **Lakeside Cafe and Creamery**, 408 Bridge Avenue, (507) 377-2233. With that in mind, the backseat gang should settle down and enjoy peering out at all the various architectural styles seen around Albert Lea.

GAZING BACK IN TIME

Before you begin the tour, check out the **Albert Lea Convention and Visitors Bureau** in the former City Hall, 202 North Broadway, (507) 373-3938 or (800) 345-8414. The venerable two-story structure was built in 1903 and served the community as its political center until the new city hall on East Clarke Street was constructed in 1967. The building is easily recognizable with its heavy stone arches across the facade.

The city, named after early explorer Albert M. Lea, is the county seat of Freeborn County. It was founded in 1856 and incorporated as a city in 1878. In Albert Lea's early years, the community was noted for its diversified economic base that included the manufacture of wooden barrels and electric fences. Today, Albert Lea, at the junction of I-90 and I-35, is surrounded by rich farmland dotted with lakes, a scene that offers a patchwork of pasture greens and sparkling blues when viewed from overhead.

The oldest building in town, at 105 South Broadway, was built in 1874. The vintage structure once housed a drugstore and then a variety store. An outside staircase on its north side lead to a barbershop in the basement. Another interesting structure, the **Freeborn County Courthouse**, was constructed in 1887 at 411 South Broadway. Topped by a large tower, the building sports a sculpture entitled *Dogs of the Nile*. See if the kids can find the hounds, which seem

A few of the 19th-century farm implements and buildings at the Freeborn County Museum and Historical Village. —Courtesy of the Albert Lea Convention and Visitors Bureau

about ready to jump down and chase a ball. Unfortunately, some additions to the grand old building make it look like it's wearing a suit that's too tight.

An antique and gift shop, **The Heart of the Artichoke**, now occupies 222 East Clarke Street, in a building dating from 1915. The structure went through many changes over its lifetime. First it was the Rogers Hotel, then the Hotel Goodwin and the Hotel Dorman before morphing into a print shop, followed by a manufacturing firm and even several restaurants. To reach today's antique and gift shop, call (507) 373-4258. Another shop, **Something Special in the Nest**, is situated in Albert Lea's oldest church, built in 1867 at 501 West Main Street. Gifts and home accessories are displayed around the church, which really elevates shopping to a religious experience. The building still has its original doors, planked floorboards, and a towering, curved ceiling. Call (507) 377-2954.

Tell the kids to hang on for one more visit, to the **Turtle Dove Tea House**, 510 West Main Street, originally a private home built in 1880. The first owner was a Norwegian jeweler, who loved woodwork and stained glass. But there is a bonus here. Settle the gang in at the coffee room where everyone can wolf down a pastry and revel in the perfume of freshly baked scones. Scattered around the building are antiques, pots, clothing, and other exotica for sale. Now that the kids' appetites have been whetted, it's time for that ice-cream cone.

Next, take the crew to the **Freeborn County Museum and Historical Village**, 1031 Bridge Avenue, a complex resembling a frontier hamlet. In Pioneer Village, children can ramble through a one-room schoolhouse and wriggle into the desks. They can check the general store and marvel at what seems to be the low, low pricing for a bolt of cloth and foodstuffs. All the place needs is a blue-light special to be an up-to-date discount store. A blacksmith shop and other buildings of the era

The Origins of Albert Lea

Surveyors laid out the city of Albert Lea in 1856, working around several large lakes in the vicinity. Originally called Fox Lake, because early explorer Albert Lea saw a fox when he first came into the region, the town was later renamed in his honor.

bring sparks of life to what can be dry history to youngsters. Inside the museum proper are old-fashioned dentist's drills and other artifacts culled from attics, basements, and backrooms of Freeborn County residents over the years.

The museum and its library are open year-round, while the village is only open Tuesday through Friday from May through September. Subsequently, plan a vacation accordingly if an outside visit is in the offing. Call (507) 373-8003; or log on to www.smig.net/fchm.

The **Story Lady Doll and Toy Museum**, 131 North Broadway, is a natural draw for any young lady under 11 years old. The museum is the only one of its kind in southern Minnesota, with more than 1,500 dolls of all shapes and sizes. They range from antiques through storybook characters and limited-edition designer dolls. Century-old dancing dolls are among the most popular items in the funky little facility. Other antique toys are also on exhibit, and there is a gift shop for browsing. The Story Lady is only open from noon to 4 p.m., Tuesday through Saturday. Call (507) 377-1820.

Another venerable structure, the **Albert Lea Civic Theatre**, 147 North Broadway, attracts audiences of all ages to its exciting array of programs. The building was built in 1909 and refurbished in 1995. The grande dame of the town is now the comfortable home of the Albert Lea Community Theatre and the Minnesota Festival Theatre. Locals who want to learn

New dolls, as well as old ones, on display at the Story Lady Doll and Toy Museum.
—Courtesy of the Albert Lea Convention and Visitors Bureau

about directing, sound, set design, sales, acting, and other aspects of the theater world can volunteer their time, sweat, and blood to help. When considering a visit to Albert Lea, block out a production slot sometime during the theater's season between October and May. At least one performance each year is geared toward families with small kids. Call (507) 377-4371 to confirm shows and schedules.

The **Minnesota Festival Theatre** is the only summer equity professional theater in Minnesota. Performers come from around the country to participate in the celebration's always-exciting range of drama each season, one that runs from mid-June through July. Plays include tried-and-true classics, as well as innovative and avant-garde contemporary works. Youngsters certainly enjoy the theater and are usually mature enough to see any of the productions. Call (507) 377-4371.

The final stop on your tour of Albert Lea's rich architecture and lively cultural scene is the former opera house and music conservatory, the **Albert Lea Art Center** building at 224 South Broadway Avenue. It was built in 1916 as the Rivoli Theater and the B&B Music Academy. After a stint as a movie house and a mini-mall, this French classical structure—with its elegant three-tiered facade—received a new lease on its multipurpose life when the art center moved here in the mid-1980s and renovated the place. The center hosts at least 12 major exhibits each year, ranging from children's artwork to the creations of professionals from around the country. The center sponsors a Christmas Tree Review from the end of November through December, in addition to exhibits such as Winter Art and Art on Broadway. All the shows are free. Call (507) 373-5665.

Speaking of art and architecture, when it comes to colors, Albert Lea was lucky to have artist Lloyd Herfindahl as a long-time resident. The painter, who died in 1966, brightened up his hometown by painting huge murals at the Naeve Hospital–Mayo Health Systems building, city offices, and the Freeborn County Courthouse. His themes most often were patriotic and soul stirring.

ALBERT LEA OUTDOORS

After all that art and inside culture, a bit of outdoor fun could be on the family's getaway calendar during an Albert Lea vacation stopover. **Myre-Big Island State Park**, three miles southeast of Albert Lea, 19499 780th Avenue (Exit 11 on I-35), offers hiking, camping, cycling, bird-watching, and canoeing, along with snowshoeing and cross-country skiing in the winter. Just open the car door and turn the kids loose. They can run, jump, and yell to their heart's content. Maple sugaring is fun in March, with tapping available under supervision on the last two Saturdays of the month. Dress for the weather: Put the gang into waterproof boots and thick socks to ward off the chill and dampness. Call (507) 379-3403 or (800) 246-2267.

Be sure to bring bikes to Albert Lea, along with fishing poles, tennis racquets, and all sorts of other outside sports gear. After all, that is what a roof

National Prohibition

The National Prohibition Act, or Volstead Act, was named after Congressman Andrew Volstead of Minnesota. Passed in 1919, the act created the Eighteenth Amendment, which outlawed the manufacture, selling, and possession of intoxicating liquor in the United States. The amendment was repealed in 1933.

carrier is for when on a vacation. The **Blazing Star Bike Trail** starts at the city's aquatic center and follows Albert Lea Lake to the east. While pedaling along, watch the fishing fans and sailboaters on the water. And if plans for a lake excursion are in your back pocket, you can access the lake from Frank Avenue at the south end of the channel. There is also a concrete ramp for put-ins along South Shore Drive. The lake is 2,654 acres, with a 26-mile shoreline, and it is just one of several large bodies of water within the city limits.

South Shore Drive, in fact, is one of the best scenic routes to get a sampling of Albert Lea's many sights, which flow along the roadway from urban to rural, from wild ducks to wildflowers. Another good way to see Albert Lea Lake is aboard the bi-level *Pelican Breeze* cruise boat, which offers public excursions Saturday and Sunday. A pizza cruise on Friday evenings is much in demand with the under-16 set. Call (507) 377-5076 for departure times during the summer sailing season.

Each summer, the **Albert Lea Water Ski Association** presents shows in Edgewater Park, with loads of heart-stopping jumps and trick skiing that the kids will applaud. The group was established in 1975 and is one of the city's most popular seasonal attractions. You can get a good view of the action from just about anywhere in the park.

For a slower look at life, the **Audubon Nature and Wildlife Preserve** is a 12-acre sanctuary in southwestern Albert Lea, just north of West Ninth Street between Lincoln Avenue and South Broadway. Once an apple orchard, the site is slowly reverting back to a more natural state, with colorful prairie flowers and native grasses to sooth the harried soul of a tired vacationer. The preserve is free and open to the public, with mowed trails providing easy walking, even for the smallest hiker. Have the kids keep on the lookout for deer, rabbits, and other wildlife.

They might also spot some critters in one of the city's 38 parks scattered around the community: Albert Lea is a town that really appreciates its green space. Pick a place for a picnic in **Edgewater Park**, at Edgewater and Lakeview, where there are shelters, a well-used playground, and a boat launch. The park features live music in the band shell each summer. Nature walks are popular in **Bancroft Bay Park**, while tennis, swimming, and volleyball are the sports of choice at **City Beach**. Be careful here, however, when the kids are swimming.

Getting into the swing of things with hot Dixieland music at the Doc Evans Memorial Jazz Festival. —Courtesy of the Albert Lea Convention and Visitors Bureau

There aren't any lifeguards. **J. M. Snyder Park**, at Bridge Avenue and Riverland Drive, has five lighted softball diamonds. The park also has four large sandlot volleyball courts for a bit o' bounce.

The **Albert Lea Aquatic Center**, 321 James Avenue, has a large pool with a diving area, as well as a shallow pool with play equipment for the small kids. Whether teen or toddler, they all enjoy the 230-foot-long water slide. The public pool is open from early June until the end of August. Beach umbrellas are available for use on the deck, where parents can doze, watch their kids splash around, or read a good vacation potboiler. The pool is accessible to the physically challenged. Call (507) 373-3328.

Now that the gang has checked out the city sites and sights, what's next? The answer to that question depends on the time of year because Albert Lea packs a lot of activities into a mere 365 days. On the second weekend in February, residents dressed in colonial-era attire set up booths in the **Northbridge Mall** to peddle their pots, books, woodwork, clothes, and other items. Also in February, Stories from the Heartland story-telling festival, which is considered one of the state's top 25 events by the Minnesota Office of Tourism, draws a wide range of national talent. Call (507) 373-4748 or (800) 345-8414.

On the third weekend in June, bring the family to the **Eddie Cochran Weekend/Low Bucks Car Club Weekend** to make a leap back in time. The kids will get a kick out of the music their grandparents were dancing to and the cars they were cruising in back in the 1950s. The festival honors Cochran, a local rockabilly musician who had a couple of big hits back then. A car show, swap meet, dance, rally, and lots of cruising are on tap for the event. Cochran was born in Oklahoma and came with his family to Albert Lea as a young boy before leaving for California as a teenager. He made his name on the club and band circuit before being killed in a London taxicab crash in 1957. Cochran's big hits were "Summertime Blues," and "Sittin' in the Balcony." He also had parts in several films, including *The Girl Can't Help It*.

For more music fun, the **Doc Evans Memorial Jazz Festival**, named after a Minnesota Hall of Famer noted for his musical prowess, is usually held in early July in Fountain Lake Park. The state's top jazz and Dixieland bands are booked for a full day of concerts. Also in June, families flock to the **Festival of Bands**, with marching bands from throughout the state. As expected, there is plenty of high-stepping enthusiasm on the part of the participating kids, to say nothing of their parents and the attending crowds.

Over Labor Day weekend, a major **Arabian Club horse show** also attracts out-of-towners from around the Midwest to the Freeborn County fairgrounds. This is a perfect, last-getaway-before-school short vacation, where the horse lovers in the family can watch the English and Western riding competitions. What's best, the event is free. Call the Albert Lea Chamber of Commerce/ Convention and Visitor's Bureau at (800) 345-8414 for details. Then on the first full weekend in October, the **Big Island Rendezvous** brings in "traders" and "mountain men" who reenact a typical 1800s gathering to swap furs and tall tales. This activity is a marvelous draw for vacationing kids who can ask all the questions they want about frontier life. To make life easier, hop onto one of the shuttle buses running between the county fairgrounds and the rendezvous-staging site. Call (507) 373-3938 or (800) 658-2526.

In December, one of Minnesota's largest model railroad shows is held at Northbridge Mall. Call (507) 377-3185 for the scoop on the tiny trains and the dates of their "arrival at the depot."

Reenacting what life was like for Minnesota's early settlers at the Big Island Rendezvous.
—Courtesy of the Albert Lea Convention and Visitors Bureau

PLACES TO STAY

AmericInn, 811 East Plaza Street, (507) 373-4324 or (800) 634-3444; www.americinn.com

Budget Host, 2301 East Main Street, (507) 373-8291 or (800) 528-1234

Comfort Inn, 810 Happy Trails Lane, (507) 377-1100

Countryside Inn, 2102 East Main Street, (507) 373-2446

Holiday Inn Express, 821 East Plaza Street, (507) 373-4000

Super 8 Motel, 2019 East Main Street, (507) 377-0591 or (800) 800-8000; www.super8.com

PLACES FOR FOOD

Abrego's Cafe, 120 South Washington Avenue, (507) 373-5469

Cafe Don'L, 4588 Bridge Avenue, (507) 377-8831

Elbow Room, 310 Eighth Street, (507) 373-1836

Kaffee Hus, 522 South Broadway, (507) 377-2951

Skyline Restaurant, 1609 West Main Street, (507) 377-3570

Trail's Travel Center, 820 Happy Lane, (507) 373-7747

Trumble's, 1811 East Main Street, (507) 373-2638

Turtle Dove Tea House, 510 West Main Street, (507) 377-4200

PLACES TO SHOP

Adams Originals Shop, 1322 Fountain Street, (507) 373-4153

Northbridge Mall, 2510 Bridge Avenue, (507) 377-3185

Skyline Mall, 1701 West Main Street, (507) 373-1610

Up North Gifts, Northbridge Mall, 2510 Bridge Avenue, (507) 377-3448

FOR MORE INFORMATION

Albert Lea Convention and Visitors Bureau, 202 North Broadway Avenue, Albert Lea 56007, (507) 373-3938 or (800) 345-8414

Albert Lea/Freeborn County Chamber of Commerce, 143 West Clark, Albert Lea 56007, (507) 373-3938

ROCHESTER AND NORTHFIELD

Rochester is consistently ranked among the nation's "most livable cities" by such noted publications as *Money* and *Redbook* magazines. The city gets kudos for its lifestyle, location, services, cultural and sports venues, restaurants, and accommodations. But this city of 82,000, founded in 1854 along the Zumbro River amid the rolling hills of southeastern Minnesota, would probably have been a pleasant but undistinguished community had it not been for the arrival of Dr. William Worrall Mayo in the 1860s.

The rolling farmland north of Rochester, extending over to the Mississippi River, is a delight to painters, photographers—and travelers. Small towns spring up alongside the byways, with nearby fields dotted with silos and red barns. The area's rich soil seems able to grow just about anything, from corn to soybeans to everything natural in between. Herds of Holsteins, horses, and hogs graze on the lush pastureland and populate feed lots, a testimony to the state's agricultural prowess. About 60 miles northwest of Rochester, you'll find the bucolic college town of Northfield, a community with an interesting past and enough activities to please the entire family.

ROCHESTER: THE HOME OF MAYO

The huge medical facility that bears Mayo's name today is the centerpiece of Rochester. People from all over the world flock to the renowned **Mayo Clinic** for top-notch medical treatment. The facility is the driving force behind the city's strong economy and social conscience. The clinic is now the world's largest private medical center. Dr. Mayo, joined by his sons William James and Charles Horace, established the clinic in 1883, laying the foundation for the highly respected institution it is today. It boasts of 47 buildings, most of which are in downtown Rochester. The main facility is located at 200 First Street S.W., (507) 284-2511.

It all began when the elder Mayo came to the city to examine recruits for the Union Army during the Civil War and then stayed to set up a private practice. Two decades later, a windstorm devastated much of Rochester, with the armory serving as an emergency hospital. As a result, Mayo led the commu-

Two of the many buildings in the Mayo Clinic complex in Rochester. By permission of Mayo Foundation for Medical Education and Research.

nity drive to build a permanent medical facility. The complex eventually burgeoned into the clinic that handles more than 240,000 patients a year.

All this may not initially impress your children, but the story of the clinic can show them how great things can be achieved from humble beginnings. And a tour of the facility might provide the spark that inspires your boy or girl to become the next great neurosurgeon or gene researcher.

The clinic's international flavor makes Rochester a mini–United Nations, with more than 20,000 medical and support personnel from dozens of countries living and working in the city. Rochester is also a welcoming home to hundreds of refugees from other countries, especially Ethiopia and Somalia.

The clinic offers two public tours daily, Monday through Friday, in addition to an art-and-architecture tour on Tuesdays and Thursdays. One of the most impressive art pieces for the family to see is the brilliantly colored-glass *Wind Wall*, which shelters the entrance to the clinic. Artist Yaacov Agam produced a mobile sculpture entitled *Welcome* in the spacious clinic lobby. Other internationally known artists have also contributed works to brighten the many clinic buildings, among them are Therman Statom, Ivan Mestrovic, and Dale Chihuly. Two 60-foot photomurals in the subway level of the clinic depict the lives and times of Drs. William J. and Charles H. Mayo

Rotating medical exhibits can be seen in the **Patient Education Center**. Many families enjoy poking around behind the scenes here, which can be enlightening for older kids and teens who may be in town visiting sick relatives. A tour can be a welcome break from a day of bedside sitting.

Self-guided tours are also available at two hospitals closely affiliated with the clinic, **Rochester Methodist** and **St. Mary's**. Adults must accompany kids on all of these excursions. Both facilities have tour brochures and other information about their services at the entrance information booths.

Unfortunately, not all families that come to Rochester are just touring the sites. Sick youngsters have their own facility on the Mayo campus. The **Eugenio Litta Children's Hospital** is an 85-bed unit with age-specific areas, designed to meet the particular needs of each sick child. The staff here makes it easier for concerned parents to stay with their children, and for the kids to interact with others as medically appropriate.

The hospital is named after Eugenio Litta, who immigrated to America with his family in 1949. He died soon afterward with a ruptured appendix, "a condition which need not be fatal today," according to Dr. E. Rolland Dickson, the development director at the hospital. Mayo Eugenio Litta Children's Hospital was funded almost entirely by private gifts, including a substantial donation from the Switzerland-based Litta Foundation that was arranged in 1995. The hospital opened in 1996. The facility is within easy walking distance of the Ronald McDonald House, a hospitality facility that is available for families requiring extended stays.

SOME LEISURE-TIME ACTIVITIES

There are plenty of recreational activities for families while in Rochester, and young sports fans have some great options for fun experiences. One of the favorite choices is taking in a game at Rochester's premier baseball facility, **Mayo Field**. Named in honor of the clinic's founders, it's the home field of the Rochester Honkers baseball team. The Honkers consist of top college ball players recruited from around the country who want to keep up their skills during the summer after their collegiate seasons are over. Mayo Field is also home base for the Rochester A's, an American Legion amateur baseball team, and the Rochester Royals, another summer baseball team. Many families from around southern Minnesota, western Wisconsin, and northern Iowa trek to the various games to cheer on their heroes. A baseball-centered outing makes for a great quick getaway for the whole family, especially when combined with a restaurant stop and a night away from home. The field is located at 403 East Center Street.

Lots of Tourists

Each year, Minnesota welcomes more than 20 million tourists, who put more than $9.1 billion into the economy annually. The tourism industry employs about 170,300 Minnesotans.

Over the winter, the Rochester Mustangs hockey club provides more exciting action for young and old sports fans. The team plays from November through May at the **Rochester-Olmsted County Recreation Center** on the city's far north side.

For sports-minded family members who would rather "do" than "see," Rochester has several golf courses that are challenging enough for all skill levels. Young and old golfers wishing for relief love the accessibility of these links. There aren't any water hazards at **Eastwood Golf Course**, 3505 Eastwood Road S.E, but watch out for the hilly terrain. Call (507) 281-6173. For a quick round, **Northern Hills**, 4800 West Circle Drive N.W., is only eight minutes from downtown, carved out of the city's surrounding farmland. Call (507) 281-6170. The Root River ambles through the Maple Valley course, making the site one of the most scenic of the state's many golf facilities.

The links-style course at **Meadow Lakes**, 70 45th Avenue S.W., is merely five minutes of easy driving from Mayo Clinic, if a stress-reducing game is required after visiting hospitalized relatives. Call (507) 285-1190. **Oak Summit**, 2751 Airport Highway 16 S.W., is one of the most challenging in the Rochester area, where golfers brag that they get to use not just one, not just two, not just three, but all of their clubs in making their way across the rolling terrain. And a serious player, regardless of age, knows what that means. Call the course at (507) 252-1808.

Soldier's Memorial Field, 244 Soldier's Field Drive, is a short, easily walkable course over a relatively flat landscape fronting the Zumbro River. While the first nine holes at Willow Creek are across pancake-smooth links, the second nine take the dedicated duffer into the woods and along a creek. Thank heavens there is a lounge at the course for soft drinks and tall tales. Call (507) 281-6176. The **Rochester Country Club**, 3100 Country Club Road, is private; however, if vacationing guests are hosted here by a member, they can also take advantage of the swimming pool, platform tennis, driving range, and tennis courts. So, as the oldsters in the family get lost in the rough, the younger kids can cavort in comfort. Call (507) 282-3170.

Rochester is rightfully proud of its parks and public recreational facilities. Be sure to pack tennis racquets for any weekend visit. Courts can be found at John Marshall and Mayo high schools, the Rochester Athletic Club, the Rochester Tennis Center, the Rochester Indoor Tennis Club, and numerous parks.

Don't forget the swimsuits, either. In addition to several lodgings with indoor pools such as the Best Western–Apache, the Courtesy Inn, Super 8 Lodge South, and others, public swimming is part of the summer fun at Foster-Arends Park, Soldier's Field Pool, the Silver Lake Pool (with its kiddy splashing area), and the Rochester-Olmstead Recreation Center.

OUT AND ABOUT IN NATURE

Seven miles west of the city on Highway 14, **Chester Woods Park** has a swimming beach and bathhouse with showers and dressing rooms. Be aware, however, that no lifeguards are on duty so parents need to keep a close watch on the smaller fry. A park entrance permit is necessary. The **Skyline Raceway and Waterslide**, 2250 40th Street S.W., (507) 287-6289, is open from May through September, with enough water activities to satisfy any Pisces.

The **Quarry Hill Nature Center** is another outdoor outlet guaranteed to keep the tykes busy admiring nature's wonders. Hiking, biking, cross-country skiing, and snowshoeing are among the activities for families on this 270-acre site with its five miles of trails. An indoor facility offers displays on southeastern Minnesota's wildlife. Anglers in the family will press their noses against the glass of the 1,700-gallon aquarium and wish they brought along a fishing rod. The site is on the east edge of the city, about 12 to 15 minutes from downtown, at 701 Silver Creek Road N.E., (507) 281-6114. The center is free but donations are accepted. Get there now before the city's approaching sprawl encircles this haven of quiet.

AN ACTIVE ARTS SCENE

For the culturally and artistically inclined, Rochester offers up **Civic Music**, 201 Fourth Street S.E., a city-managed umbrella organization consisting of Rochester Civic Music Concert Band, the Concert Choir, Community Band, and the Summer Festival Choir. Each group performs at many of the above-mentioned events. Call (507) 281-8076. For theater, there are the **Rochester Civic Theater**, 220 East Center Street, (507) 282-8481, and the **Rochester Repertory Theater**, 314 1/2 South Broadway, (507) 289-1737. The **Masque Youth Theatre**, 14 Fourth Street S.W., (507) 287-0704, produces shows geared toward kids. The **Southeast Minnesota Youth Orchestra** regularly presents concerts around the community. Call (507) 282-1718 for schedule information.

Now, for a literary experience removed from the playing field or golf links, escort the family to the **Chateau Theater**, 15 First Street, S.W. This dazzling old building was built in 1927, with an outside marquee featuring 636 light bulbs. See if your mathematically inclined children can count that many. Refurbished in 1994, the old theatre has subsequently been turned into a luxurious Barnes and Noble Bookstore and Café. Enter through the theater's old lobby and aim for the kids' section with its extensive book selection. Authors regularly show up at the bookstore for readings and signings. Nobody minds if the kids curl up in the store's reading area to peruse a book before purchase.

For art, the free **Rochester Art Center** has a variety of programs and cultural events throughout the year, as well as ongoing exhibits. Just the thing for researching school art projects, the center's Sunday and Thursday series of videos focusing on major artists and their work are always popular. The center is at 320 East Center Street, (507) 282-8629.

The **Southeast Minnesota Visual Artists Gallery**, located on Peace Plaza in downtown Rochester, is a fine showcase for area painters and sculptors and just might give that budding young Picasso in your family some artistic inspiration. The gallery's selection of fabrics and clothing usually attracts the eye of even the most discerning teen shoppers. They often gravitate to the silk, hand-painted wearables by Mary Elizabeth Sheehan or to Anne Black-Sinak's jewelry. Dave Dunn's spinning tops and other wooden items are of interest to the younger crowd.

For every panel they utilize, the 70 or so artists renting space in the gallery each donate two four-hour shifts a month working in the shop. It makes a good lesson on co-operative economics for kids taking business classes. The gallery is at 16 First Street S.W., (507) 281-4920.

Peace Plaza was created when First Street was cordoned off by the construction of the Galleria shopping mall at the east end of the block. A plaza fountain with a flock of brass doves emphasizes the peace theme. The Chateau Theater, with its bookstore, is directly across the plaza from the gallery.

The **Olmsted County Historical Center and Museum**, 1195 West Circle Drive, (507) 282-9447, is another interesting place to spend part of a vacation weekend. The museum is open year-round, with exhibits relating Rochester's colorful past. Take note of the displays tracking the city's medical heritage. From Memorial Day through Labor Day, you can also explore the William Dee log cabin, a refurbished pioneer home, and the Hadley Valley School House, a one-room school with all the pioneers' teaching trimmings, which will surely astound youngsters more used to computer keyboards.

The younger set will love scurrying along the pathways through the formal gardens of the **Plumber House of the Arts**, a 49-room mansion built by Dr. Henry S. Plumber at 1091 Plummer Lane S.W., (507) 281-6160. There is a bird trail, quarry, and water tower on the grounds, as well. The mansion is open for self-guided tours on Wednesday afternoons from June through August.

Tax Break, Kinda

In Minnesota, there is no sales tax for items like groceries, clothing, and medicine. However, there is a tax of 6.5% for everything else, plus a local tax of 0.5%, and a lodging tax of 3%.

Finally, there is yet another attraction bearing the Mayo name that is worth a look-see. **Mayowood Mansion**, 3720 S.W. Mayowood Road, was home to three generations of the family and is open for tours from May through October. It has over 40 rooms full of European and American antiques. Call (507) 289-5481 for a tour schedule; or e-mail businessoffice@olmstedhistory.com.

Rochester is a city full of year-round events. Among the many family-oriented events to consider are the Arts and Crafts Show and the Rochester Figure Skating Club Ice Show in April; Rochesterfest in June; a Greek Festival, Down by the Riverside concerts, and a Blues Fest in August; the Three Rivers Ren-

The 40-room Mayowood Mansion, home to three generations of the Mayo family. Minnesota Office of Tourism photograph.

dezvous and the Fall Harvest Festival at Quarry Hill in September; a Festival of Trees and Mayowood holiday tours in November; and Yule Fest in December.

NASTIES IN NORTHFIELD

The kids will certainly get a kick out of Northfield's main claim to fame and the attendant activities that are planned around it. The story goes that on September 7, 1887, Jessie James and a bunch of his thievin' cohorts rode into Northfield and shook up the quiet community with gunfire, murder, and general mayhem. The James-Younger Gang had thundered into town to rob the First National Bank, then hightailed it out of the place in only seven minutes, leaving behind the bodies of two townspeople and two robbers . . . and all the money. Up to 1,000 men joined a posse in hot pursuit, capturing a couple of the gang members in a bog north of town. Jesse himself, however, made it out of the state and into the Dakota wilds.

Even though the incident took place more than a hundred years ago, it still makes the home folk proud. So, why not celebrate? Subsequently, the **Defeat of Jesse James Days** festival is held the first September weekend following Labor Day. The four-day fest is perfect for a visiting family looking for a little weekend excitement and wanting to do it inexpensively. The event features colorful reenactments of the bank raid, a rodeo, tractor pull, carnival, art fair, and concerts.

Bad guys galloping through Northfield during the city's annual Defeat of Jesse James Days.
—Courtesy of the Northfield Area Chamber of Commerce

Motorists can also follow the gang's trail with a handy driving guide provided by the Northfield Area Chamber of Commerce. Trace the route from Mankato through the small towns on the way to Northfield and follow the track taken when the desperados retreated.

The city, of course, now offers many more events that capture the spirit of the local residents. Tops on the list are the **Rice County Steam and Gas Engine threshing show** on Labor Day weekend and the **Music City Minnesota Winter Festival** in February, with its variety of musical acts, along with a softball tournament. Every Thursday evening in the summer, much of the town gathers at **Bridge Square** for concerts, an ice-cream social, variety shows, and even the occasional pie-baking contest. In addition, **St. Olaf College**, 1520 St. Olaf Avenue, (507) 646-2222, presents an annual Christmas festival, which draws thousands of guests to town to see a show usually broadcast on public radio. Concerts and plays are also offered at **Carleton College**, 1 North College Street, (507) 646-4000, Northfield's second fine institution of higher learning.

The city distributes maps for walking tours around town, earmarking historical buildings and other attractions. You can get a map from the Northfield Area Chamber of Commerce at 205 Third Street West, or by calling (507) 645-5604 or (800) 658-2548. Take in the museum that is located next to the restored **First National Bank** from which James and company attempted to make a major withdrawal those many years ago. Both buildings have rotating exhibits, highlighting the city's past. Contributing to the displays are the Northfield Historical Society, the Minnesota Historical Society and other research outlets. A small museum store has loads of kid-oriented goodies earmarked for the souvenir trade. The museum and shop are located at 408 Division Street, (507) 645-9268.

Or take a walk past 319 Water Street South where portions of a gristmill have survived as part of the **Malt-O-Meal cereal plant**. Northfield is the only city where the popular hot breakfast dish is produced. Another Malt-O-Meal plant is on Highway 19 West.

The city parks offer a wide range of activities, so be sure to bring hiking boots, snowshoes, skis, or whatever else is appropriate for the season. **Odd Fellows Park** on Forest Avenue offers 20 pleasant acres of open and wooded space with a playground and nature area. **Riverside**, **Babcock**, and **Sechler Parks** also provide the perfect getaway spot for a bit of rest and recuperation for the harried traveler and children. The **Cannon River** flows through town and is a popular draw for canoe lovers. For those who enjoy trees and flowers, the **Carleton Arboretum** has 13 miles of trails on which to enjoy Minnesota's best flora and a bit of fauna.

Naturally, if the teens offer a golf challenge to the older folks in the vacation crew, Northfield's courses are ready for any level of familial competition. The **Northfield Golf Club**, an 18-holer at 707 Prairie Street, is on the eastern edge of the city. Call (507) 645-4020. **Willingers**, 10 miles west of Northfield at 6900 Canby Trail, is another fine public course. Contact the facility at (952) 652-2500.

If hot and sweaty after a round of holes-in-one, head to the outdoor public swimming pool at East Fifth and Elm Streets. Shower first and then jump in. The tiny tots will love the wading pool.

Finally, what would the James boys say if they came back to Northfield today and saw the sign outside the **Jesse James Lanes and Lounge**, 1700 U.S. Highway 3 South, and all the folks having a great time inside here. Well, they'd probably park their horses, check their spurs, and bowl away the evening, winding down with a pizza. Call (507) 645-6062 to see if the desperadoes are there.

Now would the James guys have had as much fun if they had stuck around? At least they'd be close to good medical care.

PLACES TO STAY

NORTHFIELD
AmericInn Motel and Suites, 1320 Bollenbacker Drive, (507) 645-7761 or (800) 634-3444; www.americinn.com

College City Motel, 875 U.S. Highway 3 North, (507) 645-4426 or (800) 775-0455

Country Inn, 300 U.S. Highway 3 South, (507) 645-2286

Riverview Legacy Motel, 205 St. Olaf Avenue, (507) 645-9980 or (800) 787-5337

Super 8 Motel, 1420 Riverview Drive, (507) 663-0371 or (800) 800-8000; www.super8.com

ROCHESTER

AmericInn Hotel and Suites, 5708 U.S. Highway 52 N.W., East Frontage Road, (800) 634-3444; www.americinn.com

Best Western-Apache, 1517 16th Street N.W., (800) 552-7224

Best Western–Soldier's Field Tower and Suites, 401 Sixth Street S.W., (507) 288-2677 or (800) 528-1234; www.bestwestern.com

Days Inn–South, 111 S.E. 28th Street, (507) 286-1001 or (800) 325-2525

Kahler Grand Hotel, 20 S.W. Second Avenue, (507) 280-6200 or (800) 533-1655; www.sunstonehotels.com. Reservations, www.kahler.com

Radisson Plaza Hotel, 150 South Broadway, (507) 281-8000 or (800) 333-3333, www.radisson.com/rochester

Rochester/Marion KOA Campground, 5232 65th Avenue, (507) 202-7005 or (800) 562-5232, rochesterkoa@qwest.net

Ronald McDonald House, 850 Second Street S.W., (507) 282-3955, mhickey@ronhouserochmn.org

Super 8 Motel South, 106 21st Street, (507) 282-1756 or (800) 800-8000; www.super8.com

Travelers Hotel, 426 Second Street S.W., (507) 289-4095 or (800) 255-3050

PLACES FOR FOOD

NORTHFIELD

Byzantine Cafe and Catering, 201 Water Street South, (507) 645-2400

Diamond Dave's Mexican Restaurante, 302B Division Street, (507) 663-1056

Hogan Brothers Acoustic Cafe, 415 Division Street, (507) 645-6653

Mandarin Garden Restaurant, 107 Fourth Street East, (507) 645-7101

Ole Store and Cafe, 1101 St. Olaf Avenue, (507) 645-5558

ROCHESTER

American Table Restaurant, 1635 Highway 52 North, (507) 289-9020

Broadstreet Cafe and Bar, 300 First Avenue N.W., (507) 281-2451

Cheap Charlie's, 11 Fifth Street N.W., (507) 289-9591

Colonial Inn House Cafe, 114 Second Street S.W., (507) 285-0714

Daube's Bakery-Pavilion Subway, 155 First Avenue S.W., (507) 252-8878

Grandma's Kitchen, 1514 Broadway Avenue North, (507) 289-0331

Michael's Restaurant and Lounge, 15 Broadway Avenue South, (507) 288-2020

Newt's, 216 First Avenue South, (507) 289-0577

Roscoe's Root Beer and Ribs, 4180 18th Avenue, (507) 281-4622

Wong's Cafe, 4 Third Street S.W., (507) 282-7545

PLACES TO SHOP

NORTHFIELD

The Art Store, 314 Division Street, (507) 663-0021

Bows and Britches, 508 Division Street, (507) 645-2772

Cocoa Bean Confectionery, 302 Division Street, (507) 645-5322

Fine Grove Records, 509 Division Street, (507) 645-7146

Hodge-Podge Que, 309 Water Street South, (507) 645-0760

Jacobsen's family store, 419 Division Street, (507) 645-4672

Oolala Gifts, 320 Division Street, (507) 645-5275

Present Perfect, 411 Division Street, (507) 645-9131

ROCHESTER

Antique Mall on Third Street, 118 S.W. Third Street, (507) 287-0684

Apache Mall Shopping Center, 702 Apache Mall, Highways 14 and 52, (507) 288-8056

Galleria Centerplace Mall, 111 South Broadway, (507) 281-1364

Kahler Complex, First Avenue S.W. and First Street S.W. (in the Kahler Grand and Marriott Hotels), (507) 280-6200

Old Stonehouse Antiques, 1901 Bamber Valley Road S.W., (507) 282-8497

FOR MORE INFORMATION

Northfield Area Chamber of Commerce/Convention and Visitors Bureau, 205 Third Street West, Northfield 55057-1098, (507) 645-5604 or (800) 658-2548

Rochester Convention and Visitors Bureau, 150 South Broadway, #A, Rochester 55904, (507) 288-4331 or (800) 288-4331

THE GREAT RIVER ROAD

Motoring along the Mississippi River from Hastings to Wabasha and beyond is one of the loveliest trips in Minnesota, no matter what the season. Highway 61 and the various state and county roads that spin off from the main artery lead the vacationing family to neat places that are historic and exciting. You could even say it's "romantic," but that might get rolling eyeballs and groans from the backseat gang. Yet go ahead and be a bit gushy anyway. After all, you're in the front seat.

The river forms a major backdrop for a marvelous journey, with secrets around almost every curve. Be sure to stop and look at the passing waters from the many observation points along the way. Lake Pepin, where the Mississippi broadens to more than a mile across in some places, is a draw for sailboaters, fishing fans, and anyone else who loves this ancient flowage.

Drive slowly southward to Wabasha. Remember, it's not cheating to hop-scotch across the river once in awhile to the Wisconsin side and drive along Highway 35 where there are other neat communities. They're all part of the Mississippi Valley Partners tourism promotional program: Maiden Rock, Stockholm, Pepin, Nelson, and Alma are the major communities to explore. They can be reached via the Highway 63 bridge in Red Wing or the Highway 25 bridge at Wabasha.

Both Highway 61 in Minnesota and Highway 35 in Wisconsin are part of the **Great River Road Scenic Byway** system, hailed by travel writers and tourism officials as "America's Great Undiscovered Scenic Drive." Spend a day, weekend, or week exploring the drive's not-so-secret secrets. Follow the green-and-white pilot-wheel signs to all sorts of family adventures.

HOP TO HISTORICAL HASTINGS

Hastings abounds in historical charm; however, the town's past shows no evidence of having been invaded by Jesse James and crew, as was the case with Northfield, 27 miles to the southwest. As a result, the kids might need some motivation to get them enthused about a visit, but that shouldn't be hard to find. Hastings, the seat of Dakota County, started as a trading post in 1833 and was incorporated in 1857 when it had about 1,918 people. Compare that with

Downtown Hastings, a city chock full of historic charm.
Minnesota Office of Tourism photograph.

St. Paul's population of 1,700 in the same year. The folks here did very well for themselves over the years in the wider world of business, politics, and the arts.

Today, the city has 62 buildings on the National Register of Historic Places, including 34 business buildings and 28 private homes. A heritage map, with details on a self-guided walking or driving tour around town to see these places, is available at city hall 101 4th Street East, or at the chamber of commerce and tourism office, both located in the same building at 111 Third Street East. The stroll is easy on a pleasant day, so even the kids could manage it without much fuss.

Some of the places seen on the walkabout include the Olson House, 4124-416 West Second Street, a neat Victorian building with a gabled roof, and the **Octagon House**, 209 West Second Street. Orson Squire Fowler, who believed that a house was a "machine built for living," built the Octagon House in 1857. Fowler said that he wanted "less wall to surround more space, a concentration of water, waste and heat through a central stack system and no wasted hall space." He built his place out of concrete blocks, but added a wraparound porch for a little bit of comfort. At least his kids didn't break anything if they bounced off the walls.

Hastings is the place to find porches in all their glory. It seems like most of the homes in the older section of the city sport expansive verandas with all the appropriate swings and furniture suitable for enjoying the lazy days of summer. Several times throughout the past few years, Hastings has sponsored front porch festivals or a history/heritage program, usually in May, where families can admire the carpentry craftsmanship that went into the construction of verandas and similar distinguishing architectural appendages. Check with the chamber of commerce, however, for dates of any such programs because they are held irregularly.

Located about 20 miles southeast of St. Paul, Hastings has long been a commercial hub because of its location on the Mississippi River where it is joined by the free-flowing Vermillion and St. Croix Rivers. The city's annual **Rivertown Days** in mid-July brings back memories of the good old days when the rivers were the mercantile lifeblood in these parts. Most of the activities occur in Jaycee Park off the Lock and Dam Road, a few blocks from downtown. A fishing competition is held in Lake Rebecca, along with an arts-and-crafts fair at Vermillion Falls Park. Shuttle buses link the sites, preventing a parking stampede. A brilliantly lighted flotilla of boats cruises past the Hastings harbor on Saturday evening, which is sure to elicit some "ooohs" and "aaaahs" from the kids.

These days, instead of steamboats picking up and delivering goods, the city is a merchandising hub for the surrounding smaller towns. Shoppers have a grand time exploring the downtown; Westview, with its mall and adjacent stores; the Midtown shopping area at the junction of Highways 35 and 55; and Southtown, which hosts antique stores, as well as the Civic Arena and a number of good restaurants.

THE GREAT OUTDOORS

Rather than shop, the kids would probably prefer to poke around outside at any one of several area parks. Within the city, the visitor can find Roadside Park, Vermillion Falls Park, Lake Rebecca with its "Idlers' Island" in the middle, Jaycee Park, and the downtown riverfront Levee Park. Scattered throughout the system are tennis courts, ball diamonds, and picnic areas.

Dakota County's **Spring Lake Park Preserve**, on the northwest side of town, has cross-country ski trails in the winter and hiking opportunities during the other three seasons. Picnickers flock to the preserve's Schaar's Bluff for its views overlooking the river valley. The preserve also has a wide field used by local model-airplane clubs. Call (651) 438-4660. Also nearby is the 11-acre **Vermillion Falls Park**, located off Highway 61 on 21st Street East. The park is a perfect place for still more picnicking, as well as hiking and biking. The little park offers a grand view of the falls and its 75-foot drop. The park is located south of a rank of towering grain elevators, 60 to 80 feet tall and capable of holding 26,000 to 32,000 bushels each, temples to the wheat industry of Minnesota.

Afton State Park remains another big draw, especially for the Twin Cities set because getting there is easy via I-94. Nine miles east of St. Paul, take County Highway 15 for seven miles, then another three miles east on County Road 20. The park is north of Hastings along the St. Croix River bluffs. Hikers and cross-country skiers appreciate the rolling hillsides guaranteed to

Big falls in a small park at Vermillion Falls Park. —Courtesy of Hastings Chamber of Commerce

loosen tight muscles. Kids find it fun to hike to the 24 primitive campsites at Afton. It is about a three-quarter mile walk to the sites from the parking lot beneath the towering shade trees and across some broad grassy openings splashed with sunlight.

Yet some folks—who don't want to do all that trekking—simply enjoy the picnicking opportunities in the park. Yet be sure to get the required daily Minnesota state park pass, or, wiser yet, go for the annual permit for year-long admission to state parks all over Minnesota. For more information, contact Afton State Park, 6959 Peller Avenue South, (651) 436-5391.

The **Carpenter St. Croix Valley Nature Center** has an extensive menu of things to do for nature lovers, especially youngsters. Located across the river at 12805 St. Croix Trail South, Hastings, the center has an outstanding two-mile, self-guided hiking route that takes walkers through wooded ravines, an oak savanna, and an old orchard. There are several longer trails, as well. Children enjoy visiting the wildlife rehabilitation hospital, which nurses sick and injured birds and animals back to health. On the Sunday closest to the Fourth of July, the center hosts Summerfolk, a festival highlighting folk singers and children's games. Call (651) 437-4359 for more information and details on programs and courses that can fill a day or so on a short visit to the region.

A stop at the **Alexis Bailly Vineyard**, 18200 Kirby Avenue, is a good way to conclude a visit to the Hastings area. The jolly ol' vintner offers regular tours and a major open house in June. In 1973, Minneapolis Attorney David A. Bailly purchased a 20-acre plot of rye and replanted it with French grapes. He selected hardy varieties that could withstand Minnesota's frosty winters. The results of his maturing vintages have been impressive, as his wines have won at least 45 awards. Bailly's daughter Nan is now the master winemaker. The kids will learn about grapes and growing, while the grownups can check the labels. The winery makes several varieties, including Mar'chal Foch, a fine dry red; Hastings Reserve, a lip-smacking, heavy dessert wine; Syval Blanc, a crisp, dry white; and several other wines. Hmmm, good. Call (651) 437-1413.

RECONNOITER RED WING

The family can get a foot up on scouting the Great River Road in Red Wing, home of the fabled shoe company that still bears the city name. Red Wing Shoes was established in 1905, and the company's quality lives on. The **Red Wing Shoe Museum**, with photographs and a vintage 1925 film showing how the footwear was made, is in the front lobby of the company's corporate office in the Riverfront Centre. A shoe store is also located there, serving mostly an adult market. But if a teen has big enough feet, there should be a pair or two on the shelves that fit. The actual shoe factory is a block to the south of the Riverfront Centre. The museum and store are located at 314 Main Street, (651) 388-8211.

Red Wing Stoneware Company and **Red Wing Pottery** also take the visiting clan back to the days when the city was a center for making bowls, dishes, and related kitchenware. The renovated Pottery Place, once the huge factory where the potters worked, is now a warren of antique shops. Historic displays are scattered around the mall, located on the west side of town. Red Wing Stoneware is at 4909 Moundview Drive, four miles west of town on Highway 61, (651) 388-4610 or (800) 352-4877. Red Wing Pottery is at 2000 Old West Main Street, (651) 388-3562 or (800) 228-0174; www.redwingpottery.com.

The historic, Italianate-style **St. James Hotel**—constructed in 1875—brings up visions of long-ago paddle wheelers. Guests in those good old Victorian days used to dock at the boat landing and stroll up a hill to reach the hotel, where they could be assured of a wonderful meal and a grand night's sleep. Occasionally, one of today's staffers dresses up in 19th-century garb to greet visitors. Be sure the kids stroll along the halls to look at all the old riverfront photographs. In fact, each room is named after a different riverboat. With this heritage, the hotel is a proud centerpiece of Red Wing's downtown refurbishment. Contact the hotel at 406 Main Street, (651) 388-2846 or (800) 252-1875, www.st-james-hotel.com.

Just below the hotel is **Levee Park** and a train depot dating from 1904, now home to the convention and visitors bureau and the chamber of commerce. Have the kids load up here on information about the community.

The **Sheldon Theatre** is another jewel in Red Wing's crown of fabled old buildings. The facility opened in 1904 and was renovated in 1987. Public tours, as well as a multimedia program on the history of the city are given from Thursday through Saturday, June to October and on Saturdays, November through May. By sitting through the informative show, the kids will learn a lot

Big Shot River

The Cannon River, which flows from Faribault to Red Wing, is included in Minnesota's Wild and Scenic River System. French explorers called it the "river of canoes" because of its calm, scenic beauty. Yet when English-speaking settlers arrived, they mistranslated "canoes" as "cannon," and the more explosive name stuck.

about the area and its businesses. The theater is located at Third Street and East Avenue, (651) 385-3667 or (800) 899-5759; www.sheldontheatre.org.

The **Goodhue County Historical Museum** is a fine place to get in touch with local history. The building, located at 1166 Oak Street, (651) 388-6024; www.goodhuehistory.mus.mn.us, overlooks the downtown and offers plenty of background on the days when Red Wing was jumping as boats from up- and downriver stopped to load and unload goods and visitors. Another scenic view of the city can be had by hiking to the top of **Barn Bluff**, with its paths and staircases leading skyward from East Fifth Street. See which of the family can reach the top first—without being too winded.

When leaving Red Wing, stop in at **Colville Park**, which is right on Highway 61, and look for bald eagles during the winter. During other seasons, mallards, great blue herons, gulls, and even such wonderful birds as common mergansers can be spotted. Hand over the binoculars and bird identification book to the youngsters and see which species they can identify.

A spectacular view of Highway 61 and the Mississippi River from the Minnesota bluffs. Minnesota Office of Tourism photoraph.

FROLIC AT FRONTENAC

One of the best overlooks along the entire drive (or any drive, for that matter) is located along the ridges that soar 400 feet over the river at **Frontenac State Park.** The park has 14 miles of hiking trails that meander off to a number of excellent viewing stations where you can gaze over miles of spectacular scenery. From Red Wing, take Highway 61 south for 10 miles, then turn east on County Highway 2, which leads into the park. For more details, contact the park manager at Route 2, Box 134, Lake City 55041, or call (651) 345-3401.

A favorite time is spring, when the prairie land in the park seems to explode in a cacophony of color. Purple, yellows, oranges, whites—bring plenty of color film and/or an artist's easel for capturing the mood. Turn the kids loose with a small point-and-shoot camera to see what images they can capture. Some photos might be silly but they are all grist for the scrapbook. A childlike eye can often capture the most dazzling scenes.

Migrating birds, as well as turkey vultures, warblers, and ducks, fill the sky and populate the ponds overhead and directly below in the river bottoms. The park has bird lists to help identify species.

In the winter, the park presents six miles of groomed cross-country ski trails, with snowmobiling allowed on eight separate miles of pathways. These trails link with another 400 miles of routes outside the park boundaries. Stuff as many inner tubes, sleds, and toboggans into the backseat as you can (but don't forget the kids) and head for the slopes at Frontenac State Park. Hardly anything can top a full Saturday and Sunday of skimming down a hill. It's similar to being aboard a Jack London dog sled. Let those imaginations rip!

Be sure to check out the nearby village of Frontenac, founded in the 1850s, to gawk at the stately homes that are more than a century old. Once dubbed the "Newport of the Northwest," Frontenac was a vacation getaway for summer visitors from Minneapolis, St. Paul, and points beyond. They were attracted by the natural beauty of the region, as well as the peace and quiet far from the maddening crowds in the Cities. The Villa Maria Center here was once a girls' school and is now a conference center.

An Early Church

A Jesuit mission at Fort Beauharnois, on the Mississippi River near today's village of Frontenac, was built in 1727. It marked the farthest reach of French exploration at the time, and the military needed a garrison to keep an eye on the frontier. Inside the fort was a chapel, now considered by historians to be one of the first "churches" in Minnesota. Flooding and warfare between the Fox and Dakota tribes drove out the French in 1729.

A boatload of pumpkins along the Great River Road.

Hanson's Harbor provides access to the river, with a full-service marina, a boat ramp if you bring your own yacht, and a store that has everything from fast food to engine oil.

TAKE A DIP IN LAKE CITY

A 2.5-mile public walkway along the Mississippi River's open shoreline offers a front-row seat to watch the fishing folk and the boaters doing their vacation thing in Lake City, a couple of miles south of Frontenac. **Roschen Park** hosts a public fish-cleaning house, just the place to show the little ones the intricacies of scaling and gutting the night's meal. The city hosts numerous fishing tournaments so there always seems to be some sort of bait-casting frenzy in the town during fishing season. Walleye and striped bass are the overwhelming game-fish favorites among the 85 or so species of fish found in the nearby waters.

This community really gets into full festival swing the last weekend of each June during **Water Ski Days**. The event attracts upwards of 20,000 folks who love the classic car parade, concerts, and carnival rides. The festival honors Ralph W. Samuelson, who invented waterskiing in 1922 when he was only 18 years old. Samuelson strapped some boards to his feet and had an old powerboat tow him across the river. And thus the sport was born. Show the kids a statue on Lake City's main drag that memorializes Samuelson. At least the teens should be impressed.

CAMP LACUPOLIS

Fishing fans from around the Midwest flock to the village of Camp Lacupolis every year to try their luck. Here, the main channel of the Mississippi and its many backwaters are home to striped bass, carp, walleye, and many other delicious species. Fishing cabins and condos range the shoreline, offering accommodations in any style for the die-hard outdoors lover.

Lacupolis is Greek for "lake city," so named because the town was once a stopover for highfalutin visitors on their way to nearby Lake City, nine miles upriver. It is now a fantastic place to watch bald eagles in the winter, while sitting near your ice-fishing shack. Bring a thermos of hot chocolate for the smallest fisherfolk in your party.

READS LANDING

Reads Landing is just a little farther south on Highway 61. The town got its start as a trading post operated by a French-Canadian/Native American named Augustin Rocque. In 1847, Charles Read, a former British soldier, bought the property and expanded the business. He was just in time to capitalize on its prime location at the mouth of the Chippewa River where it flowed into the Mississippi on the Wisconsin side. The timber trade was just picking up and the lumberjacks needed a place to party and resupply. Reads Landing became the place to be, with its 27 hotels, 21 saloons, and the second brick schoolhouse built in Minnesota.

The school now houses a large collection of Laura Ingalls Wilder memorabilia. Any child who loves reading the famed author's books about growing up on the frontier will enjoy a stroll through the facility. Wilder was born in Wisconsin, just across the river from Reads Landing. *Her Little House in the Woods* and others in her series spawned a loyal following of young readers and formed the basis for the famous television show. Today, barges are pushed by muscular towboats in the river, harkening back to the era when lumberjacks floated huge log rafts downstream from the landing.

GOOD TIME IN AN OLD TOWN

Historic Wabasha, 12 miles south of Lake City, claims it was the first real town in Minnesota, established in the early 1830s. Three museums testify to the fact that there is at least a lot of old stuff around to admire. The town is also a fun place for strolling, with plenty of refurbished old buildings to explore.

These days, Wabasha is better known as the home to the *Grumpy Old Men* movies starring the late Jack Lemmon and Walter Matthau. Each February, the Grumpy Old Men Festival celebrates these films, with ice-fishing competitions, and even a nine-hole golf course set up on ice. The weekend is topped off with a massive spaghetti dinner and dance ... if anyone can still move after all those carbs.

Lake Pepin

Lake Pepin, a wide spot on the Mississippi River between Red Wing and Wacouta, was called *Pem-vee-cha-mday* ("Lake of the Mountains") by the local Native Americans. The "lake" was formed by the Chippewa River, which enters the Mississippi 34 miles downstream. Sediment carried by the Chippewa created an underwater dam that backed up the Mississippi and formed the lake.

Eagle watching is best along the river, where they feed on gizzard shad, which are abundant during the winter. The Mississippi here seldom freezes over, as it does farther north. Subsequently, an avid eagle watcher can spot dozens of the magnificent birds drifting lazily on the updrafts before plunging down for a free lunch.

On the route, young girls will discover **The Girls**, located across from the Wabasha High School, where they can find all sorts of dolls, dollhouse furniture, and clothing. The shop is geared toward the collector, yet wide-eyed children can have a fun feast just looking over the grand array of toys.

KELLOGG

Even the smallest kid can admire the scenery around the next stop along Highway 61, tiny Kellogg. It is a visual delight, with maple-blanketed limestone bluffs rearing high over the rolling waters of the Mississippi and Zumbro Rivers. The area is rich with wildlife, perfect for bird and critter watching. So be sure to pack binoculars and cameras with telephoto lenses so everyone in the family can get a close look at the Canada geese, tundra swans, muskrats, and turtles that call the backwaters their home. Six miles southeast of town, the Nature Conservancy manages 700 acres of prairie sand dunes where budding biologists can look for the rare Blandings turtle and burgeoning botanists can check out all the wildflowers.

Kellogg is a picnic place, with a large park in the center of town that is perfect for a noonday stop while driving along the Great River Road. There are also rest areas on County Highway 18 near town, where your gang can tumble out of the minivan, stretch their legs, and release some energy. For added fun, the town has hosted the annual **Watermelon Festival**—always the weekend after Labor Day—since 1946. The festival draws vacationers and locals to its parade, truck and tractor pulls, carnival, and, naturally, plentiful supply of watermelon. Stock up on moist towelettes to "unstick" the little ones.

One of the most exciting places along this stretch of the Great River Road is the **L.A.R.K. Toy Store** with its hand-carved carousel animals, a museum, a bakery, and a gift shop. The name of the store is an acronym for "Lost Arts Revival by Kreofsky," referring to shop owner Donn Kreofsky, who started the operation in 1983. He says L.A.R.K. is dedicated to bringing back toys made of wood. There are pull toys, trucks, trains, hand puppets, dolls, craft and birdhouse kits, nesting dolls, and loads of other articles for sale, all designed with children in mind. In 1998, after seven years of work, Kreofsky finished his giant merry-go-round with 19 hand-carved and hand-painted characters. The scent of wood shavings permeates the building, where kids and adults can watch the artisans at work creating all sorts of fanciful creatures.

The accompanying **Moose Tracks Museum** is packed with thousands of toys from the early 1900s through the 1960s, a real treat for tykes, who can learn how toys have changed over the generations. There is also a large bookstore, with everything from the classics to unusual ABC books and laminated posters. Families can also eat in the Rocking Café, getting a fill of hot dogs with a view of the Mississippi River bluffs outside the windows. After lunch, save time for the mom and dad in the family. Stroll through Baby Boomer Heaven, which is stocked with toys for grownups, such as super-sized pedal cars, lead soldiers, and robots. The sprawling complex is located just north of the junction of Highway 61 and Highway 42. Call (507) 767-3387, or visit www.larktoys.com. Visitor information for Kellogg can also be found here. You can also get tourist facts on the area from the Mississippi Valley Travel Partners Web site at www. Mississippi-river.org/kellogg or by calling the Kellogg Village Hall at (507) 767-4953.

Clam Up

In the early 1900s, more than 500 clammers worked the riverbeds of the Mississippi near Lake Pepin collecting bivalves. They then sent the clams to button factories at Lake City.

PLACES TO STAY

CAMP LACUPOLIS
Camp Lacupolis campground, R.R. 4, U.S. Highway 61, (651) 565-4318; winter (507) 324-5216

HASTINGS
AmericInn, 2400 Vermillion Street, (651) 437-8877 or (800) 634-3444; www.americinn.com

Country Inn and Suites, 300 33rd Street, (651) 437-8870 or (800) 456-4000

Hastings Inn, 1520 Vermillion Street, (651) 437-3155

Super 8 Motel, Highway 61 and 25th Street, (651) 438-8888 or (800) 800-8000; www.super8.com

LAKE CITY

Lac Lani Guest Cottage, 317 Park Street, (651) 345-5756

Red Gables Inn, 403 North High Street, (651) 345-2605 or (888) 345-2605; www.redgablesinn.com

RED WING

AmericInn, 1819 Old West Main Street, (651) 385-9060 or (800) 634-3444; www.americinn.com

Best Western Quiet House and Suites, 752 Withers Harbor Drive, (651) 388-1577

Moondance Inn, 1105 West Fourth Street, (651) 388-8145 or (866) 388-8145; www.moondanceinn.com

Parkway Motel, 3425 U.S. Highway 61, (651) 388-8231 or (800) 762-0934

WABASHA

Eagles on the River, 50 Coulee Way, (651) 565-4561; www.EaglesOnTheRiver.com

Wabasha Motel, 1110 East Hiawatha Drive, (651) 565-9932

PLACES FOR FOOD

HASTINGS

The Mississippi Belle, 101 East Second Street, (651) 437-4814

Perkins Family Restaurant, 1206 Vermillion Street, (651) 437-5028

Taco Johns, 1217 Vermillion Street, (651) 437-2925

LAKE CITY

Chickadee Cottage, 317 North Lakeshore Drive, (651) 345-5155 or (888) 321-5177

The Galley, 100 East Lyon Avenue, (651) 345-9991

RED WING

Liberty's Restaurant and Lounge, Third and Plum Streets, (651) 388-8877

Maries, 217 Plum Street, (651) 388-1896

Perkins, U.S. Highway 61 and Withers Harbor Drive, (651) 385-0783

Staghead, 219 Bush Street, (651) 388-6581

Tea Room and Gift Shoppe, 204 West Seventh Street, (651) 388-2250

WABASHA

Eagle Nest Coffee House, Second and Bridge Streets, (651) 565-2077; www.eaglesnestcoffeehouse.com

Eagle Valley Cafe, 1130 Hiawatha Drive, (651) 565-2040

PLACES TO SHOP

HASTINGS

The Gift Tree, 1266 Frontage Road, (651) 437-5090

Fancy That, 110 East Second Street, (651) 437-6851

Just Thinking Bookstore, 1303 Eddy Street, (651) 438-3696

KELLOGG

Bouquet's Factory Outlet, 3818 Belvidere Avenue, (507) 767-4986

SVJ Creative Designs, 191 State Highway 42, (507) 767-3039

LAKE CITY

Bushel and Peck, 35878 U.S. Highway 61 North, (651) 345-4516 or (800) 4-BUSHEL; www.bushel-peck.com

First Mate's Gift House, 1015 North Lake Shore Drive, (651) 345-5169; www.firstmates.com

Home Traditions, 106 South Lake Shore Drive, (651) 345-2017

RED WING

Al's Antique Mall, 1314 Old West Main Street, (651) 388-0572 or (888) 388-0572

Antiques of Red Wing, 415 Main Street, (651) 385-5963

Hiawatha Valley Ranch, three miles south on U.S. Highway 61, (651) 388-4033

Hobgoblin Music, 920 State Highway 19, (651) 388-8400 or (877) 866-3936; info@stoneyend.com

Main Street Toys, 318 Main Street, Riverfront Centre, (651) 388-5900

Red Wing Antique Emporium, 420-430 West Third Street, (651) 267-0689 or (888) 407-0371

Red Wing Book Company, 406 Main Street, St. James Hotel Shopping Court, (651) 388-7274

WABASHA

The Girls, 2206 Hiawatha Drive, (651) 565-4026

Old City Hall, 257 West Main Street, (651) 565-2585

WW Mercantile, 254 West Main Street, (651) 565-2617; www.wwmercantile.com

FOR MORE INFORMATION:

Hastings Area Chamber of Commerce and Tourism Bureau, 111 East Third Street, Hastings 55033-1211, (651) 437-6775 or (888) 612-6122; www.hastingsmn.org

Kellogg City Hall, Kellogg 55945, (507) 767-4953

Lake City Tourism Bureau, 1515 Lakeshore Drive North, Lake City 55041, (877) 525-3248; www.lakecity.org.

Mississippi Valley Partners, Box 407, Pepin, WI 54759, (888) 999-2619; www.mississippi-river.org

Red Wing Chamber of Commerce, 418 Levee Street, Red Wing 55066, (800) 762-7519; www.redwingchamber.com

Red Wing Visitors and Convention Bureau, 418 Levee Street, Red Wing 55066, (800) 498-3444

Wabasha Area Chamber of Commerce, 257 Main Street West, Wabasha 55981, (651) 565-4158 or (800) 565-4158; www.wabashamn.org

BLUFF COUNTRY

Minnesota's Bluff Country is a crazy quilt of rumpled hills, thick hardwood forests, and secret hiking paths that inquisitive youngsters will find thrilling. There are calf-stretching bike routes and hidden hamlets of antique shops and marvelous little restaurants that know how to cater to vacationing families. The area, nuzzled alongside the Mississippi River near the Iowa border, includes Winona, Fillmore, and Houston Counties in the state's far southeastern corner. The Bluff Country is part of the Driftless Region, untouched by the glaciers that flattened other parts of Minnesota and Wisconsin eons ago.

Taking the clan on a short getaway to this part of the state is a marvelous way to show off a bit o' reeeealllly cool nature, far from the heat of the urban pavement and the stressful rush of traffic. The area is a perfect getaway for harried family members, a great antidote for the workweek and homework blues.

This is a part of Minnesota where "getting out and doing things" is the way to enjoy the scenery. Spiderwebbing county roads dip and roll, up and over bluffs, snaking through cathedrals of towering maples and oaks before wonderfully opening up to fields of fragrant timothy and hay. Roll down the windows, sing a road song with the backseat gang, and count the cows.

BIRD-WATCHING IN WINONA

The Mississippi River valley is one of the major flyways in the country for migrating birds, and many species of feathered fowl nest here year-round. In addition, muskrats, beaver, and mink call the river bottoms their home, and deer scamper around on the high ground.

Regardless of the season, devoted bird-watchers—of all ages—flock to the Winona area along the river. It's a thrill to search out the majestic great egret, the noisy yellow-headed blackbird, and the rare Henslow's sparrow. The latter is most often found hidden among the prairie grasses above the bluffs, hanging on to the bobbing stalks and chirping its distinctive "sssclick-ssssclick-sssclick."

Majestic bald and golden eagles are prolific throughout the area. One of the best times to bring the family to the area is during Winona's annual **Eagle Watch** held on the first weekend in March. A Saturday-evening educational program is followed by a Sunday motor-coach field trip to get "nose to beak" with the birds. An observation deck in the downtown area overlooks the river, making it easier even for the smallest tyke to spot one of those wonderful birds.

The city of Winona from on high. Minnesota Office of Tourism photograph.

In addition to eagles, observing a peregrine falcon will make any kid's day. Look for these stream-lined hunters as they roam the skies over the farmland near Winona's western edge. The birds can hit speeds of 180 mph when attacking. On a gentler note, bring the gang to Weaver Bottoms, along Highway 61 north of Winona, or to Reick's Park across the river in Alma, Wisconsin, to search out tundra swans during their spring and fall migrations.

During these seasons, when the birds are flying between their Arctic nesting grounds and their winter homes in the Carolinas, the Winona area hosts the largest concentration of these fowl anywhere in North America. The large birds concentrate along the river, and you can readily spot them from roads near the waterway. A **Swan Watch** is held each year on the first weekend in November.

HISTORIC WINONA

French explorer and adventurer Father Louis Hennepin traveled to the far reaches of the Upper Mississippi River, looking for souls to save and land to claim for France. He passed the site of today's Winona, possibly waving a bonjour to the Native Americans in the area. The next notable white man to meander through the area was Zebulon Pike who, in 1805, waxed eloquent about the river bluffs, the rich fishing, and the abundance of game.

In 1823, the steamboat *Virginia* was the first such craft to float by what would eventually become Winona, but another 28 years would pass before Orrin Smith, a retired steamboat captain, officially founded the city in 1851. The city's **Steamboat Days** at the end of June recall that era with lots of fun activities for kids and oldsters, with concerts, games, and historical exhibits. The beached *American Queen* steamboat is now a museum highlighting the life and lore of the river. You can really impress the teenagers if you follow these bits of Winona history with a hipper piece of trivia: this is the birthplace of movie star Winona Ryder. No kidding.

Speedster Caught

In 1900, there were only about 12 automobiles in Minnesota. Two years later, one motorist was arrested for exceeding the state's 10-mph speed limit. By 1910, there were more than 7,000 cars and 4,000 motorcycles registered with the state.

Most of Winona is set on an island, spilling over onto the mainland as the years progressed. Sugarloaf Mountain, a noted landmark, provided much of the stone for Winona's buildings. The structures are among those in the city's two national historic districts, made up of more than 100 sites. Kids might enjoy seeing the Egyptian Revival style of the **Winona National and Savings Bank**, which was built in the early 1900s. With all its delightfully bizarre bronze work, it looks as if it belongs in a classic mummy movie.

The city is often called the Stained Glass Capital of America because of its abundance of galleries and studios utilizing the brilliant panes of glass. Many businesses and homes in Winona have excellent examples of this ancient art, which came to Winona in 1946 when the first studio opened. Be sure the shutterbugs in the crowd have their cameras ready because the light streaming through these windows is a colorful sight.

Many Polish émigrés came to live in Winona. Their kids' kids still worship in St. Stanislaus Kostka Catholic Church, with its glistening white dome topped by a statue of the church's patron saint. The **Polish Cultural Institute** shows off artifacts and family donations that highlight the Old World roots of Winona. The museum was founded in 1976 to keep alive the Kashubian culture of the region in Poland where many early residents were born. A two-day **Polish Heritage Festival** in late April celebrates that history, making for a perfect short getaway. *Smaczne Jablka*, a Polish apple festival, honors the region's major fruit crop in mid-October. This is subsequently a good time and place to get the kids munching their requisite "apple-a-day." The Winona Polish Cultural Institute is located at 102 Liberty Street, (507) 454-3431. Kids don't have to speak Polish to appreciate the colorful exhibits.

The Winona County Historical Museum also houses interesting displays, including a major showing of antique toys and vintage clothing. The backseat gang will get a kick out of looking at the styles from a variety of historical periods. The museum is housed in a brick building originally constructed as an armory in 1915; it's located at 160 Johnson Street, (507) 454-2723; www.winona.edu/historicalsociety.

WALKS ON THE WILDLIFE SIDE

Great River Bluffs State Park is just one of the many fabulous overlooks from which the gang can view wildlife on the river. The park features expansive stands of hickory and oak trees, as well as stands of white cedar. The park has a 31-site campground, with picnic tables, fire rings, and nearby modern toilets. The family's more fastidious members can be assured of some creature comforts, even in the "wilds," 20 miles as it is, southeast of Winona near the intersection of Highway 61 and I-90. If an afternoon picnic is all you have time for, there are about 20 tables scattered along the top of the bluff in the park. It's a great place for the clan to sit and watch the natural panoply arrayed along the river far below. For specifics on park attractions and activities, contact the park manager at (507) 643-6849.

The Reno Bottoms Delta lies south of the state park, stretching six miles along County Highway 26 from the town of Reno southward to the Iowa border. To get the best view of the wildlife that calls the area home, take the levee road from Reno to Lock and Dam No. 8 on the Mississippi. Sandhill cranes and moorhens are abundant. The Reno Management Unit, part of the sprawling **Richard J. Dorer Memorial Hardwood Forest**, has a multipurpose day-use area for horseback riding, snowmobiling, and hiking—depending on the season. The management unit overlooks the river, some 500 feet below at the foot of the bluffs. Make sure to dress everyone for the weather if out roaming the forestlands. It can get cool out there in the autumn and quite warm in the summer.

Smack in the middle of Houston County, about 15 miles west of Reno, lies **Bear Creek Valley State Park**, a summer symphony of dozing cottonwoods, where the drumming of a red-headed woodpecker provides percussive background sound during a lazy getaway weekend. This 650-acre park is small enough not to be overrun by guests, yet has enough to offer any young or old biologist or woods walker. It's the site of an ongoing, major butterfly survey, and park rangers proudly show off the brilliantly hued insects to amateur and first-time counters, some as young as 12 years old. About eight miles of trails loop through the park, with several of the campsites adapted to the needs of the physically challenged. The park is five miles west of Caledonia on County Highway 1, off Highway 76.

What's in a Name?
In the Case of La Crescent, a Lot.

The town of La Crescent, on the west bank of the Mississippi River, used to be known as Manton. So heated was the town's rivalry with La Crosse, just across the river on the Wisconsin side, that Manton elected to change its name to reflect the animosity. Thinking that La Crosse was French for "the cross," Manton residents chose the crescent, a Muslim symbol, as a way to emphasize the differences between the two towns.

FUN IN FILLMORE COUNTY

Cycling along the many local trails in the Bluff Country may be the best way to get the backseat gang out among the area's flora and fauna. The trails are guaranteed to clear the senses befuddled by long office hours and studying for ACT exams. The **Root River Trail** is a favorite, one of the best in the state; it winds for 28.5 miles between Rushford and Fountain in Fillmore County, Houston County's neighbor to the west. The trail passes through the charming villages of Lanesboro, Peterson, and Whalen, with their snug bed-and-breakfasts, tucked-away inns and rustic campgrounds. The trail shadows one part of the Root River, which offers about 75 miles of lazy paddling, another great way to look over the countryside and, hopefully, spot a wild turkey or deer coming down to drink from the river.

Bring a rod, hand-tied flies, and a current fishing license, because this is trout country, with plenty of babbling brooks hiding the crafty critters. Coordinating all the arm, wrist, and elbow movements while casting is better for hand-eye coordination than all the video games in the world.

Also in Fillmore County near Preston, **Forestville/Mystery Cave State Park** presents a healthy dose of geography and history. Forestville was once a real town, dating back to 1853. It was a farming center, prior to the railroads that sliced through the state, but died slowly after the trains found alternate routes. The hamlet has been administered by the Minnesota Historical Society as a living history center since 1977.

However, at one time, the village had 200 residents, two hotels, two stores, a school, a brickyard, and other businesses. Today, the town looks as it would have in the late 1890s, with costumed interpreters acting the roles of the locals. This is a marvelous place to haul the kids for a subtle history lesson, especially to one of the stores packed with bolts of cloth, tins of food, and just about everything else needed for self-sufficiency in the good old days.

Taking in history lessons at Forestville/Mystery Cave State Park. —Courtesy of the Minnesota Historical Society

Checking out the Devil's Kitchen in Mystery Cave.
—Courtesy of Forestville/Mystery Cave State Park

Then take the crew into the deep recesses of **Mystery Cave**; the cave's 12 miles of underground caverns make it the most extensive cave system in Minnesota. The cave is dark and deep, but not dangerous. Lighted tours take about an hour along ramped concrete paths.

The cave is home to four species of bats, a fact certainly guaranteed to bring squeals out of some of the kids. But the bats are harmless, doing their nighttime best to control the outside mosquito population in the summer. The cave was purchased in 1988 as an adjunct to the state park, which was founded in 1963 and enlarged in 1977. The cave is delightfully spooky. But warn the kids not to touch the cave walls: skin's natural oils can discolor the rocks.

On the wild side above ground, ornithologists have identified more than 175 species of birds in the vicinity, making the park a special place for entire families of birdwatching fans. For more information on the park, caves, and village, contact the Forestville/Mystery Cave State Park Manager, Route 2, Box 128, Preston 55965, (507) 352-5111.

WHITEWATER STATE PARK

Back up in Winona County, be sure to check out **Whitewater State Park**, which sprawls over 2,800 acres of woods and hills three miles south of Elba on Highway 74. Kids generally enjoy interpretive talks in the visitor center auditorium, especially on rainy days when huddling in a tent quickly loses its allure. Be sure to visit the museum and environmental exhibits in the Discovery Room, where historical artifacts, as well as plant and stuffed-skunk displays, are highlighted. A live timber rattlesnake in all its splendor can also be seen in the Discovery Room, though the serpent is separated from its audience by a pane of glass. The park has one of the best naturalist programs in the state, allowing kids to call wild turkeys, fiddle with collecting maple sap, check out the eagle scene, and look for fossils—all under the guidance of trained rangers.

Lots of fishing fans then angle for rainbow trout in the Middle Branch of the Whitewater River.

The nearby **Chimney Rock Geological Center** offers a slide show and displays about the landscape of this hilly region. The facility is near the park's North Point picnic area, accessible off Highway 74, which cuts through the park. If the gang is up for it, take 'em up Chimney Rock Trail behind the center. It's a tough climb, so sturdy hiking boots are suggested rather than tennis shoes. Sandals are out.

The park is popular with weekenders from the Rochester area, western Wisconsin and northern Iowa who come here for a couple of solid days of hiking and exploring the rugged countryside. The **Dakota Trail** and **Coyote Point Loop** are two of the best walkways. For park details, contact the ranger at Whitewater State Park, Route 1, Box 256, Altura 55910, (507) 932-3007.

The **Whitewater Wildlife Management Area (WWMA)** is another fascinating local attraction for the outdoorsy set. Look for signs along Highway 74, about two miles north of Elba. The area covers most of the Whitewater River Valley, one rich in wildlife. Roads cut into the park show the multiple layers of rock stratified over the eons, with fossilized sea creatures easily seen in the rock.

Back in 1857, local farmer Nicolas Marnarch built a stone house here with walls up to 2.5-feet thick for protection from unfriendly Native Americans. The now-abandoned home is reached only by hiking or cross-country skiing about 1.5 miles west on an old stagecoach road, which today leads to the home from the parking lot of the WWMA offices on Highway 74. To seek other information, contact WWMA, Route 2, Box 333, Altura 55910, (507) 932-4133.

PLACES TO STAY

AmericInn, 60 Riverview Drive, Winona (507) 457-0249 or (800) 634-3444; www.americinn.com

Best Western Riverport Inn and Suites, 900 Bruski Drive, Winona, (507) 452-0606 or (800) 595-0606; www.bestwestern.com

Quality Inn, 956 Mankato Avenue, Winona, (507) 452-2187 or (800) 562-4544

Sterling Motel, 1450 Gilmore Avenue, Winona, (507) 454-1120 or (800) 452-1235

Winona KOA Campgrounds, Route 6, Winona, (507) 454-2851 or (877) 454-CAMP

PLACES FOR FOOD

Golden China, 411 Cottonwood Drive, Winona, (507) 454-4261

Good Harvest Cafe, 5205 West Sixth Street, Winona, (507) 452-3360

Jefferson's Pub and Grille, 58 Center Street, Winona, (507) 452-2718

Sammy's Pizza and Deli, 126 West Second Street, Winona, (507) 454-3403

Winona Family Steakhouse, 3480 Service Drive, Winona, (507) 452-3968

Winona Island Cafe, 2 Johnson Street, Winona, (507) 454-1133

PLACES TO SHOP

Bird Song, 1220 East Seventh Street, Winona, (507) 454-6711; www.bird-song.com

Kolter Bicycle and Fitness, 400 Mankato Avenue, Winona, (507) 452-5665

Pieces of the Past, 79 East Second Street, Winona, (507) 452-3722; www.pieces-qpg.com

Winona Gallery, 425 Cottonwood Drive, Winona, (507) 454-8801

FOR MORE INFORMATION

Minnesota Department of Natural Resources, 2300 Silver Creek Road N.E., Rochester 55904, (507) 285-7432

Winona Convention and Visitors Bureau, 67 Main Street, Winona 55987, (507) 452-2272 or (800) 657-4972; www.visitwinona.com

INDEX

INDEX

INDEX

INDEX